ISBN 978-1-4950-7237-6

7777 W. Bluemound Rd. P.O. Box 13819 Milwaukee, WI 53213

Visit Hal Leonard Online at
www.halleonard.com

CONTENTS

THE BARE NECESSITIES

from THE JUNGLE BOOK

Words and Music by
TERRY GILKYSON

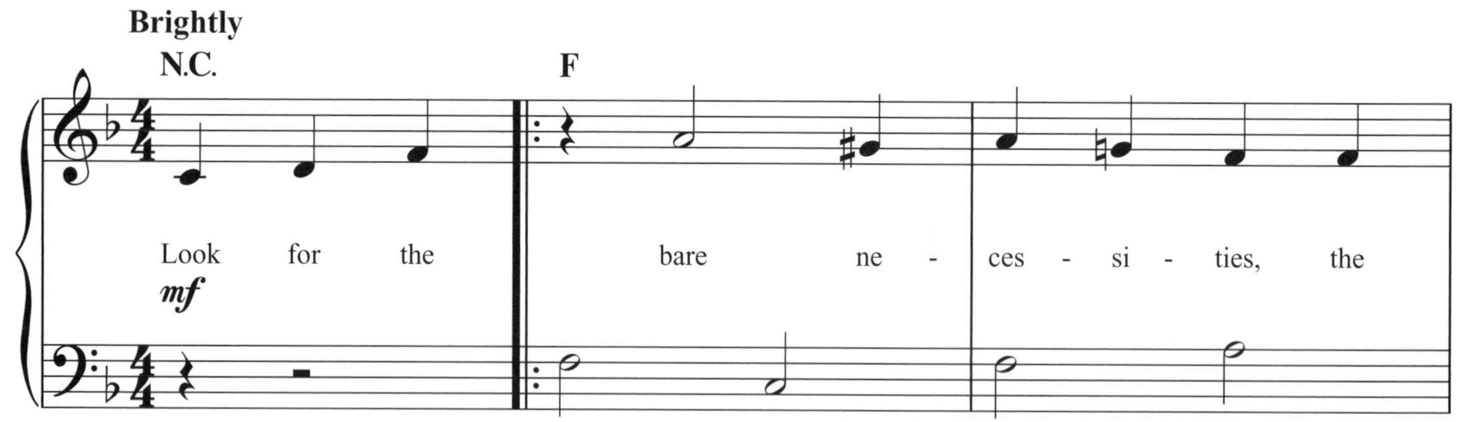

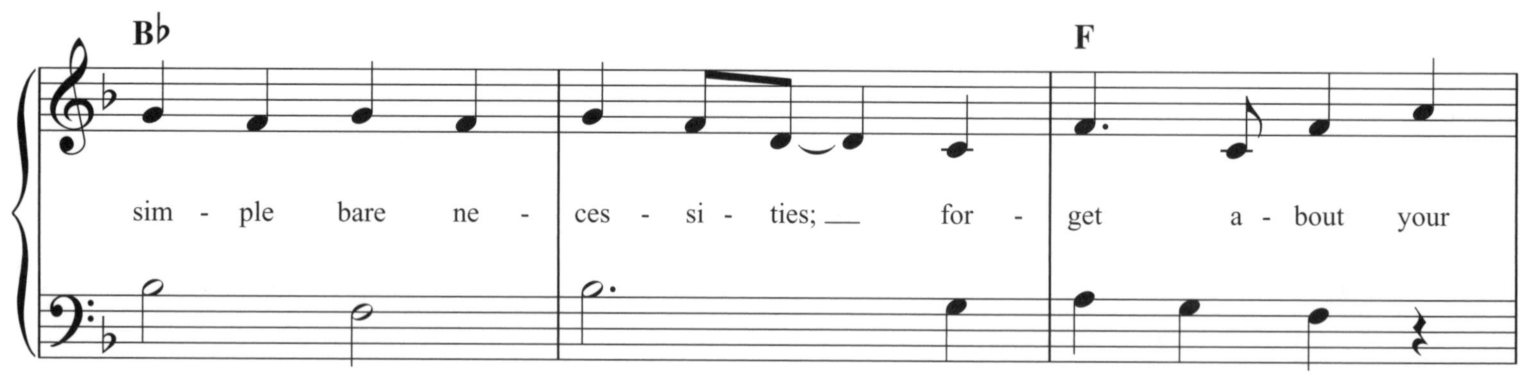

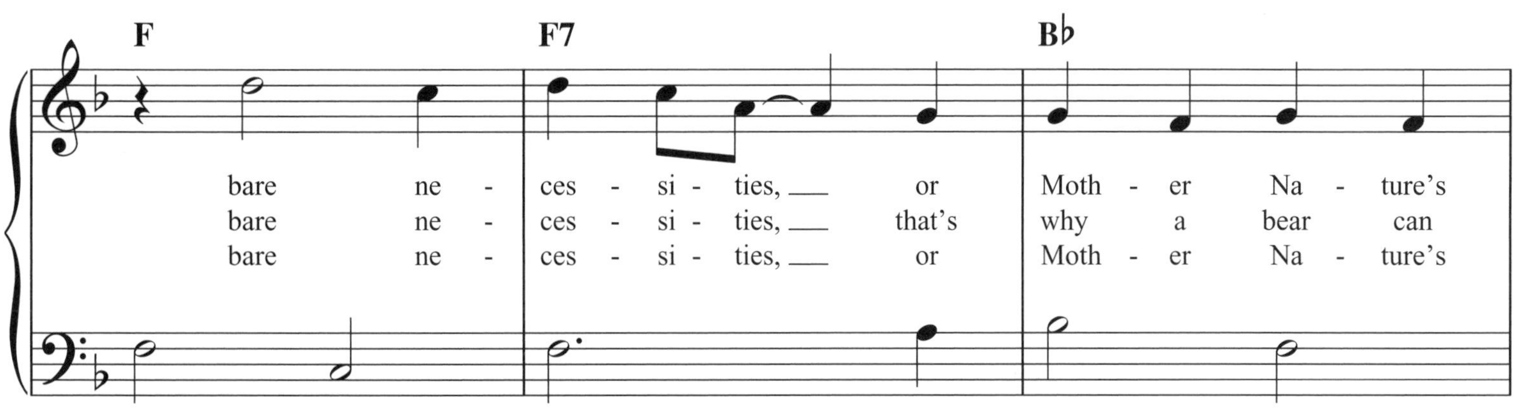
F
F7
B♭
bare ne - ces - si - ties, or Moth - er Na - ture's
bare ne - ces - si - ties, that's why a bear can
bare ne - ces - si - ties, or Moth - er Na - ture's

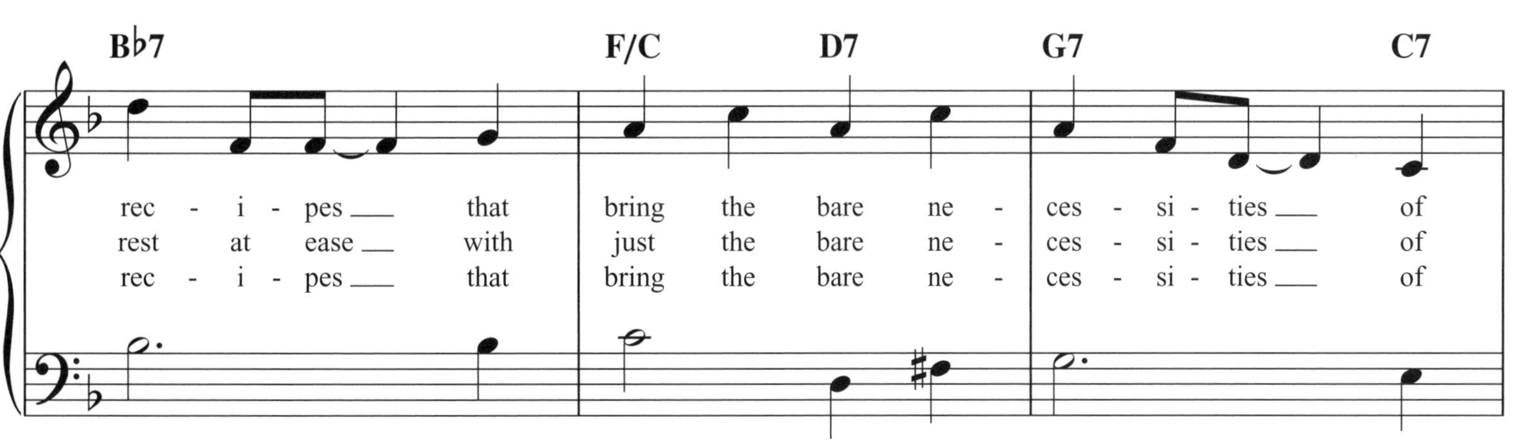
B♭7
F/C
D7
G7
C7
rec - i - pes that bring the bare ne - ces - si - ties of
rest at ease with just the bare ne - ces - si - ties of
rec - i - pes that bring the bare ne - ces - si - ties of

F
N.C.
C7
life. Wher - ev - er I wan - der,
life. When you pick a paw - paw
life. So just try to re - lax Spoken: Oh Yeah!

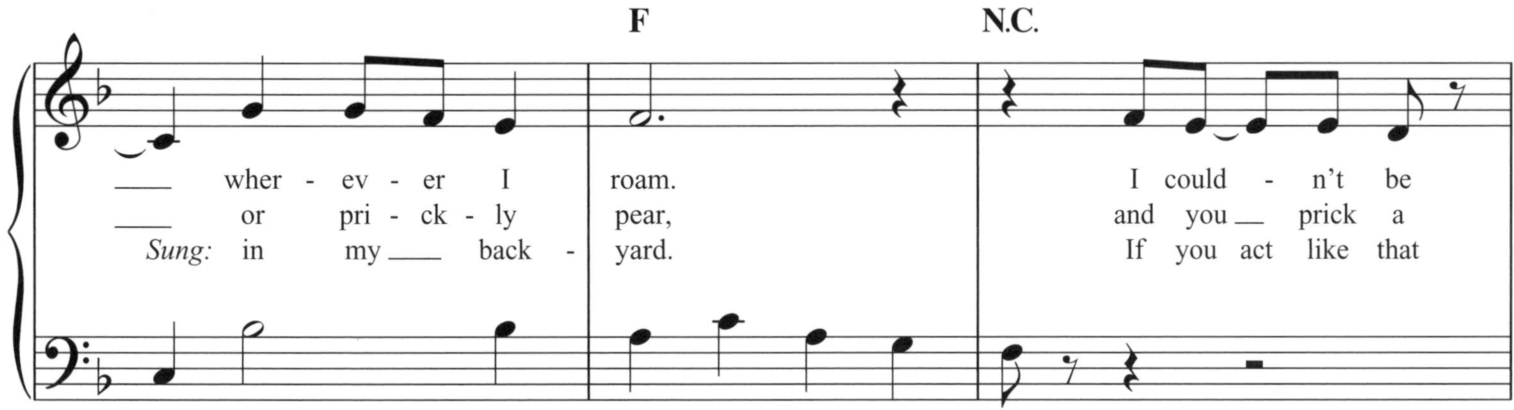
F
N.C.
wher - ev - er I roam. I could - n't be
or pri - ck - ly pear, and you prick a
Sung: in my back - yard. If you act like that

C7
F
fond - er of my big home.
raw paw, next time be - ware.
bee acts you're work - in' too hard.

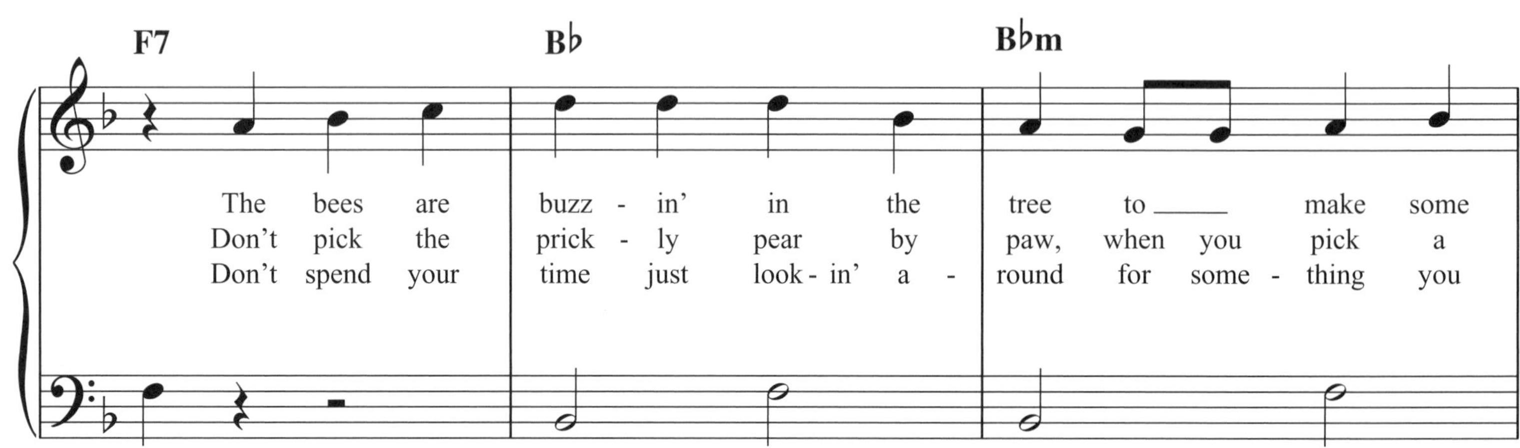
F7
B♭
B♭m
The bees are buzz - in' in the tree to make some
Don't pick the prick - ly pear by paw, when you pick a
Don't spend your time just look - in' a - round for some - thing you

F
G7
Dm7
hon - ey just for me. You look un - der the
pear, try to use the claw. But you don't need to
want that can't be found. When you find out you can

D7
Gm
rocks and plants and take a glance at the
use the claw when you pick a pear of the
live with - out it and go a - long not

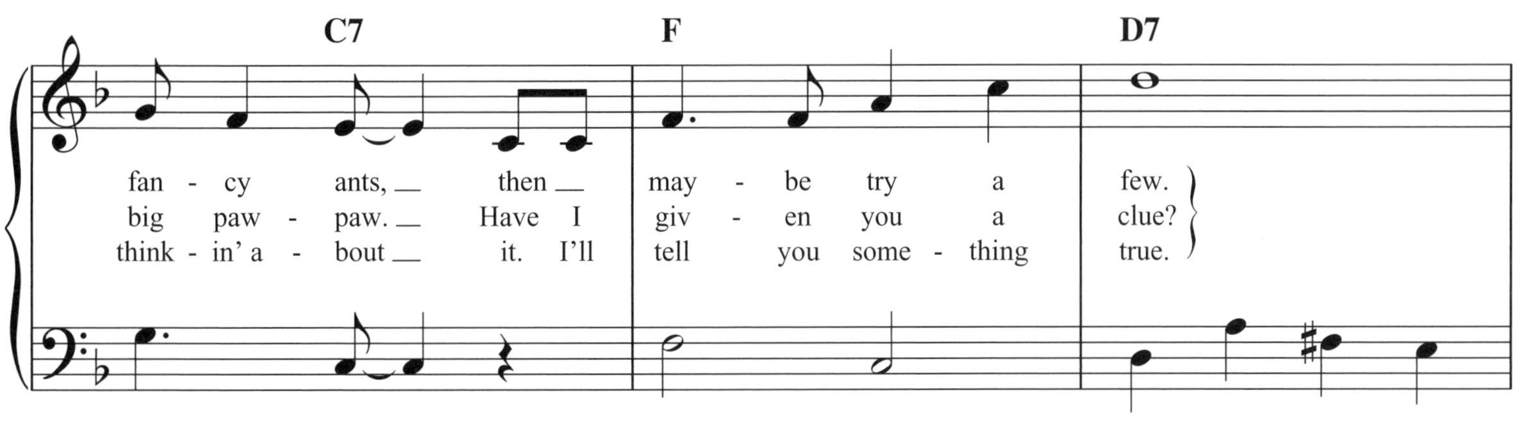
C7
F
D7
fan - cy ants, then may - be try a few.
big paw - paw. Have I giv - en you a clue?
think - in' a - bout it. I'll tell you some - thing true.

Gm7
C7
The bare nec - es - si - ties of life will come to

1., 2.
F
Dm
Gm
C7
F
you, they'll come to you!

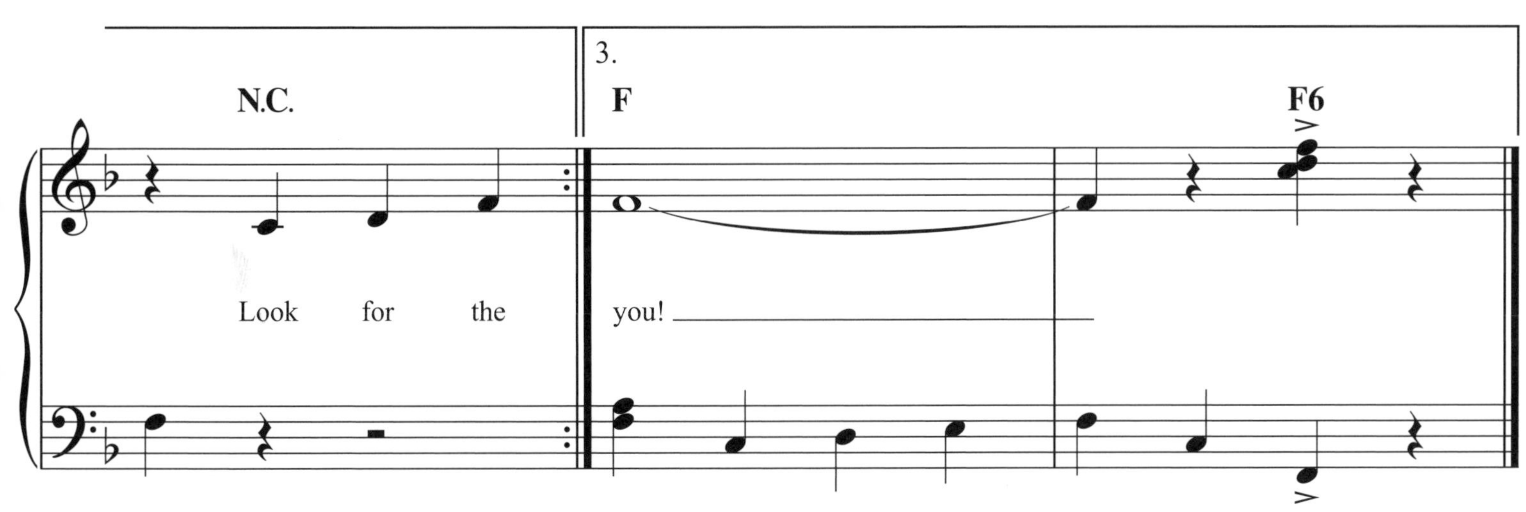
3.
N.C.
F
F6
Look for the you!

BE OUR GUEST
from BEAUTY AND THE BEAST

Music by ALAN MENKEN
Lyrics by HOWARD ASHMAN

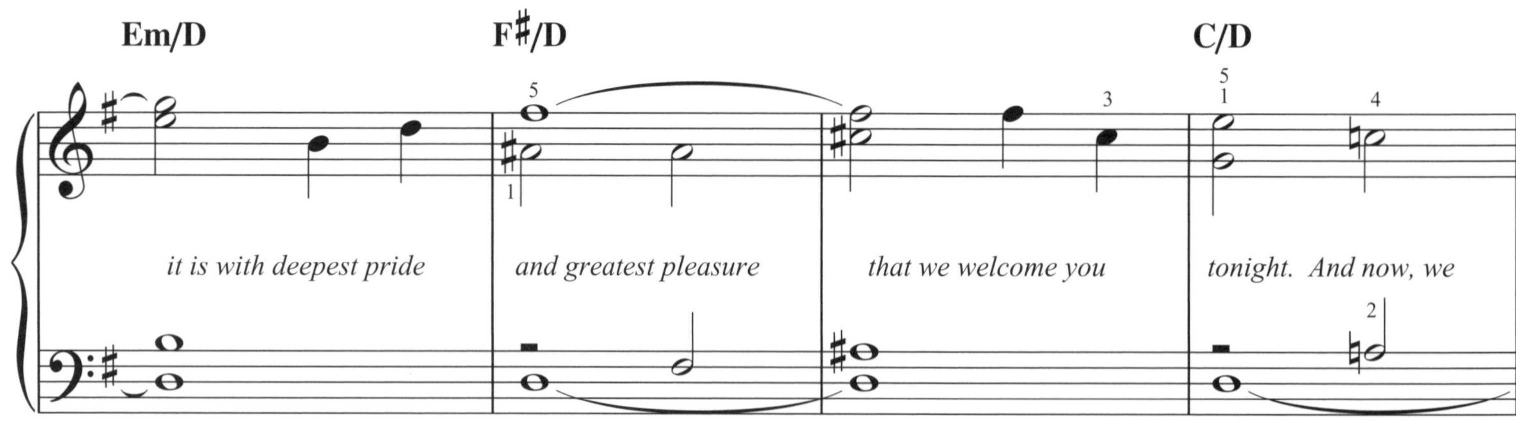

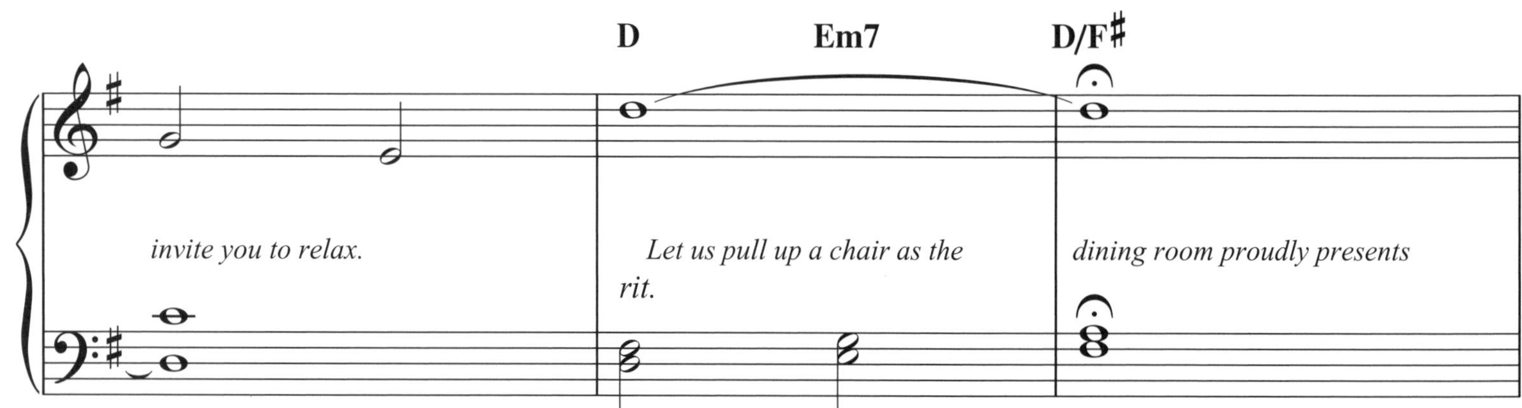

N.C.
G
Gmaj7
your dinner!
Be our guest! Be our guest! Put our
a tempo

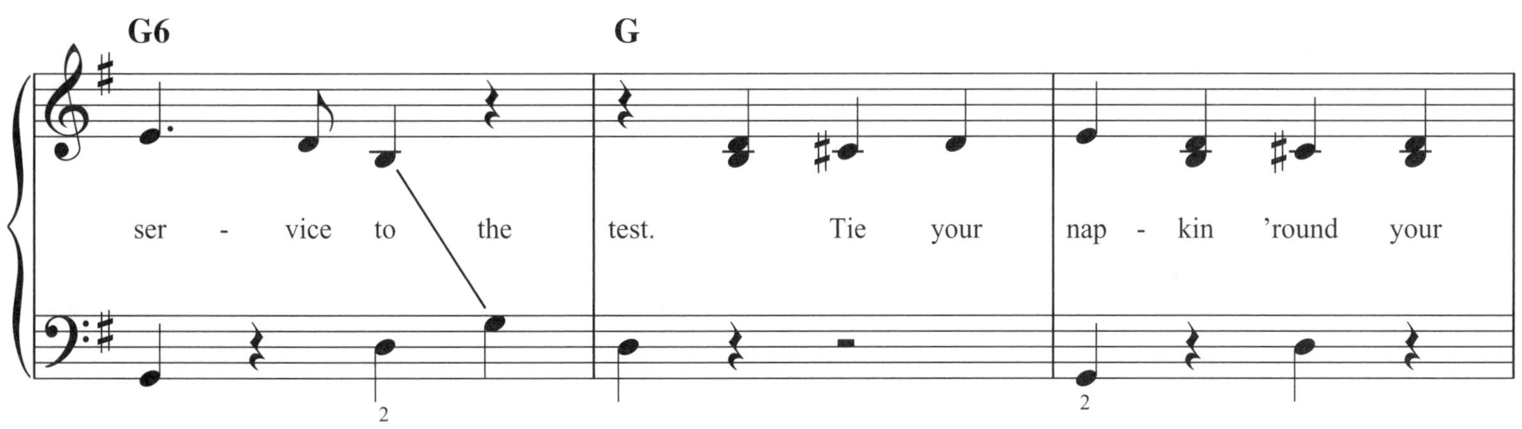
G6
G
ser - vice to the test. Tie your nap - kin 'round your

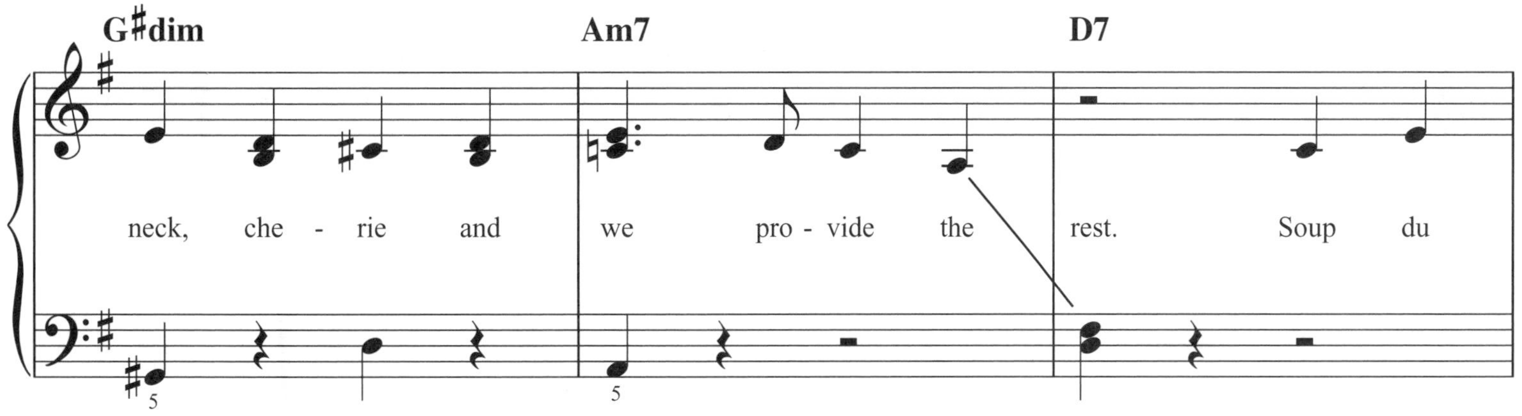
G♯dim
Am7
D7
neck, che - rie and we pro - vide the rest. Soup du

Am
Am♯7
Am7
jour! Hot hors d'oeuvres! Why, we on - ly live to

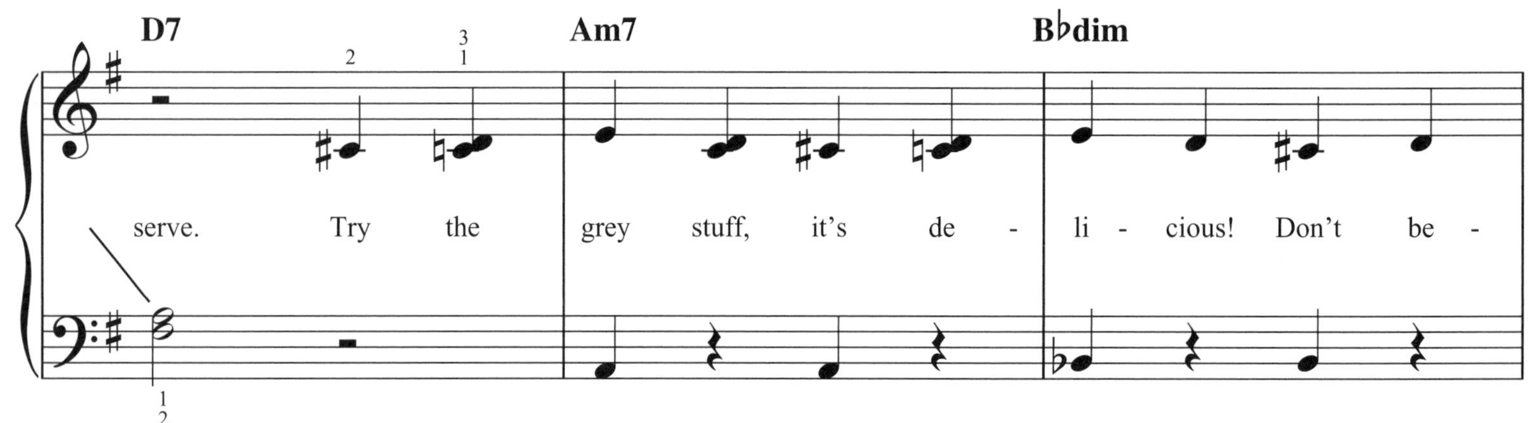
D7
Am7
B♭dim
serve. Try the grey stuff, it's de - li - cious! Don't be -

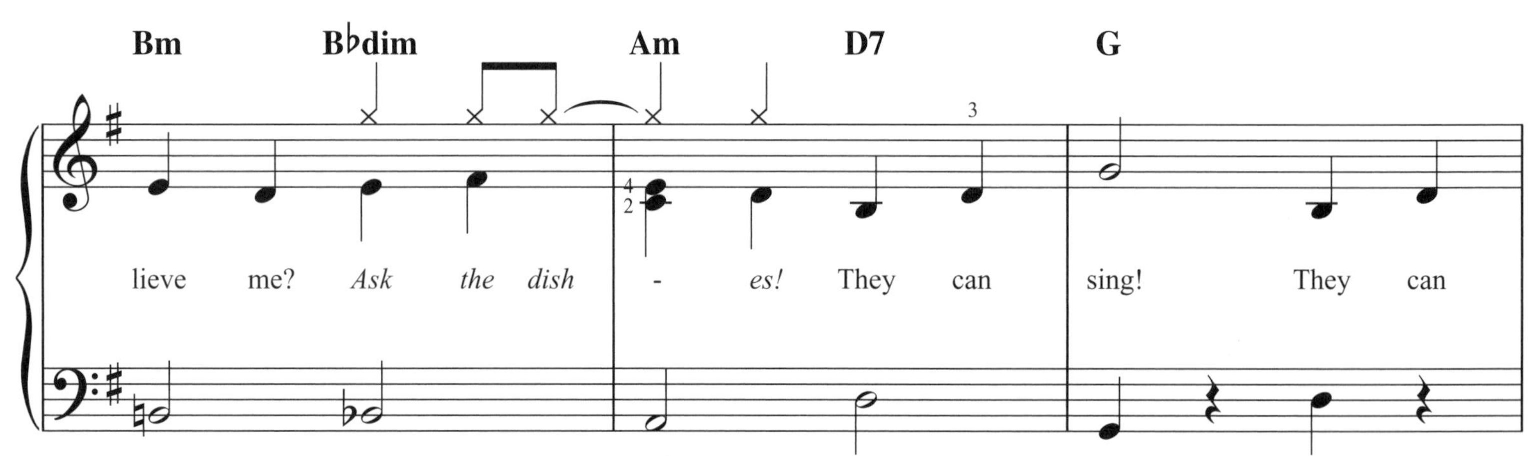
Bm
B♭dim
Am
D7
G
lieve me? Ask the dish - es! They can sing! They can

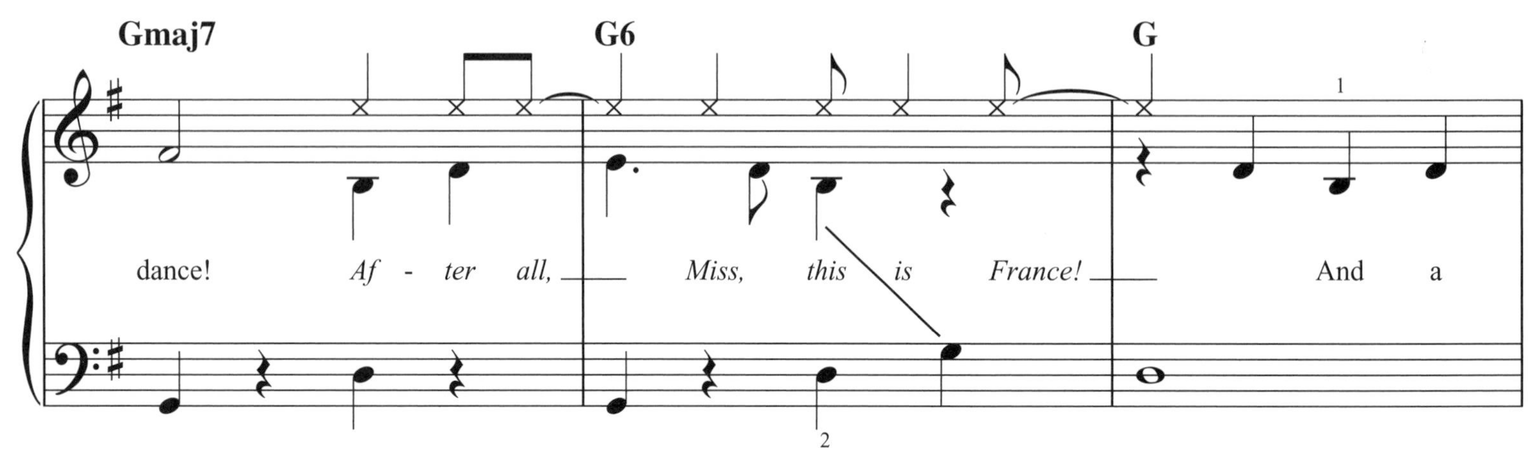
Gmaj7
G6
G
dance! Af - ter all, Miss, this is France! And a

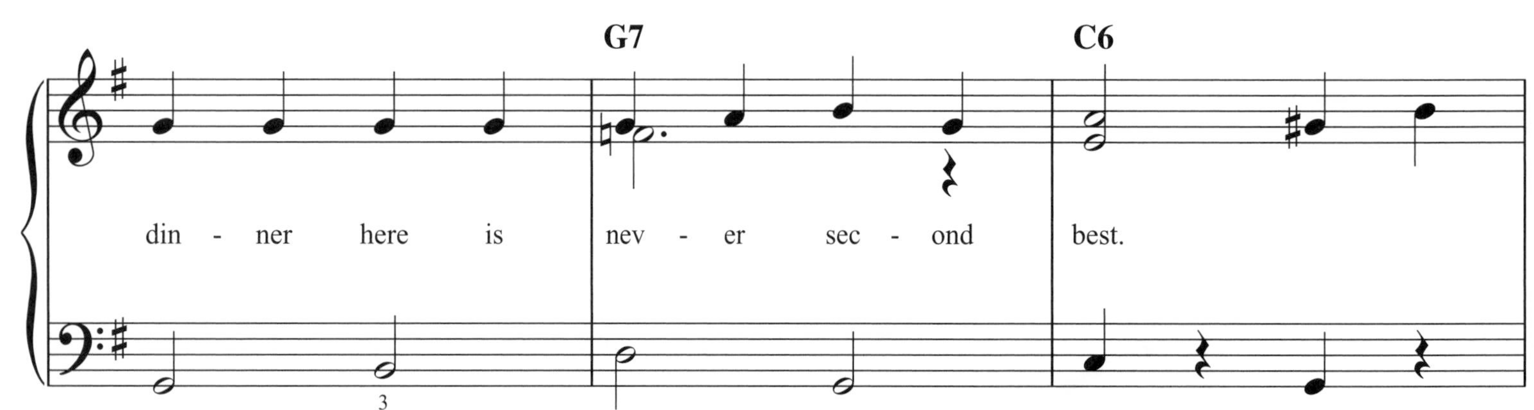
G7
C6
din - ner here is nev - er sec - ond best.

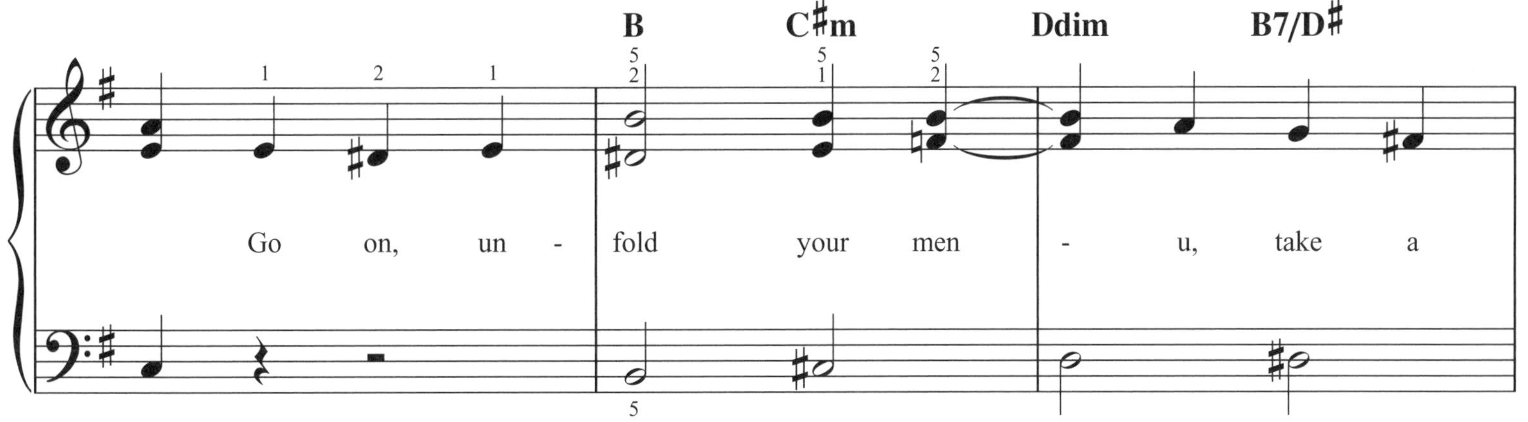
B C♯m Ddim B7/D♯
Go on, un - fold your men - u, take a

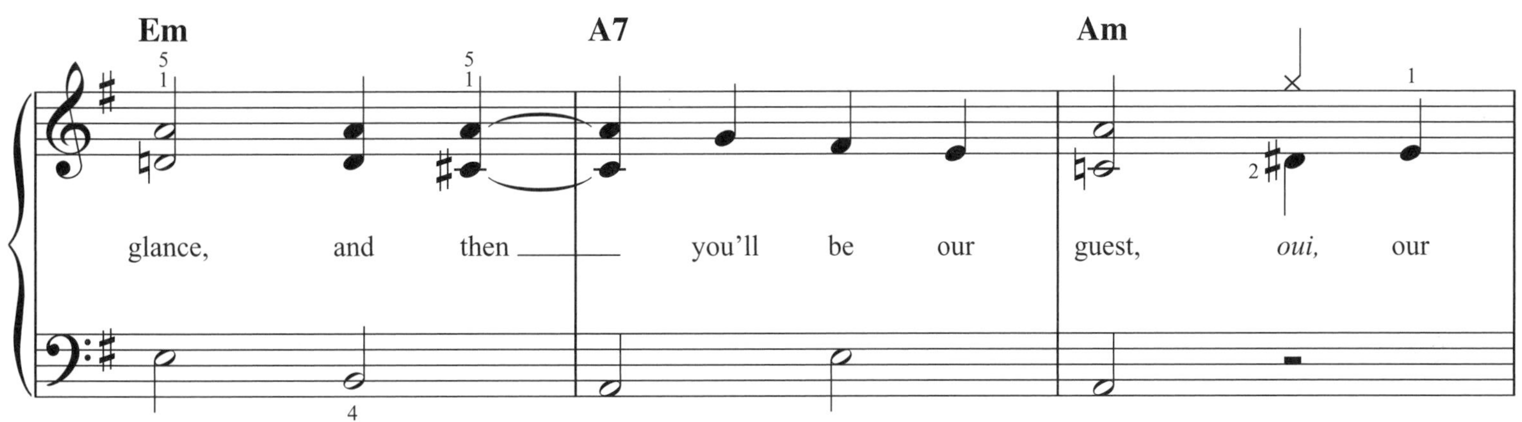
Em A7 Am
glance, and then you'll be our guest, oui, our

D7 G G7 C
guest! Be our guest! Beef ra - gout! Cheese souf -

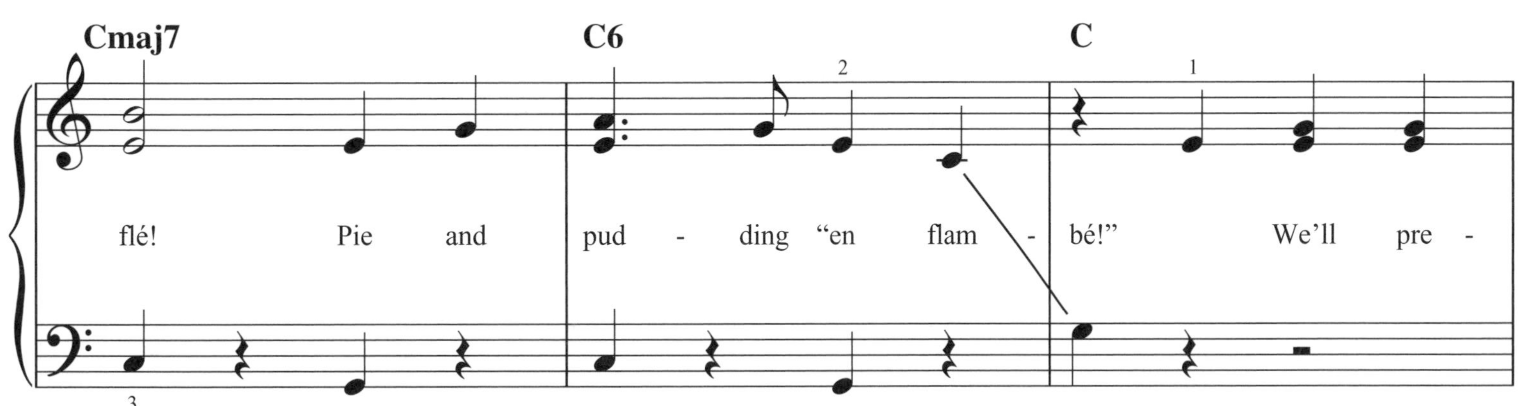
Cmaj7 C6 C
flé! Pie and pud - ding "en flam - bé!" We'll pre -

C♯dim
Dm7
pare and serve with flair a cu - li - na - ry ca - ba -
5
5
5

G7
Dm
Dm♯7
1
3
ret! You're a - lone and you're scared but the

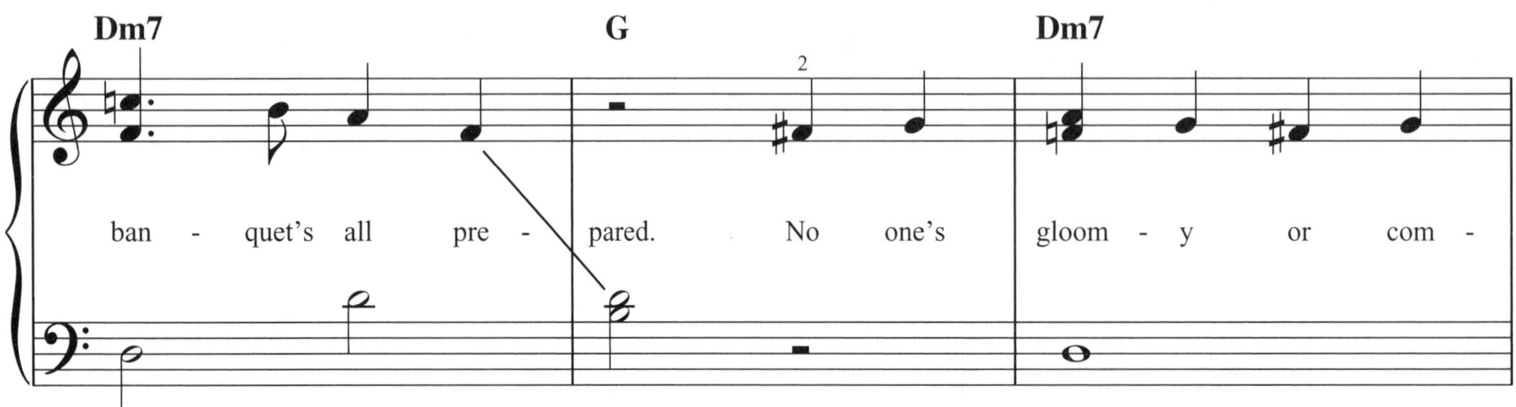
Dm7
G
Dm7
2
ban - quet's all pre - pared. No one's gloom - y or com -

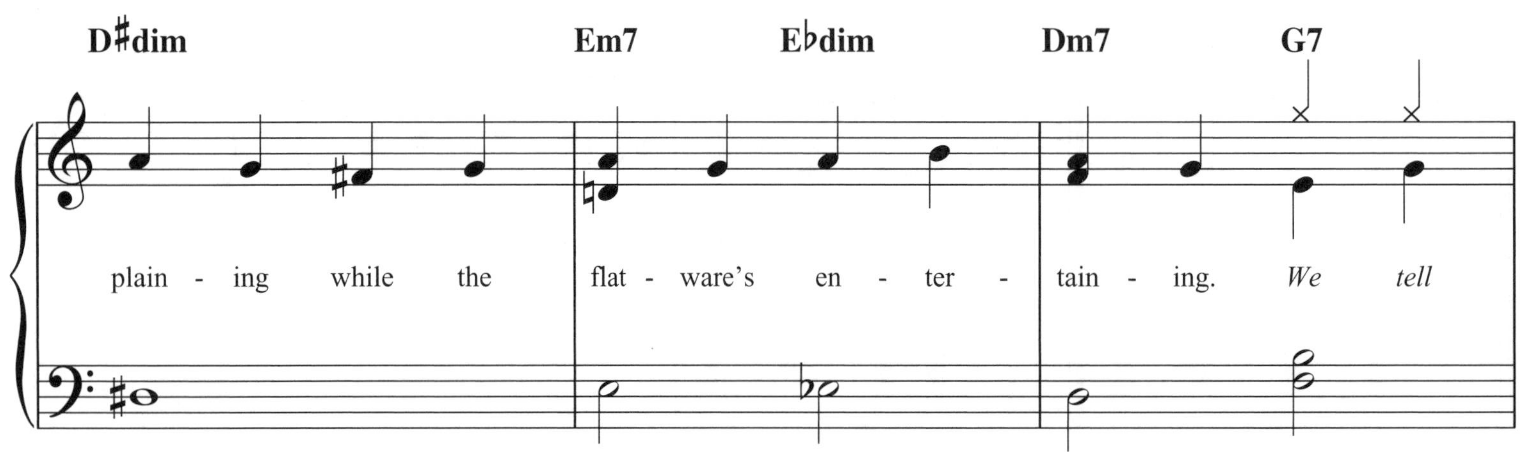
D♯dim
Em7
E♭dim
Dm7
G7
plain - ing while the flat - ware's en - ter - tain - ing. We tell

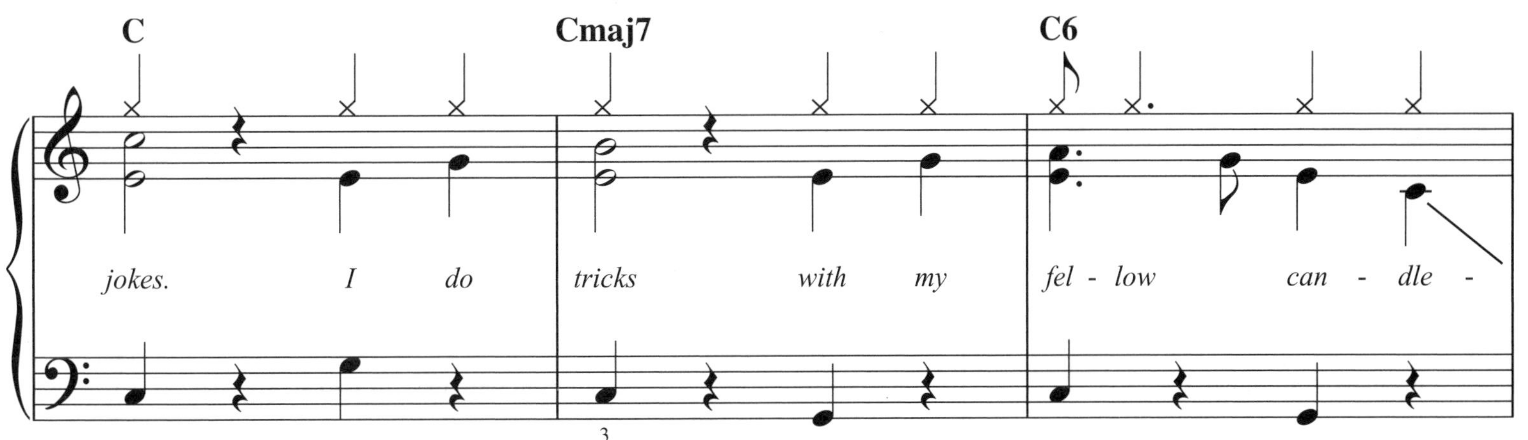
C
Cmaj7
C6
jokes. I do
tricks with my
fel - low can - dle -
3

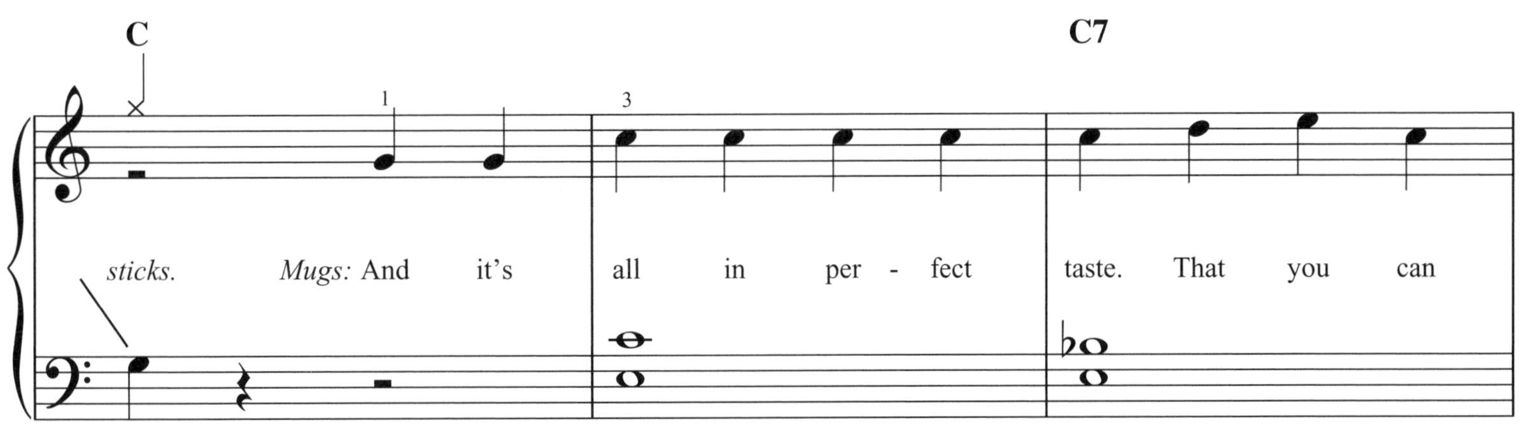
C
C7
1
3
sticks. Mugs: And it's
all in per - fect
taste. That you can

F6
E
F♯m7
Gdim
bet!
All: Come on and
lift your glass
3
5

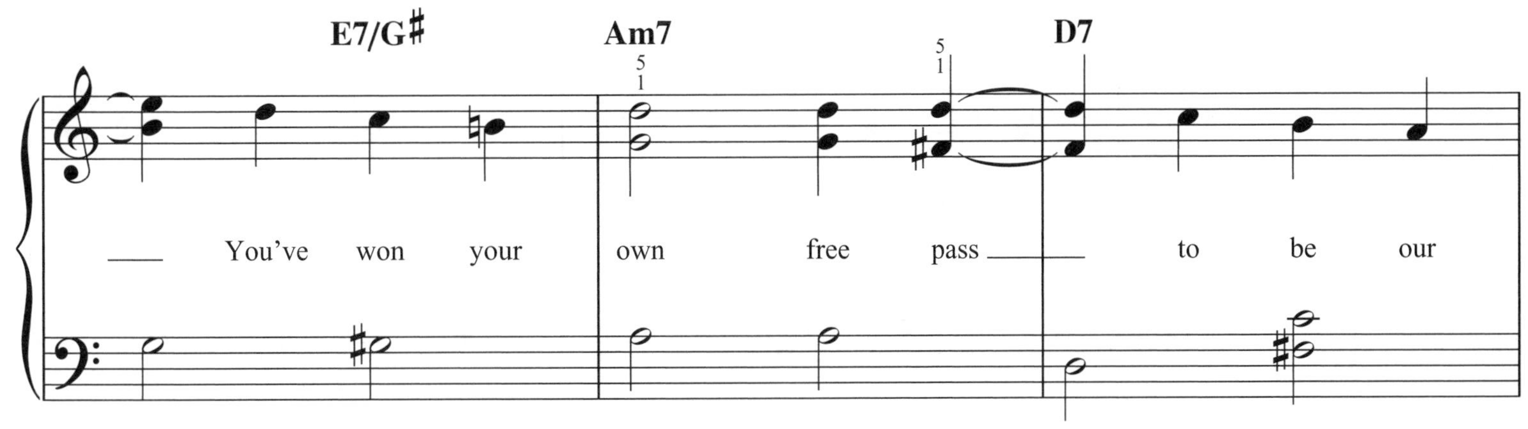
E7/G♯
Am7
D7
You've won your
own free pass
to be our

Dm7
G7
Em
guest! Lumiere: If you're
stressed it's fine
din - ing we sug -

A7#5
Dm7
G7
C
gest. All: Be our
guest! Be our
guest! Be our
guest!

Slower
E
Am
Lumiere:
mp
Freely
Life is so un -
nerv - ing for a

E/G#
Gdim
ser - vant who's not
serv - ing. He's not
whole with - out a

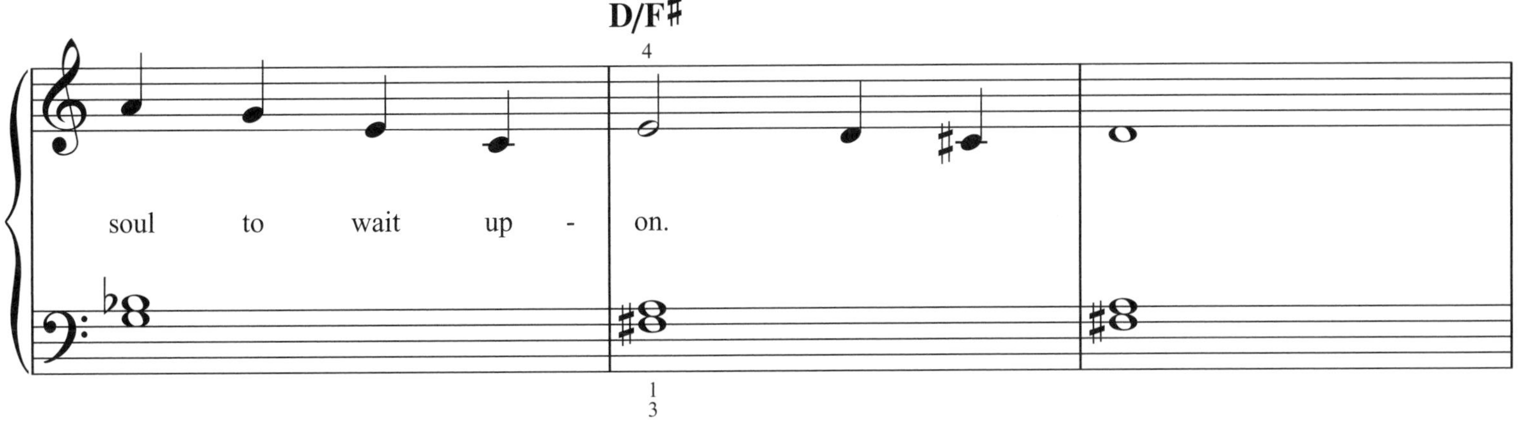
D/F♯
soul to wait up - on.

Fdim
Em
Ah, those good old days when we were use - ful.

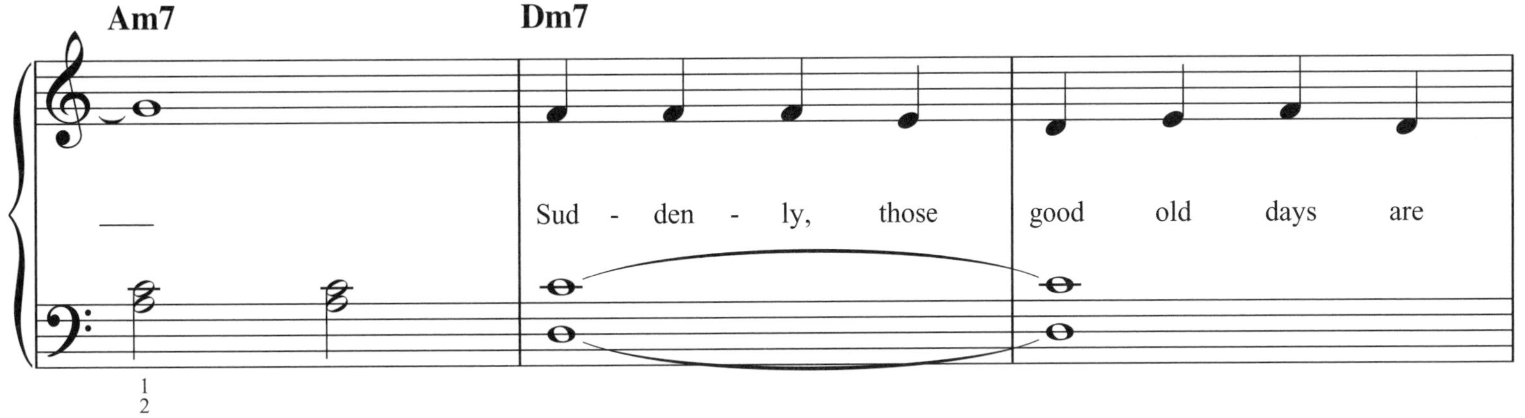
Am7
Dm7
Sud - den - ly, those good old days are

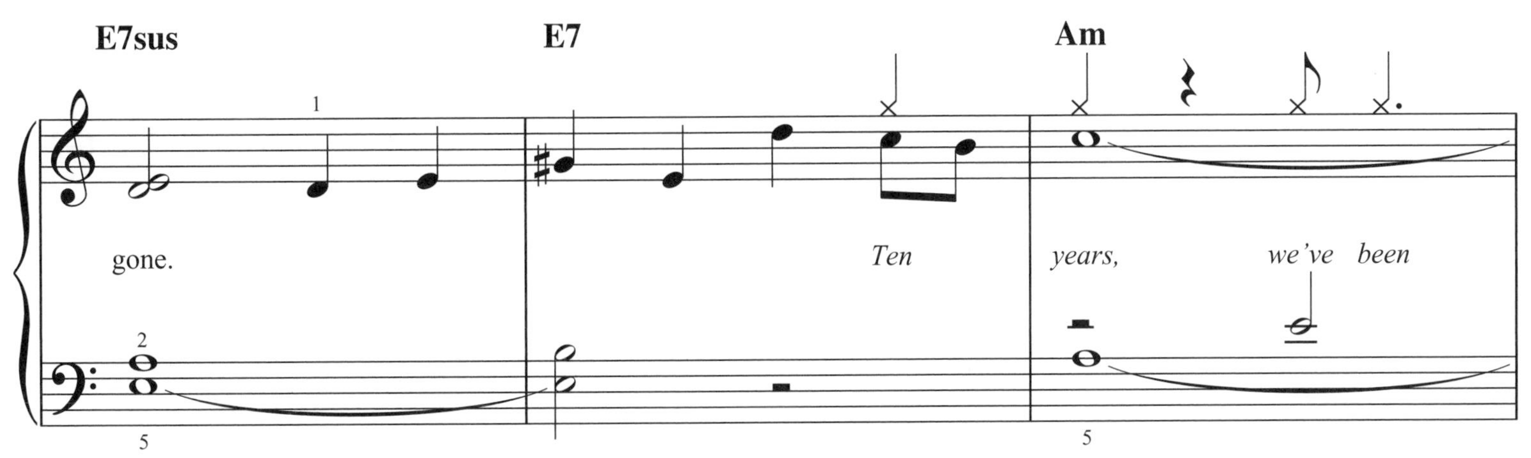
E7sus
E7
Am
gone. Ten years, we've been

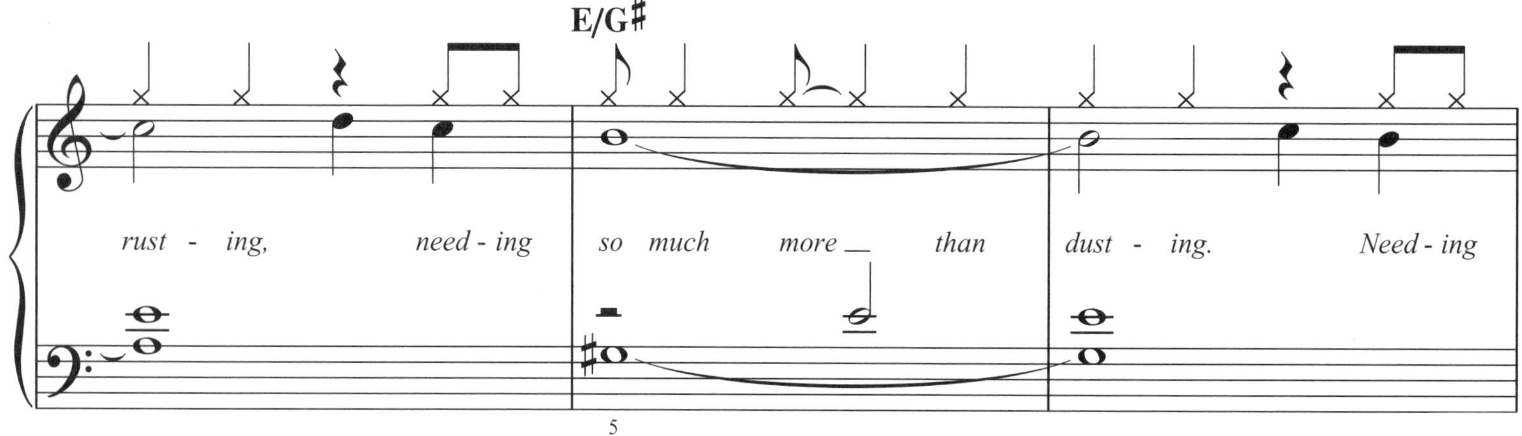
E/G♯
rust - ing, need - ing
so much more_ than
dust - ing. Need - ing
5

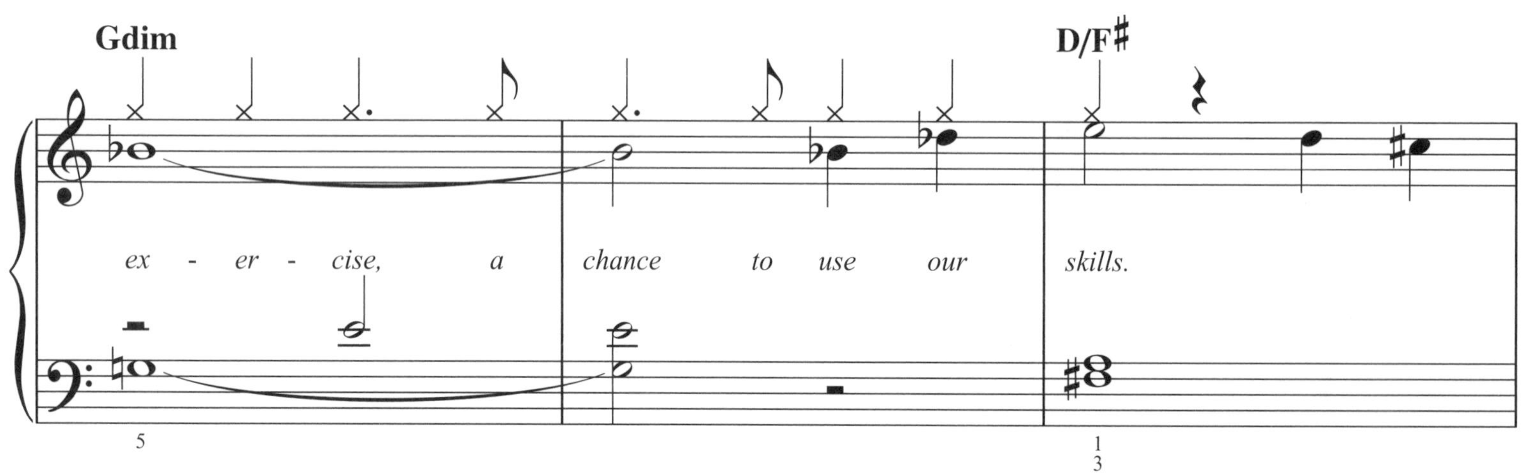
Gdim
D/F♯
ex - er - cise, a
chance to use our
skills.
5
1
3

Fdim
3
Most days, we just
lay a - round the

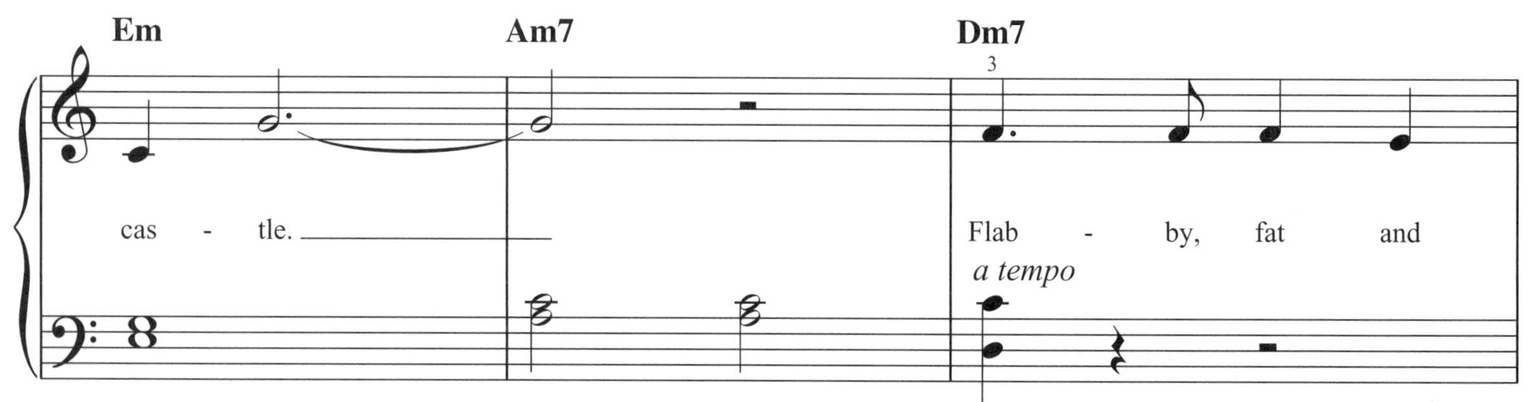
Em
Am7
Dm7
3
cas - tle.
Flab - by, fat and
a tempo

G7
la - zy. You walked in and oops - a - dai - sy! Mrs. Potts: It's a

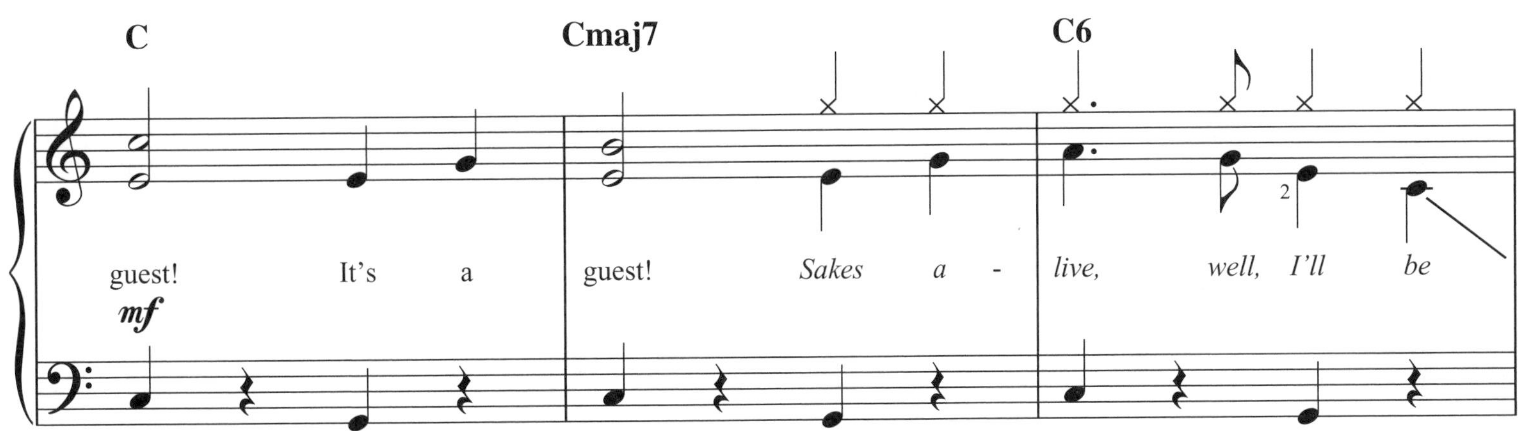
C
Cmaj7
C6
guest! It's a guest! Sakes a - live, well, I'll be
mf

C
C♯dim
blessed! Wine's been poured and thank the Lord I've had the

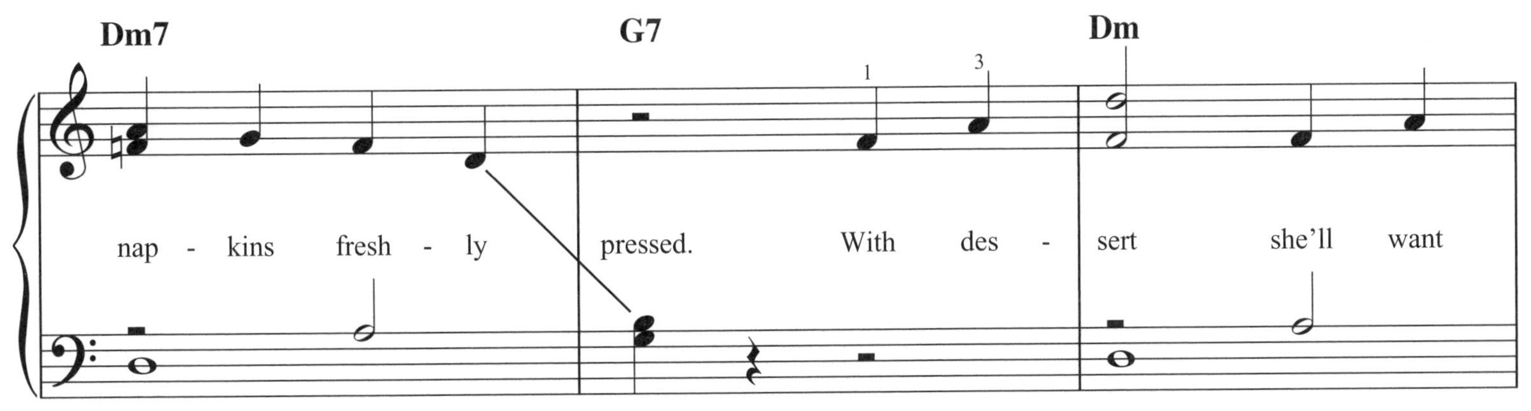
Dm7
G7
Dm
nap - kins fresh - ly pressed. With des - sert she'll want

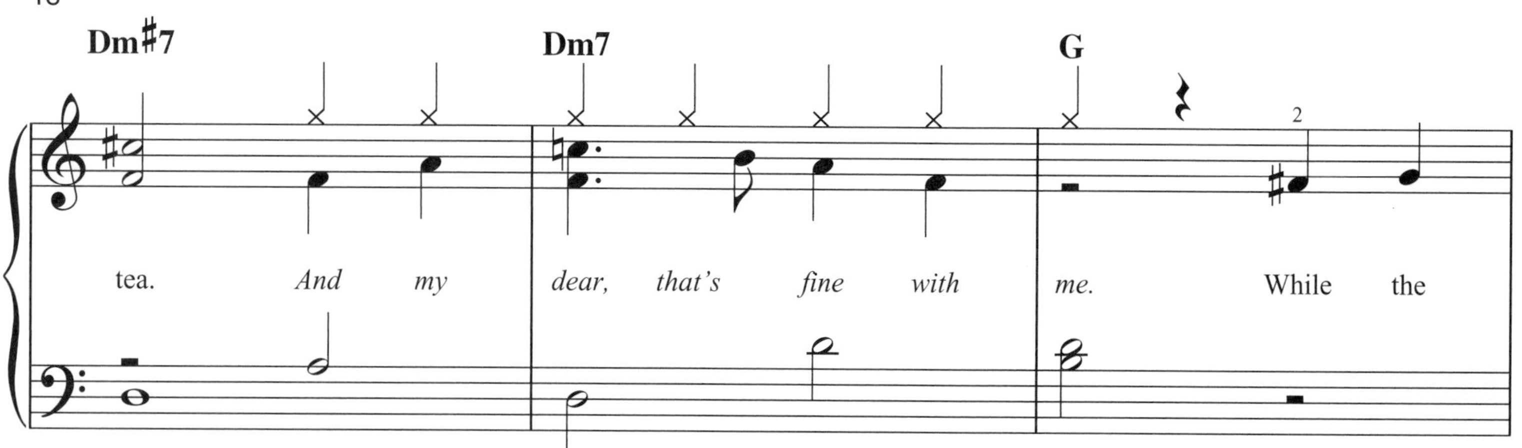
Dm♯7
Dm7
G
tea. And my dear, that's fine with me. While the

Dm7
D♯dim
Em
E♭dim
cups do their soft shoe - ing, I'll be bub - bling! I'll be

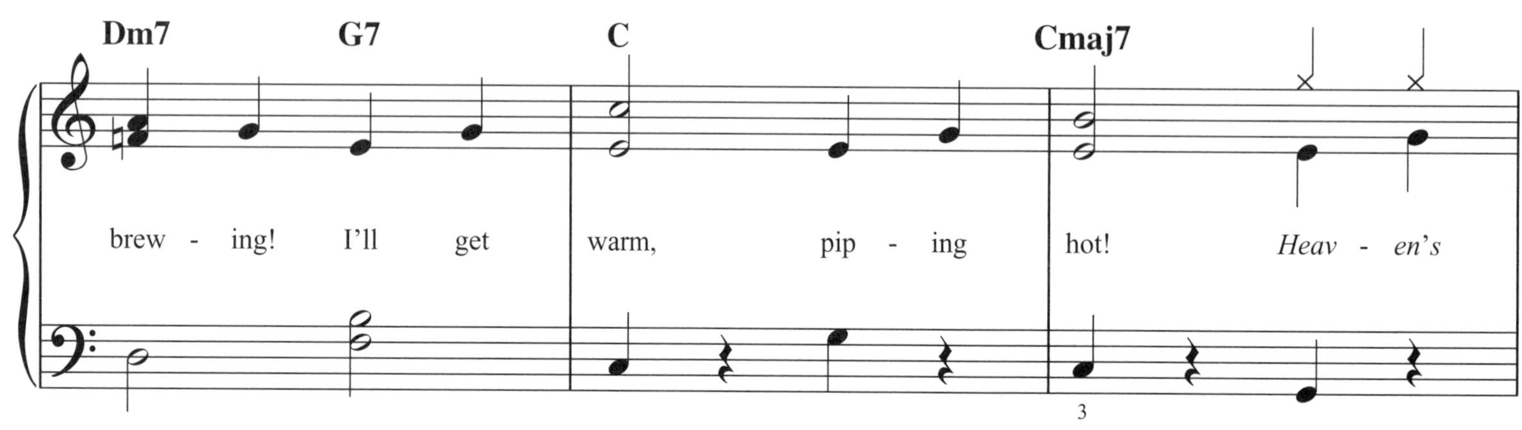
Dm7
G7
C
Cmaj7
brew - ing! I'll get warm, pip - ing hot! Heav - en's

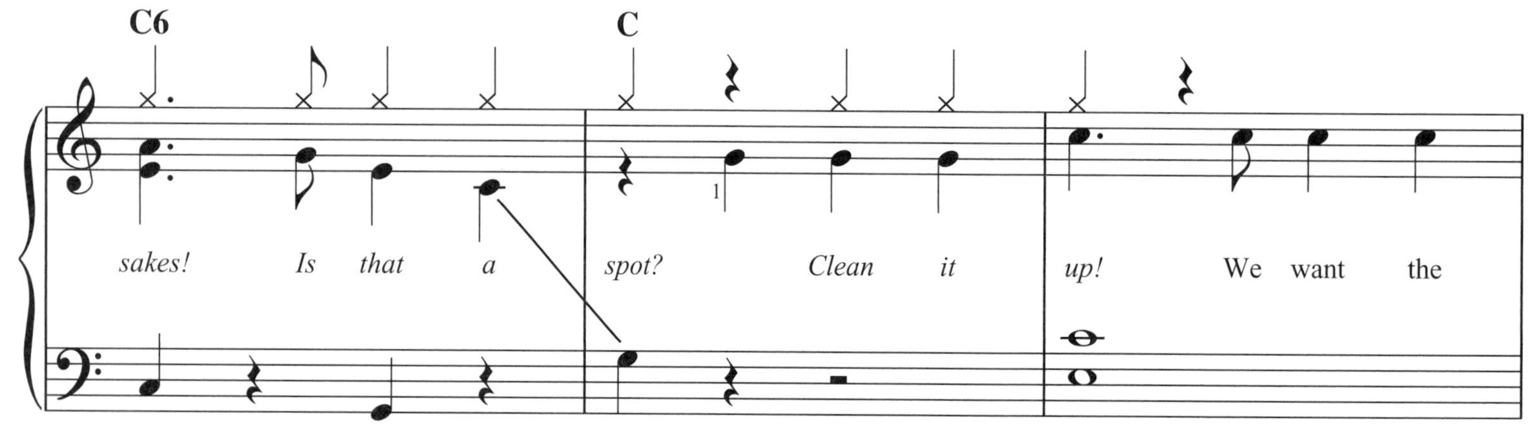
C6
C
sakes! Is that a spot? Clean it up! We want the

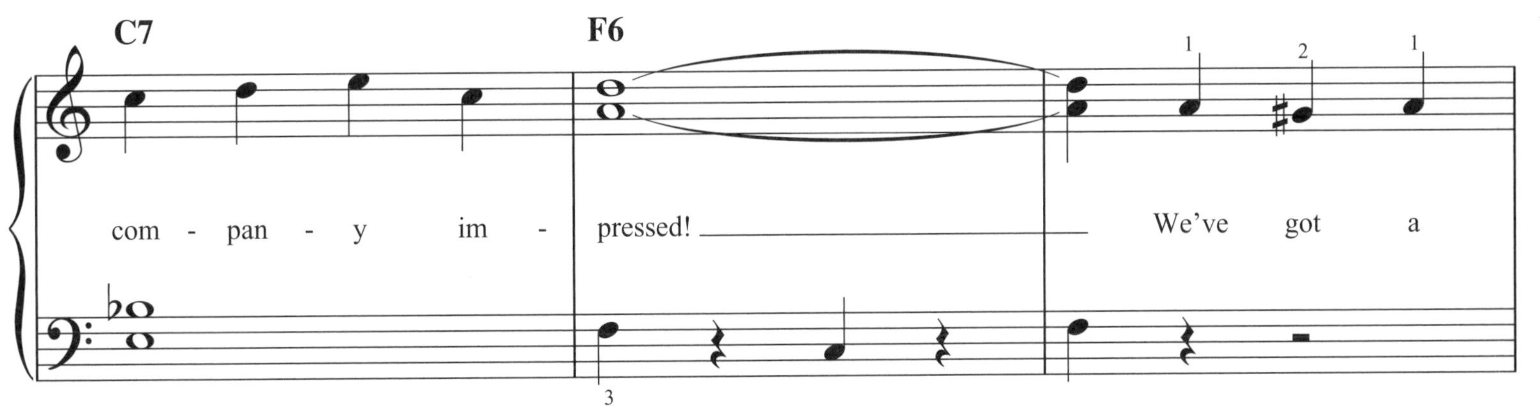
C7
F6
com - pan - y im - pressed!
We've got a

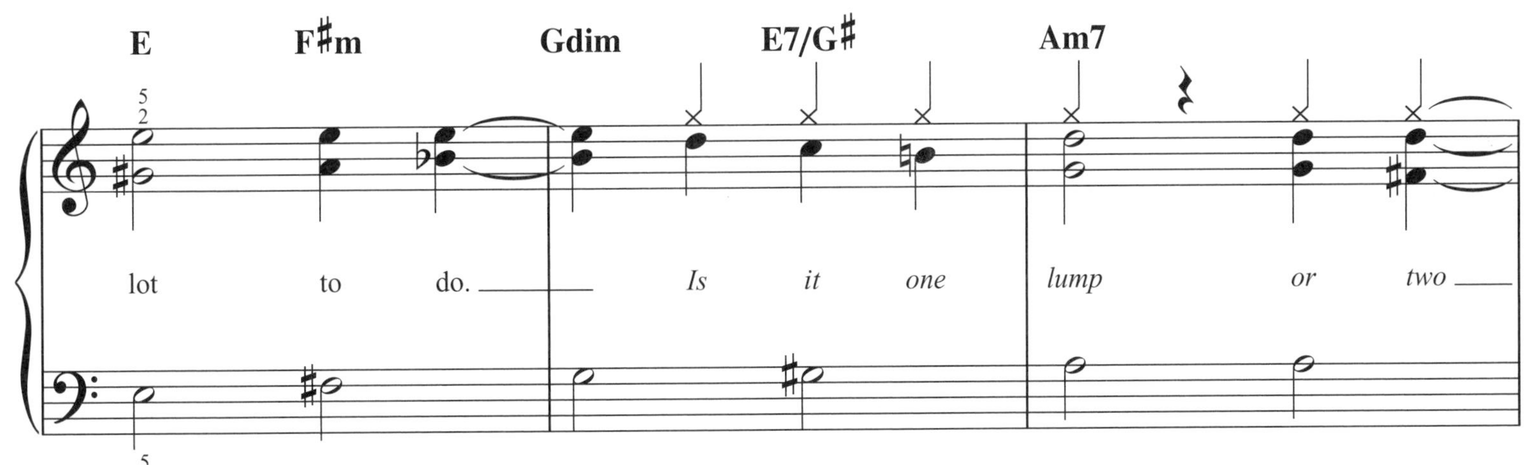
E
F♯m
Gdim
E7/G♯
Am7
lot to do.
Is it one
lump or two

D7
Dm7
G7
for you, our
guest? Chorus: She's our
guest! Mrs. Potts: She's our

Em
D7
G
guest! Chorus: She's our
guest! Be our
guest! Be our

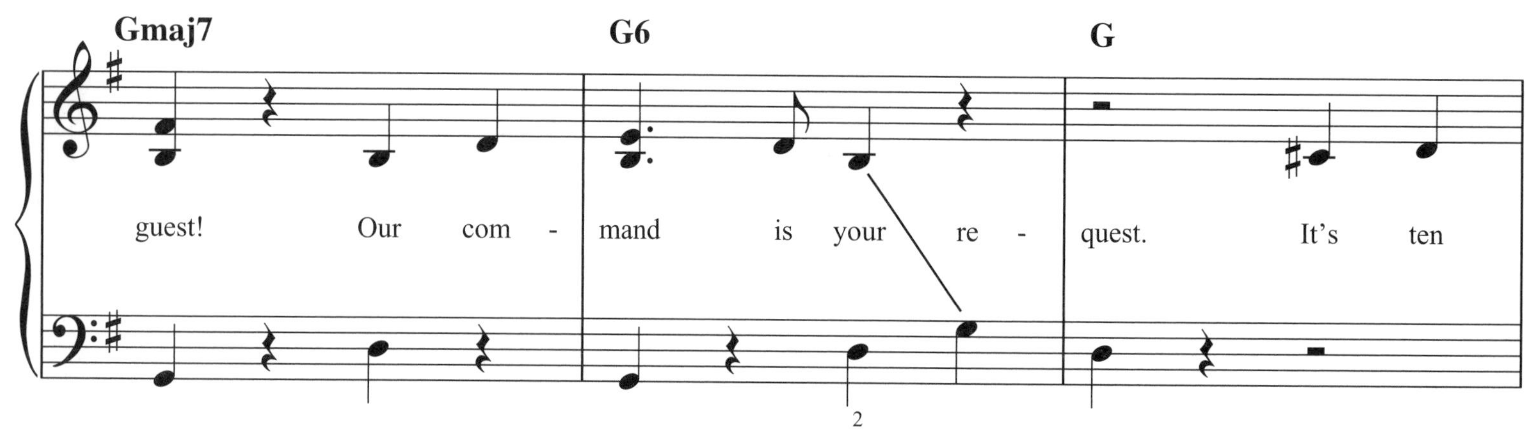
Gmaj7
G6
G
guest! Our com - mand is your re - quest. It's ten
2

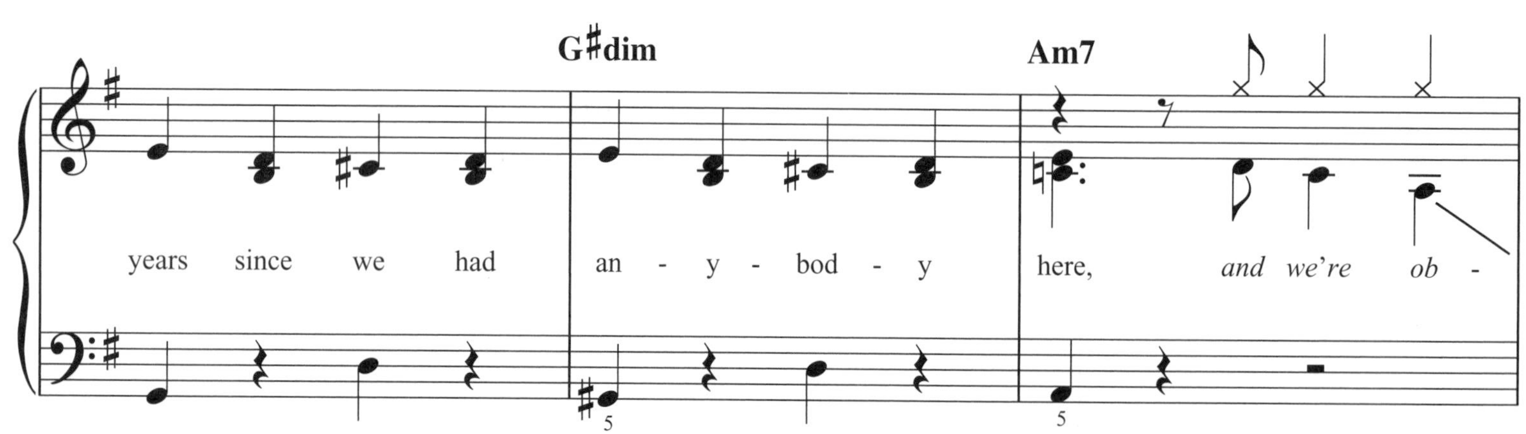
G#dim
Am7
years since we had an - y - bod - y here, and we're ob -
5
5

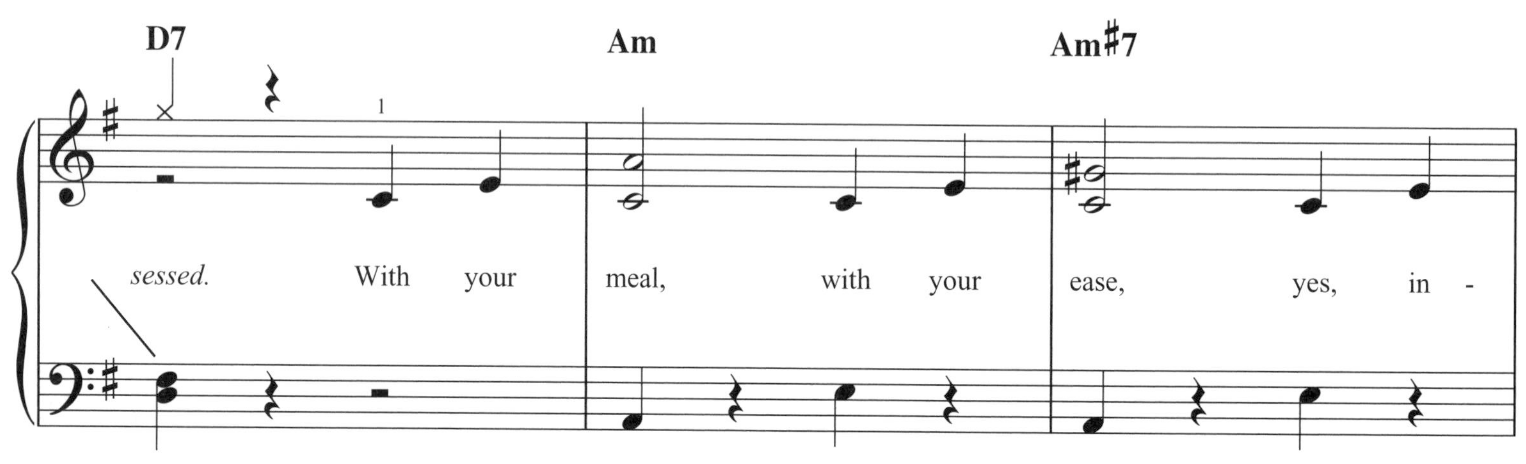
D7
Am
Am#7
1
sessed. With your meal, with your ease, yes, in -

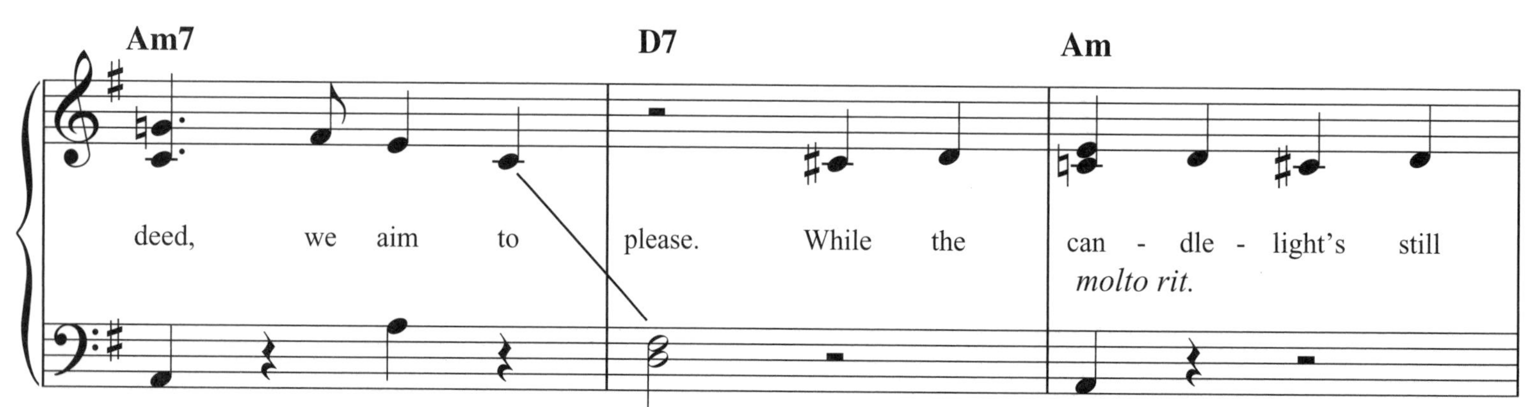
Am7
D7
Am
deed, we aim to please. While the can - dle - light's still
molto rit.

D7
G7
glow - ing let us
help you, we'll keep
go - ing course by
rit.

Much slower
C
Cmaj7
C6
course, one by
one! 'Til you
shout, "E - nough. I'm

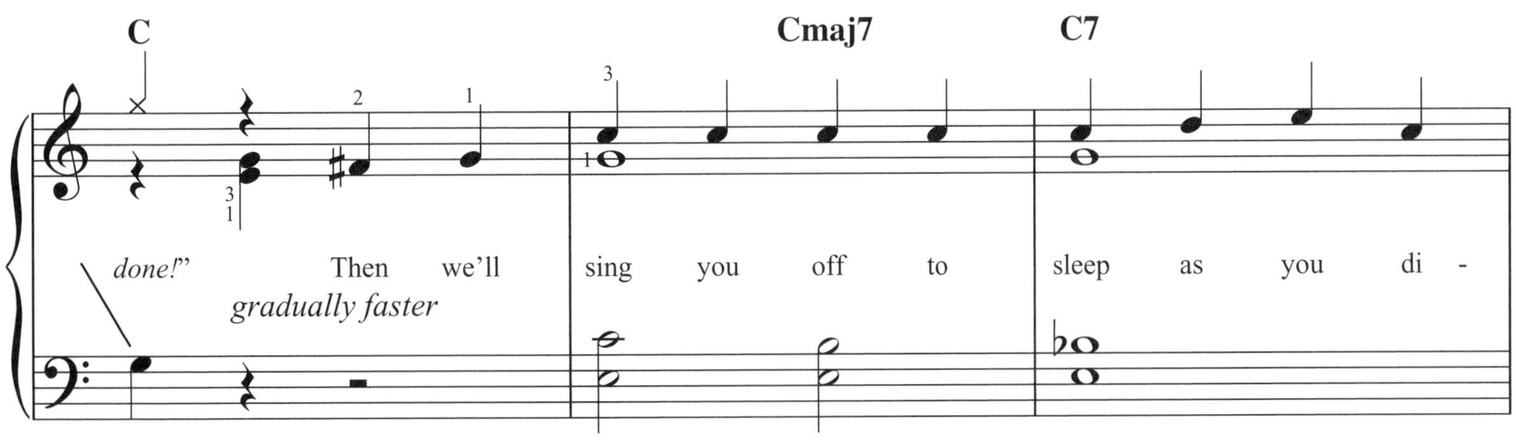
C
Cmaj7
C7
done!" Then we'll
gradually faster
sing you off to
sleep as you di -

F6
E
F♯m7
gest.
To - night you'll
prop your feet
a tempo

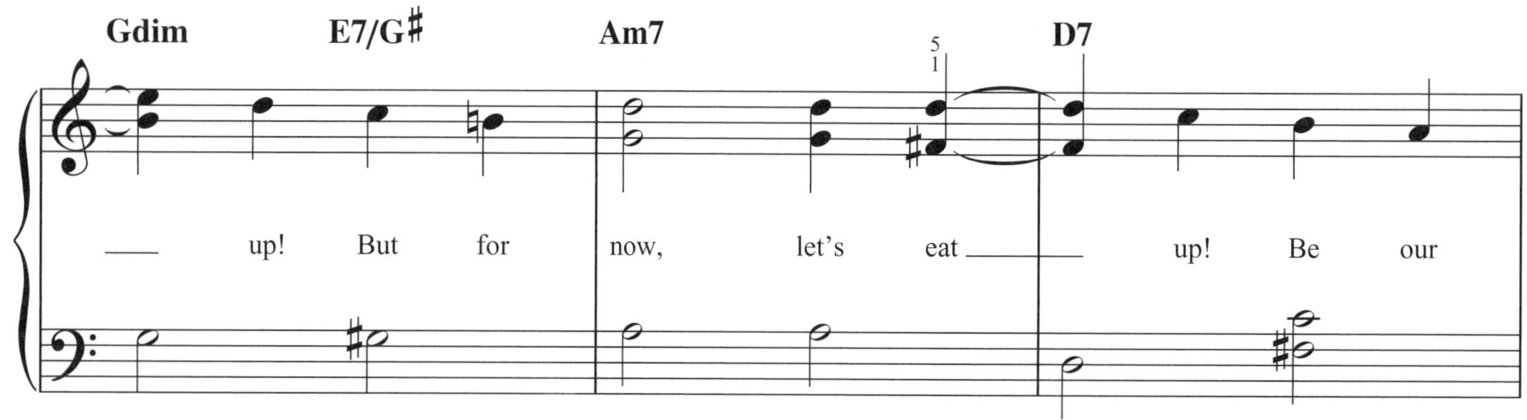
Gdim
E7/G♯
Am7
D7
up! But for now, let's eat up! Be our

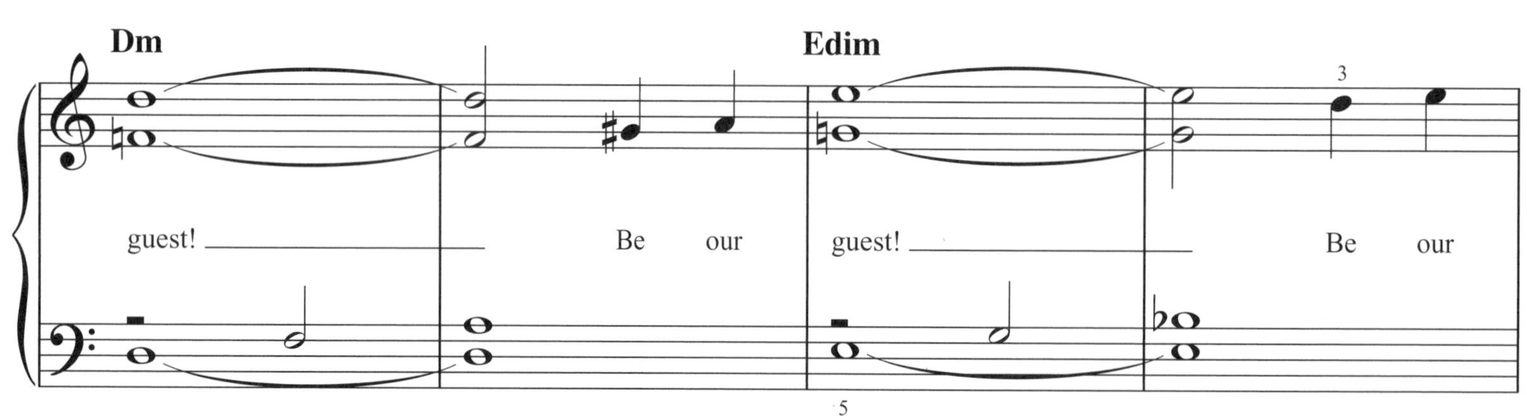
Dm
Edim
guest! Be our guest! Be our

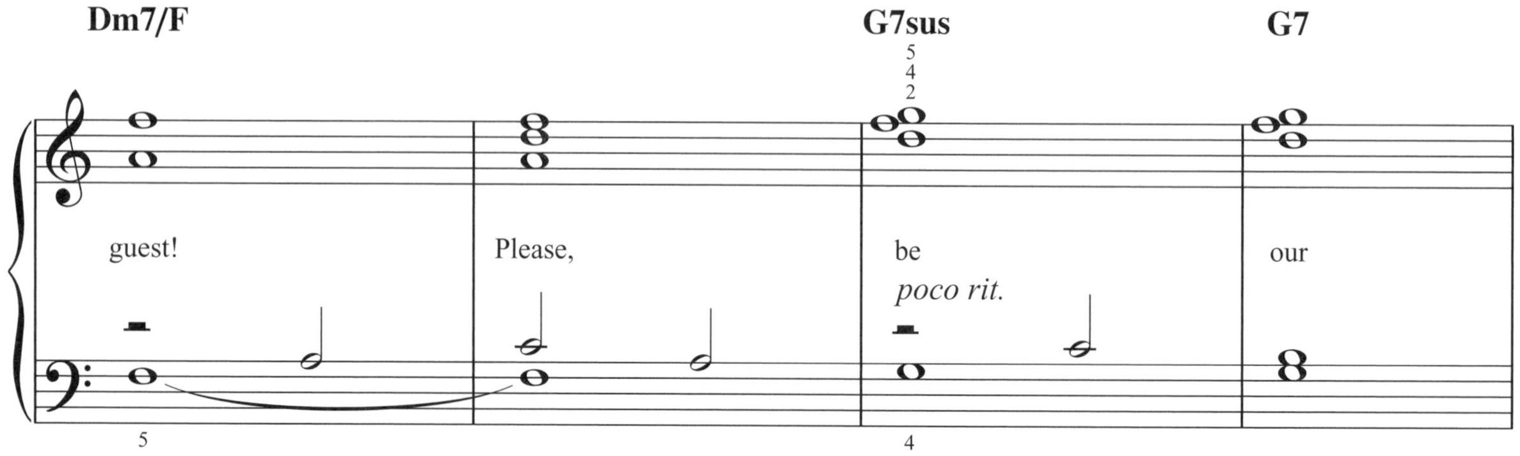
Dm7/F
G7sus
G7
guest! Please, be our
poco rit.

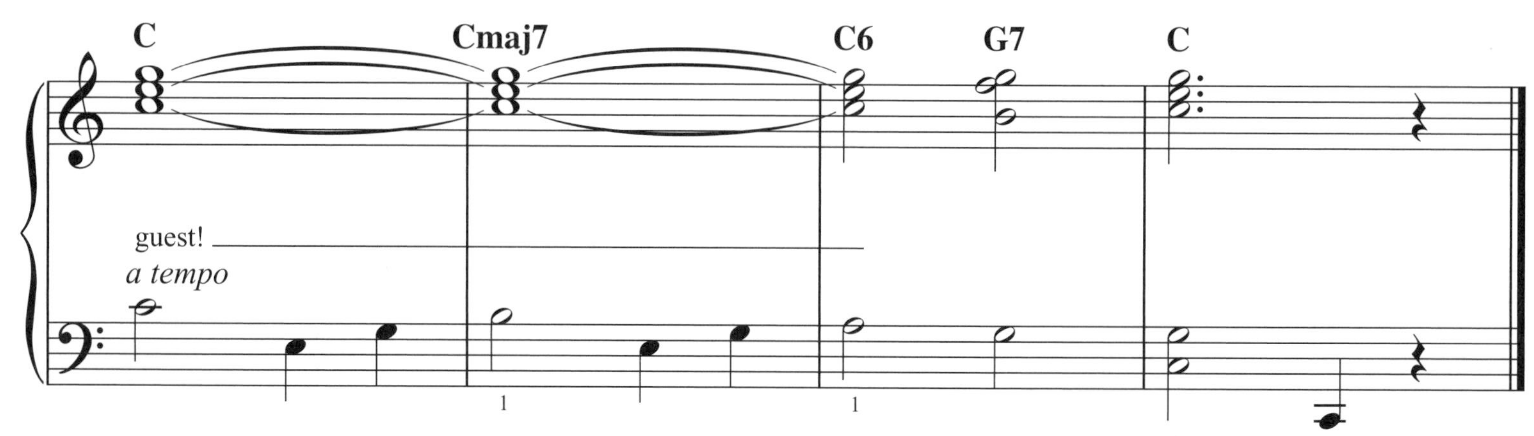
C
Cmaj7
C6
G7
C
guest!
a tempo

BIBBIDI-BOBBIDI-BOO
(The Magic Song)
from CINDERELLA

Words by JERRY LIVINGSTON
Music by MACK DAVID and AL HOFFMAN

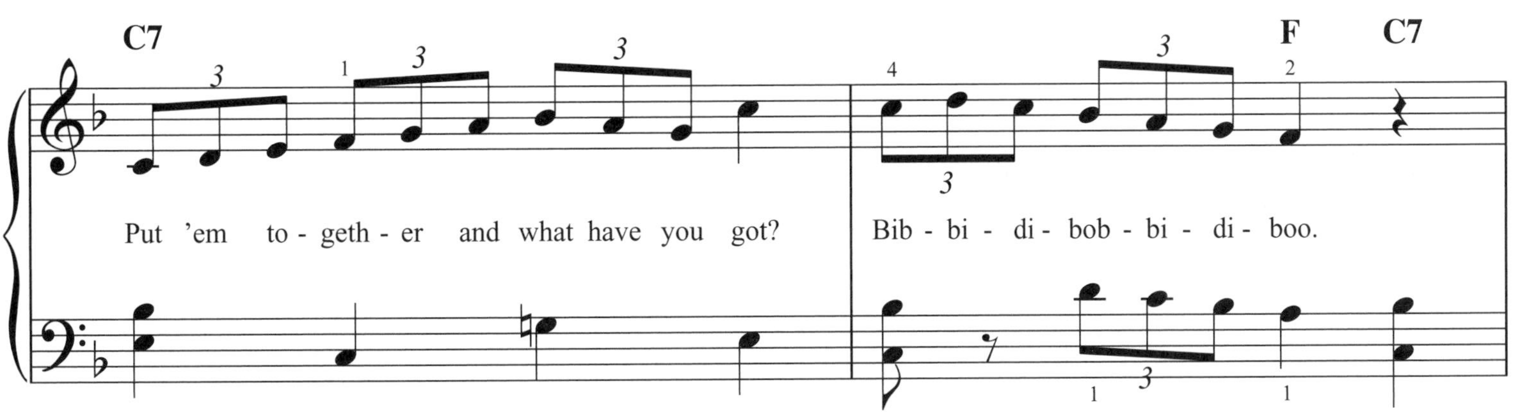

F
Sa - la - ga - doo - la men - chic - ka boo - la
bib - bi - di - bob - bi - di - boo.

C7
F
C7
It - 'll do mag - ic, be - lieve it or not,
bib - bi - di - bob - bi - di - boo.

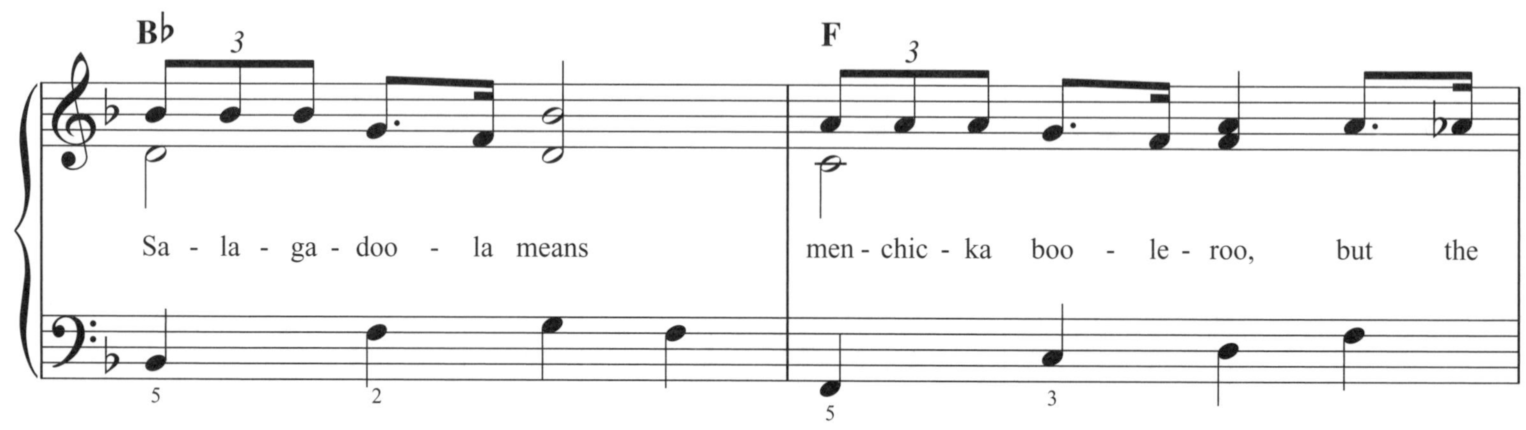
B♭
F
Sa - la - ga - doo - la means
men - chic - ka boo - le - roo, but the

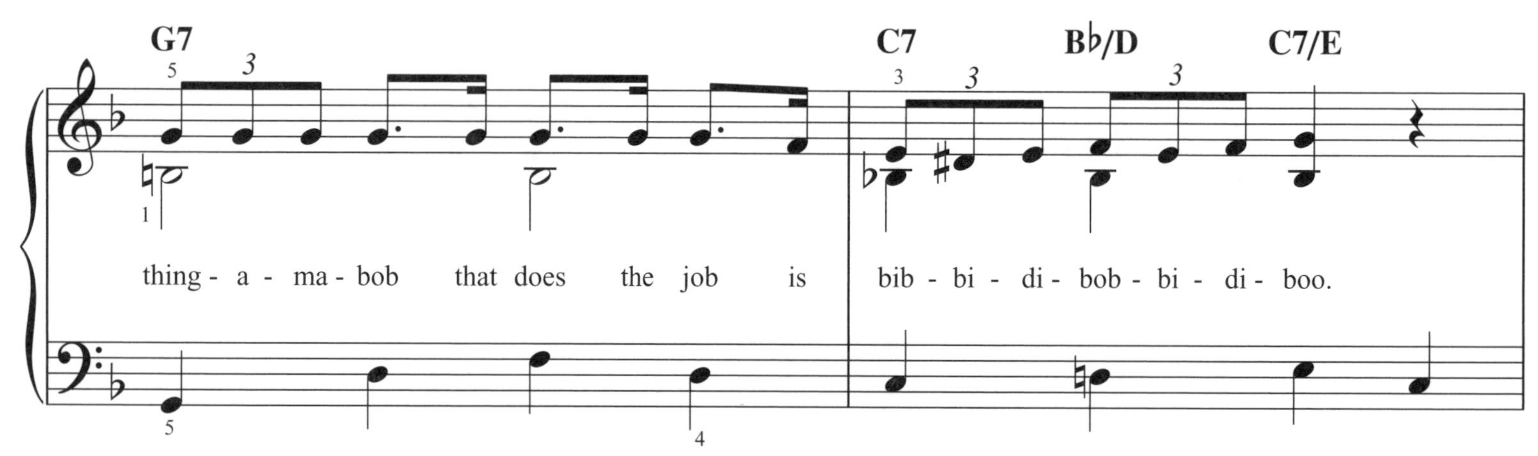
G7
C7
B♭/D
C7/E
thing - a - ma - bob that does the job is
bib - bi - di - bob - bi - di - boo.

F
Sa - la - ga - doo - la men - chic - ka boo - la bib - bi - di - bob - bi - di - boo.
C7
Put 'em to - geth - er and what have you got?
1.
F C7
Bib - bi - di - bob - bi - di - boo.
2.
C7
Bib - bi - di - bob - bi - di, bib - bi - di - bob - bi - di,
F
bib - bi - di - bob - bi - di - boo.
C7 C♯7 B♭/D C7
F

EV'RYBODY WANTS TO BE A CAT

from THE ARISTOCATS

Music by AL RINKER
Words by FLOYD HUDDLESTON

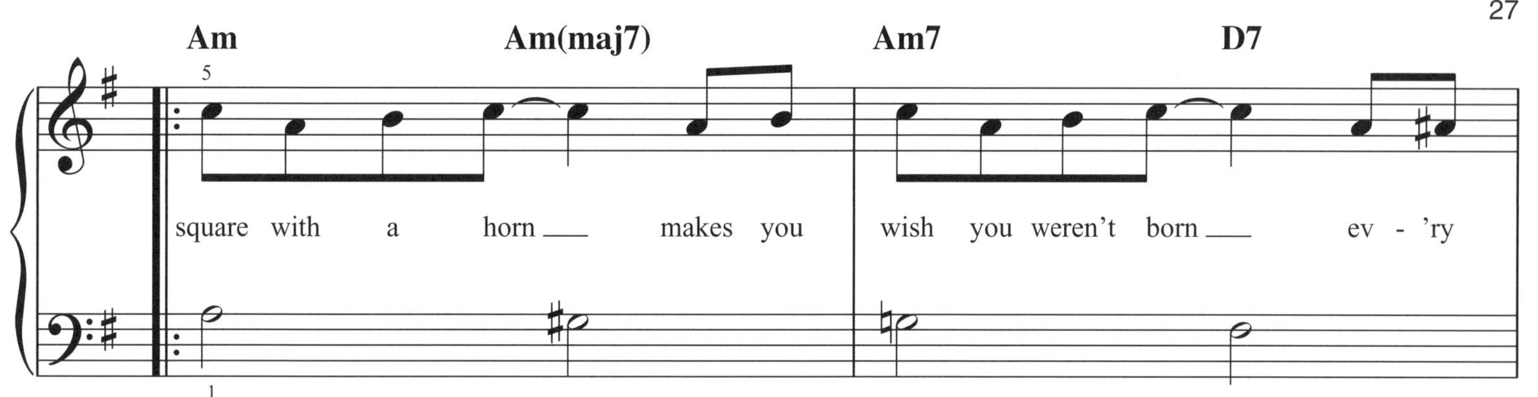
Am
Am(maj7)
Am7
D7
square with a horn makes you
wish you weren't born ev - 'ry

G
time he plays!
But with a

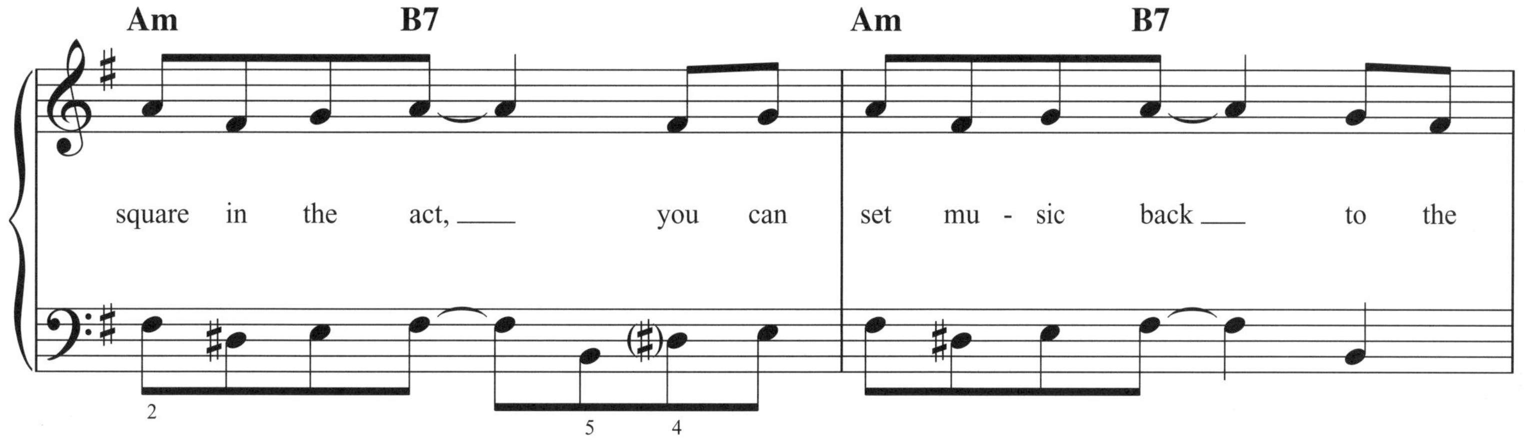
Am
B7
Am
B7
square in the act, you can
set mu - sic back to the

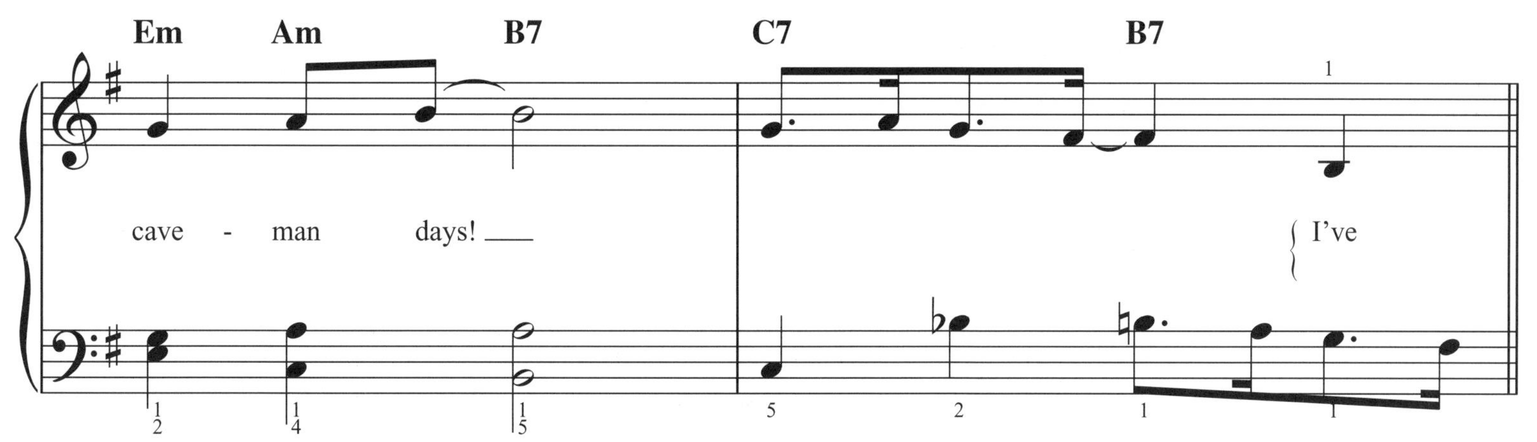
Em
Am
B7
C7
B7
cave - man days!
I've

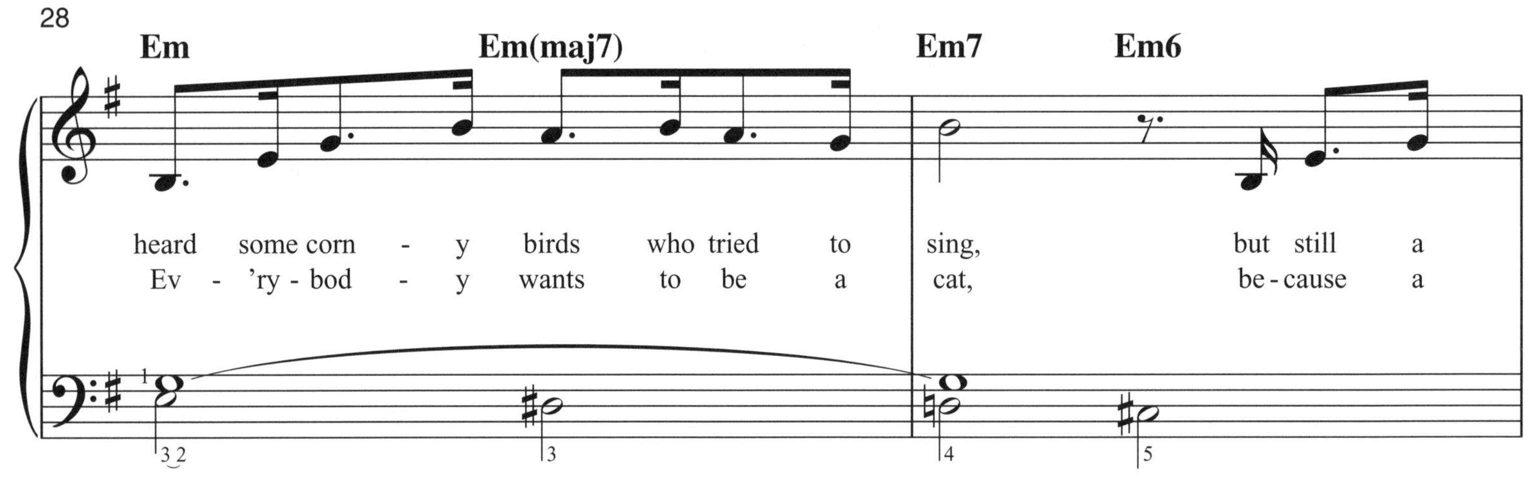
Em
Em(maj7)
Em7
Em6
heard some corn - y birds who tried to sing, but still a
Ev - 'ry - bod - y wants to be a cat, be - cause a

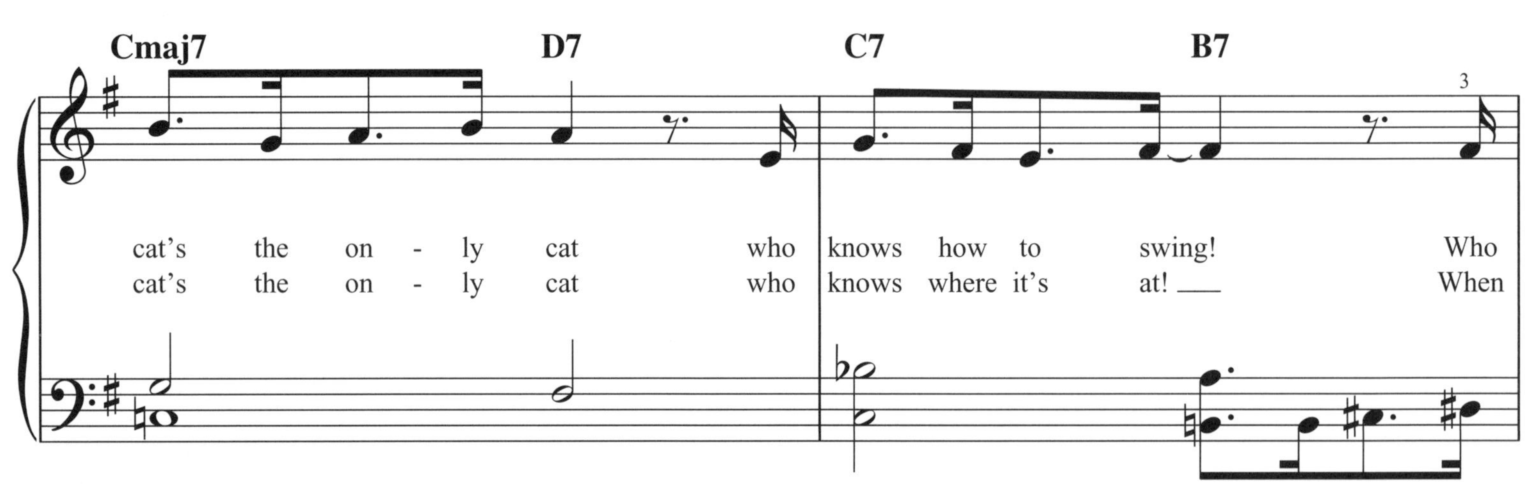
Cmaj7
D7
C7
B7
cat's the on - ly cat who knows how to swing! Who
cat's the on - ly cat who knows where it's at! When

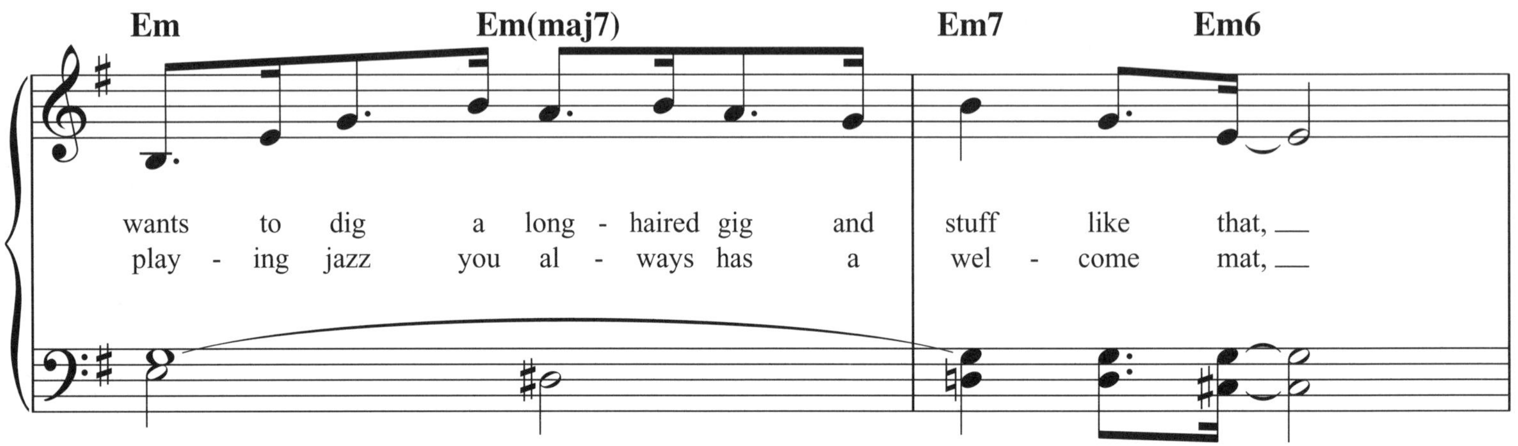
Em
Em(maj7)
Em7
Em6
wants to dig a long - haired gig and stuff like that,
play - ing jazz you al - ways has a wel - come mat,

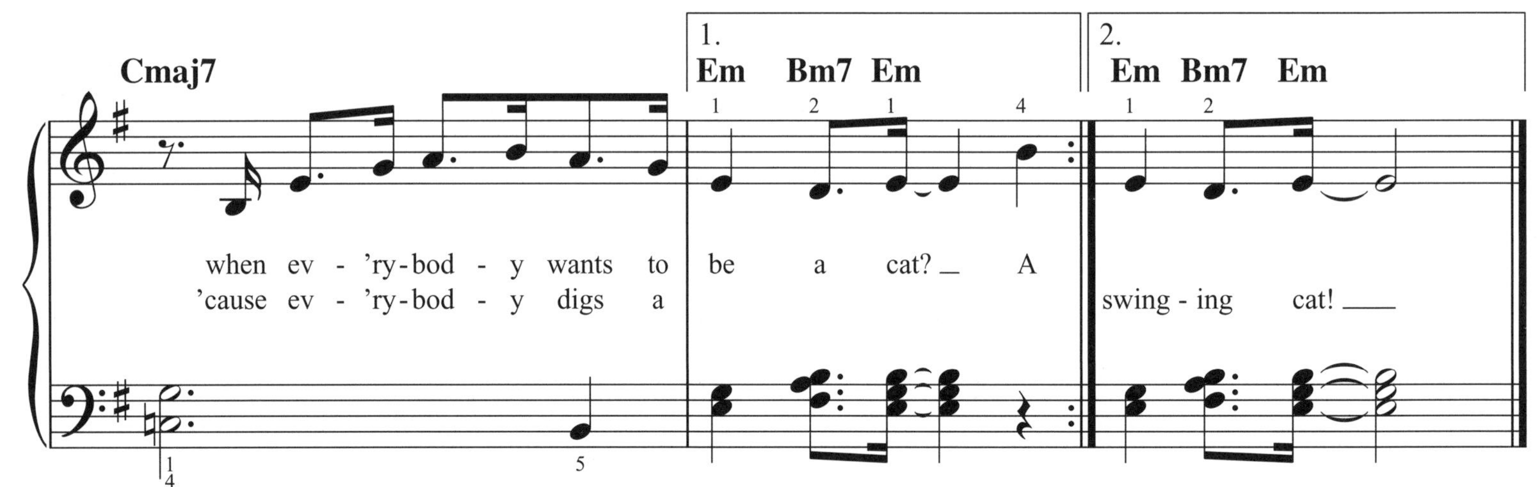
Cmaj7
1.
Em Bm7 Em
2.
Em Bm7 Em
when ev - 'ry-bod - y wants to be a cat? A
'cause ev - 'ry-bod - y digs a swing - ing cat!

HAKUNA MATATA

from THE LION KING

Music by ELTON JOHN
Lyrics by TIM RICE

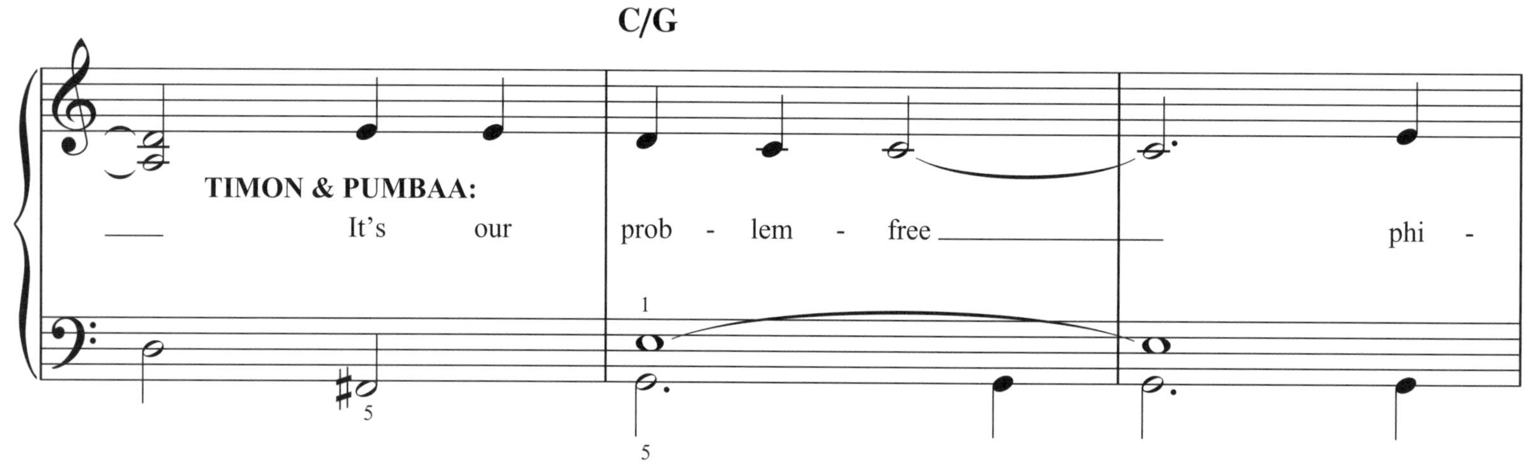
C/G
TIMON & PUMBAA:
It's our prob - lem - free phi -
1
5
5

G
C
2
los - o - phy.
TIMON: Ha - ku - na ma - ta.
rall.

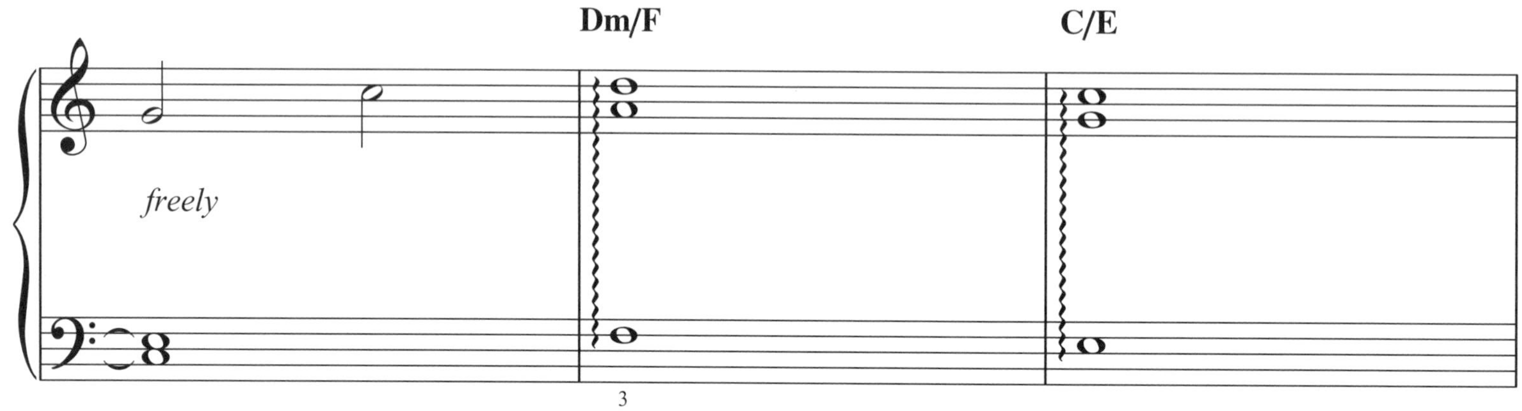
Dm/F
C/E
freely
3

G
Dm
Am
5
1
2

G
N.C.
B♭
F
TIMON: When
he was a young wart -
f

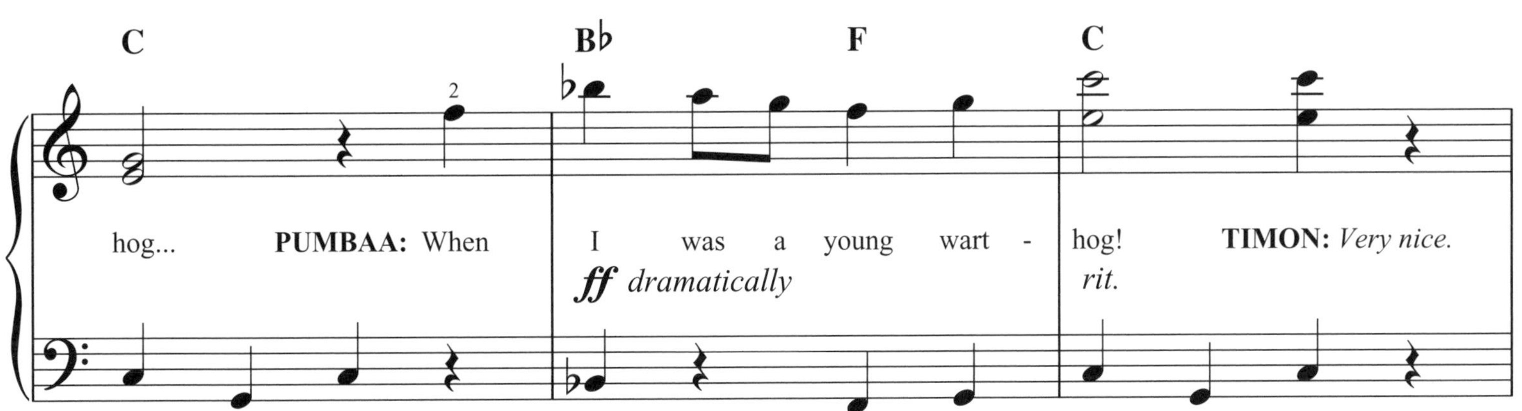
C
B♭
F
C
hog...
PUMBAA: When
I was a young wart -
hog!
TIMON: Very nice.
ff dramatically
rit.

TIMON:
E♭
F
PUMBAA:
Thanks.
He
found his a - ro - ma lacked a
cer - tain ap - peal. He could
mf
somewhat faster

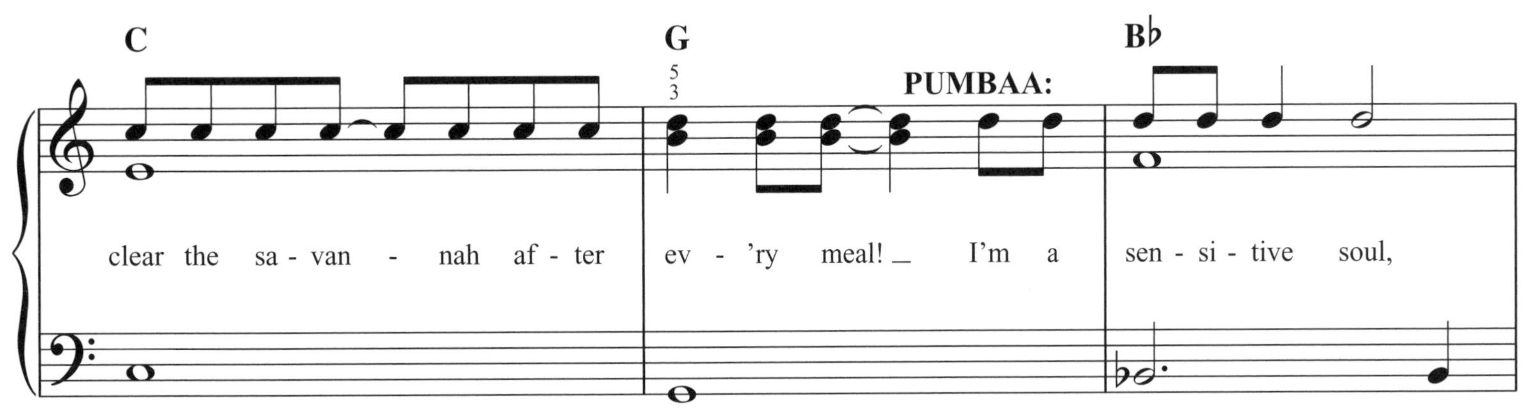
C
G
B♭
PUMBAA:
clear the sa - van - nah af - ter
ev - 'ry meal! I'm a
sen - si - tive soul,

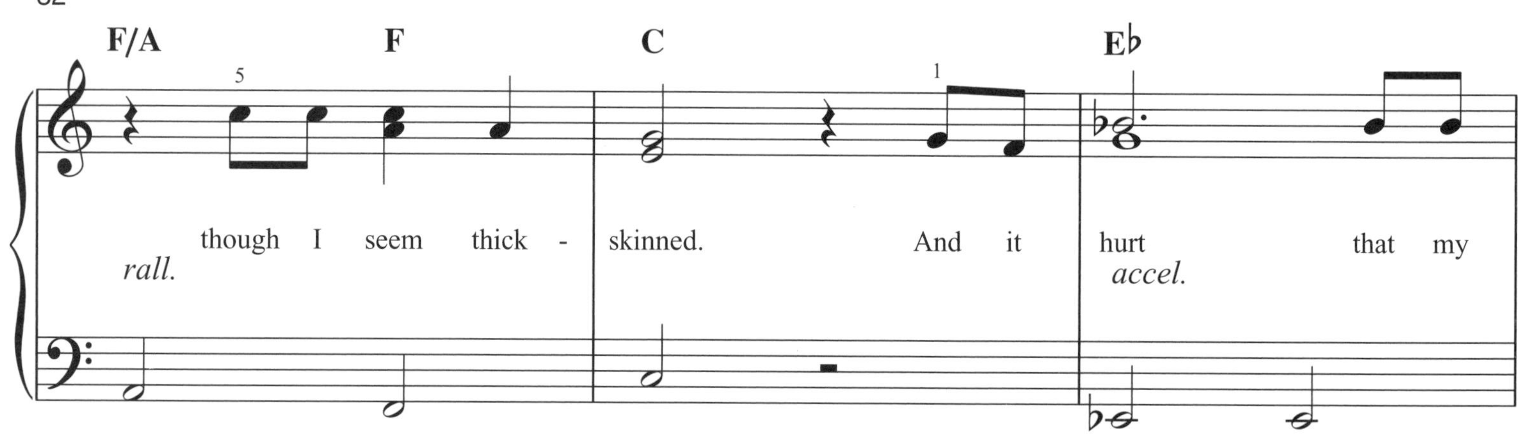
F/A
F
C
E♭
5
1
though I seem thick - skinned. And it hurt that my
rall.
accel.

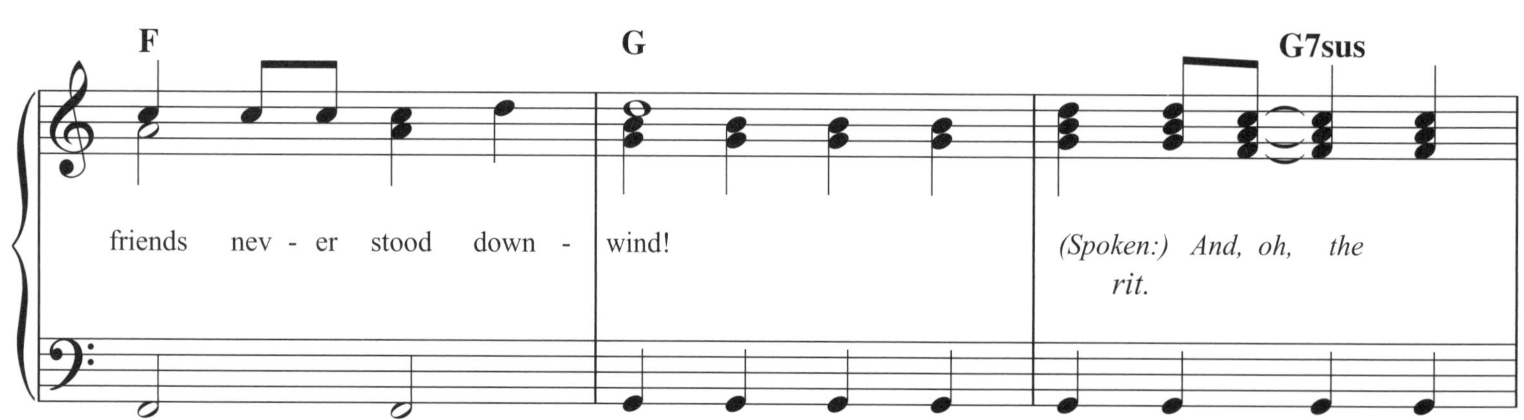
F
G
G7sus
friends nev - er stood down - wind!
(Spoken:) And, oh, the
rit.

C
F/C
C
G
C/G
5
1
3
1
TIMON:
PUMBAA:
TIMON:
shame! He was a - shamed! Thought of chang-in' my name! Oh, what's in a
a tempo

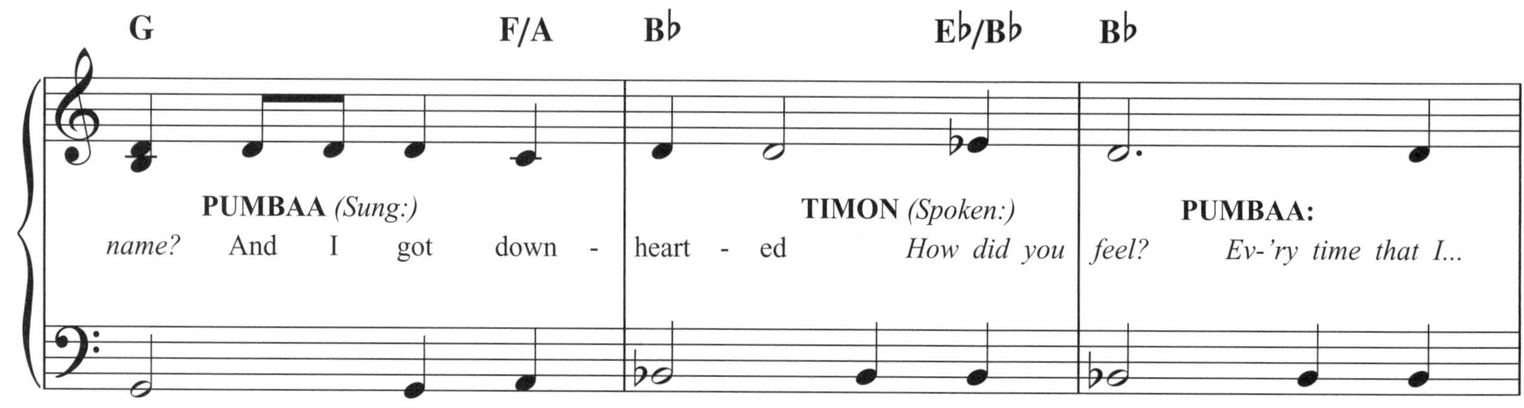
G
F/A
B♭
E♭/B♭
B♭
PUMBAA (Sung:)
TIMON (Spoken:)
PUMBAA:
name? And I got down - heart - ed How did you feel? Ev-'ry time that I...

N.C.
C
TIMON:
Hey, Pumbaa, not in front of the kids.
PUMBAA:
Oh, sorry.
TIMON & PUMBAA:
Ha - ku - na ma -
f

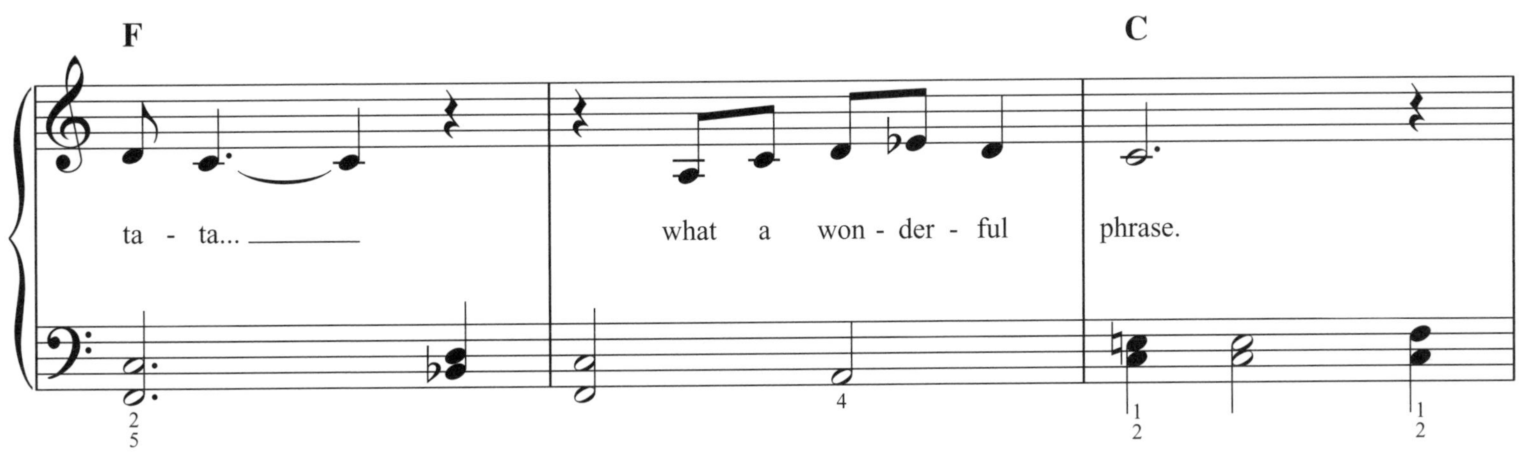
F
C
ta - ta...
what a won - der - ful
phrase.

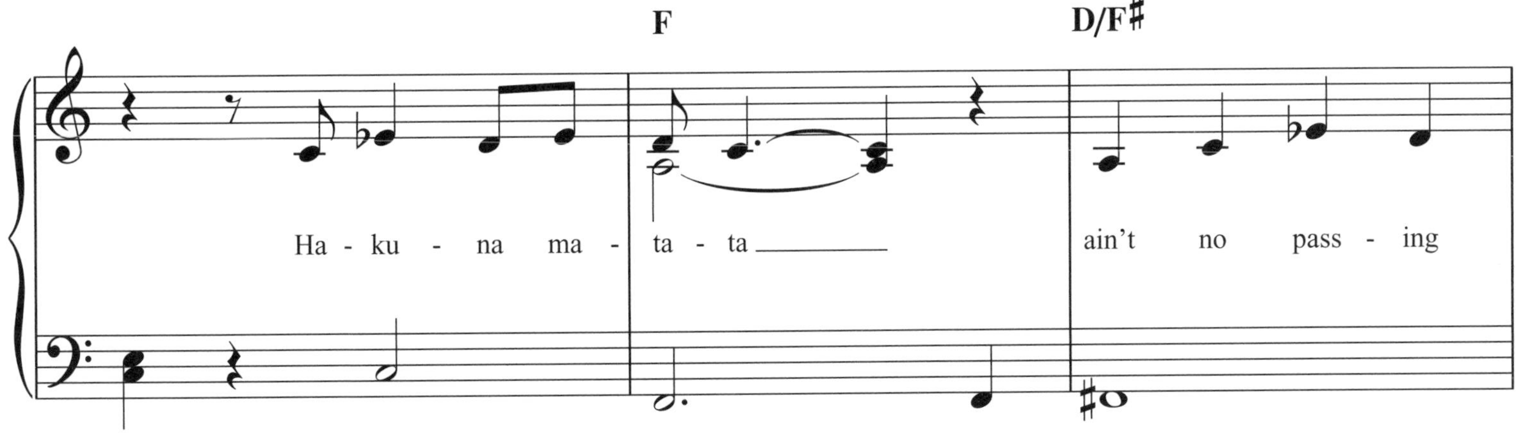
F
D/F♯
Ha - ku - na ma -
ta - ta
ain't no pass - ing

G
E/G♯
Am
craze.
SIMBA: It means no
wor - ries

34

C/E
F
D/F♯
for the rest of your days.
TIMON: Yeah, sing it, kid!
TIMON & SIMBA:
It's our

C/G
G
prob - lem - free
PUMBAA: phi - los - o - phy.

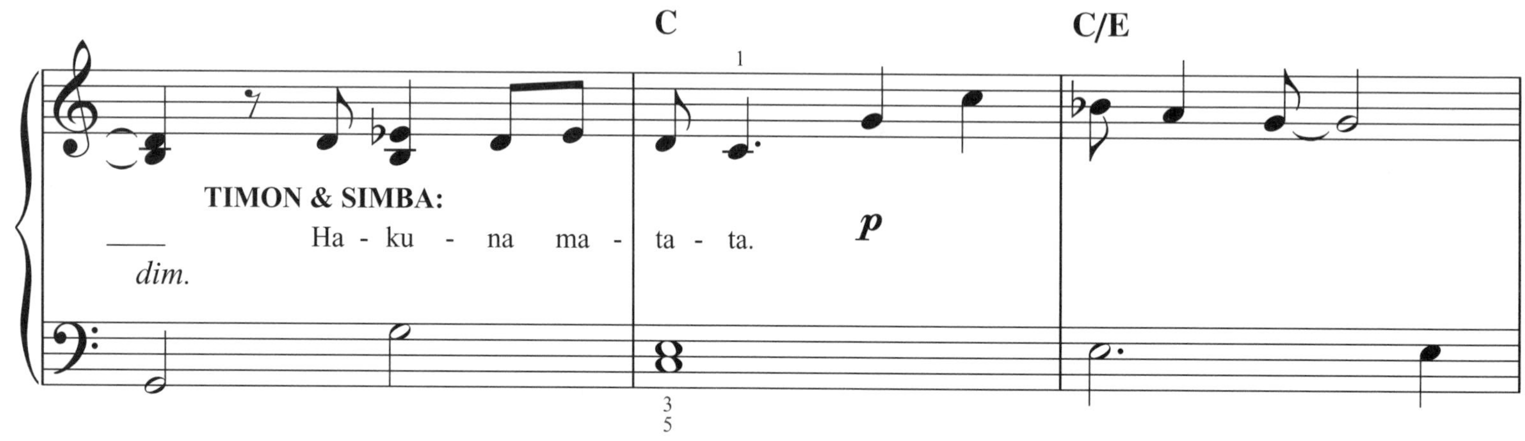
C
C/E
TIMON & SIMBA:
Ha - ku - na ma - ta - ta.
dim.
p

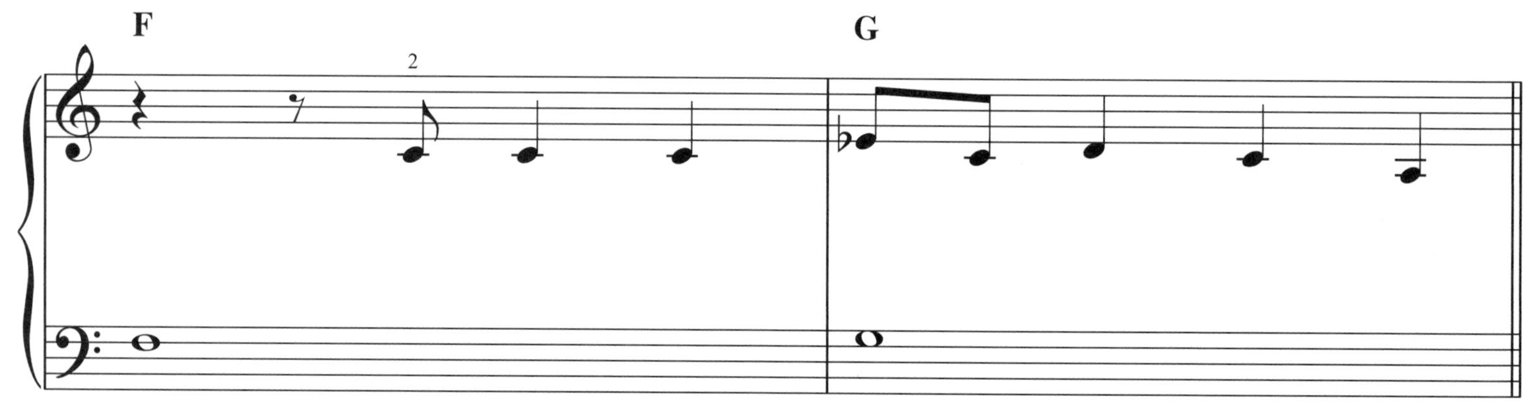
F
G

1.
C
C/E
F
G
2
2

2.
G
C
F
ALL (Spoken:)
Hakuna matata.
cresc. poco a poco
Hakuna matata.
Add pedal

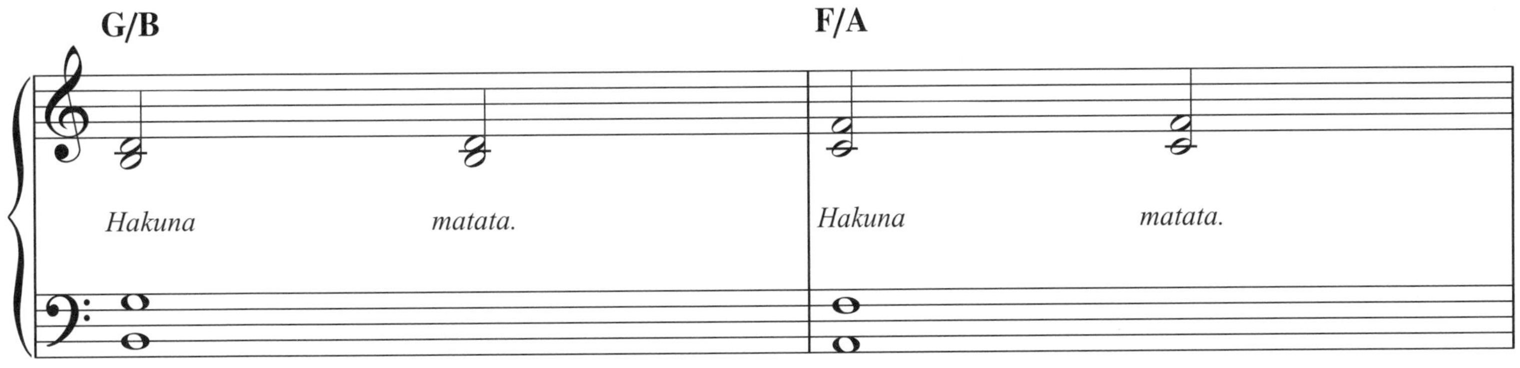
G/B
F/A
Hakuna matata.
Hakuna matata.

C/G
Hakuna matata.
Hakuna matata.

G
E/G♯
Am
4
1 2
TIMON (Sung:)
Hakuna matata.
Hakuna... It means no
wor - ries
f

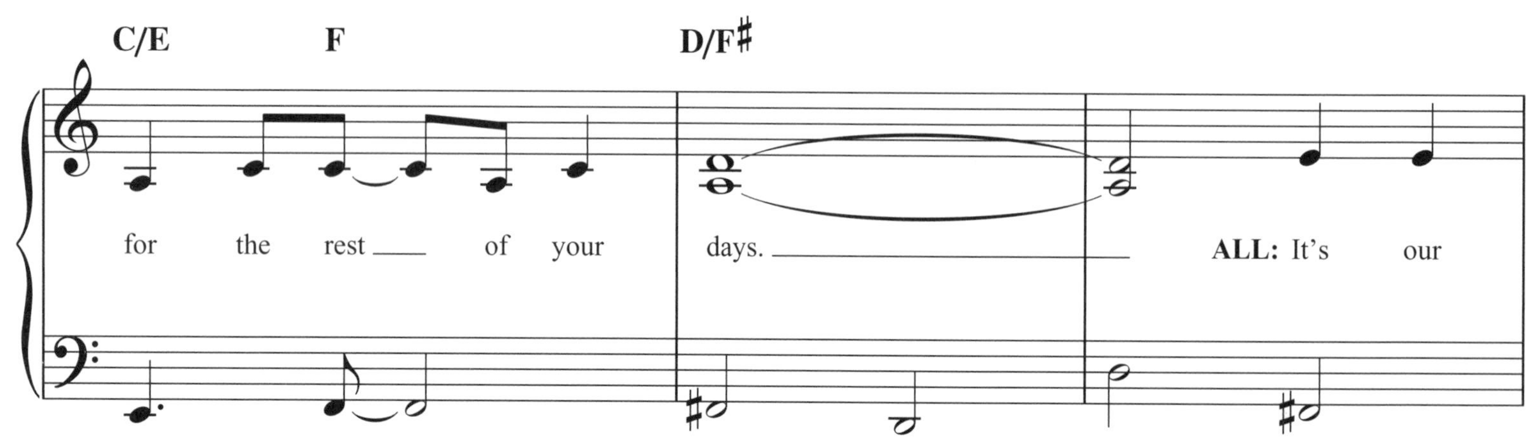
C/E
F
D/F♯
for the rest of your
days.
ALL: It's our

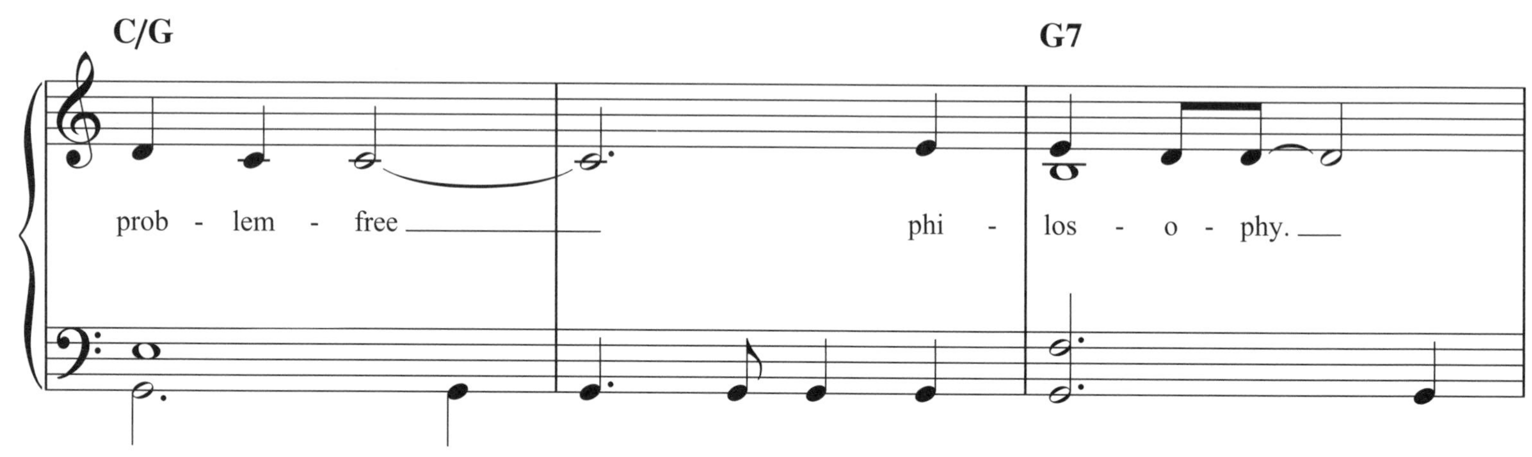
C/G
G7
prob - lem - free
phi - los - o - phy.

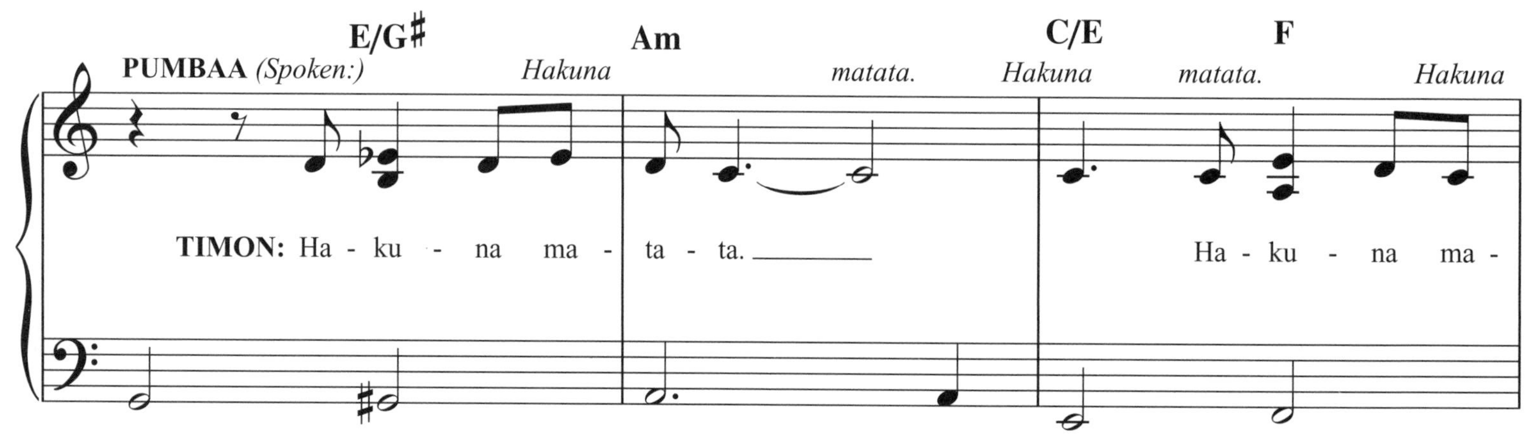
E/G♯
Am
C/E
F
PUMBAA (Spoken:)
Hakuna
matata.
Hakuna
matata.
Hakuna
TIMON: Ha - ku - na ma - ta - ta.
Ha - ku - na ma -

G
E/G♯
Am
matata.
Hakuna
matata.
ta - ta.
Ha - ku - na ma - ta - ta.

C/E
F
G
Ha - ku - na ma - ta - ta. Ha - ku - na ma -

C
C/E
F
ta - ta.
Ha - ku - na ma - ta - ta.

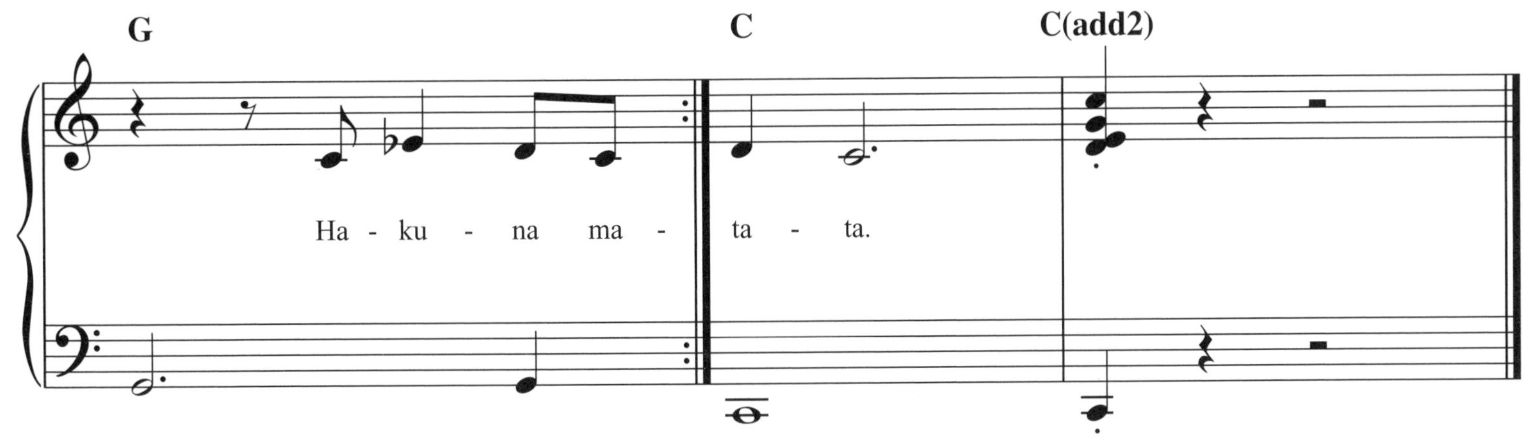
G
C
C(add2)
Ha - ku - na ma - ta - ta.

FRIEND LIKE ME

from ALADDIN

Music by ALAN MENKEN
Lyrics by HOWARD ASHMAN

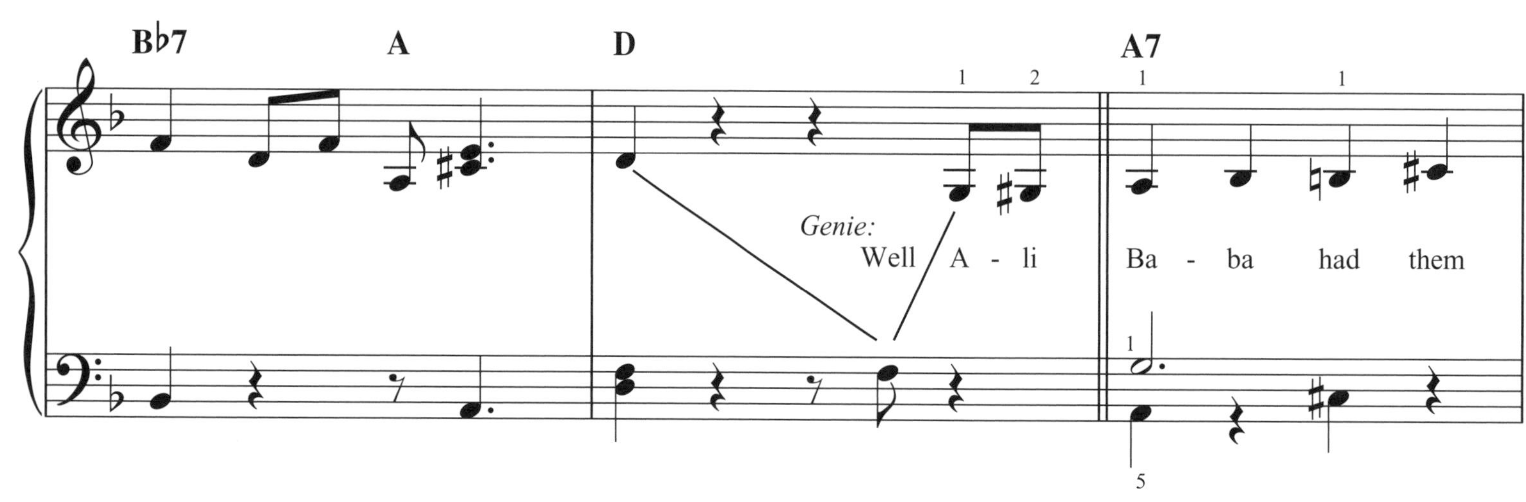

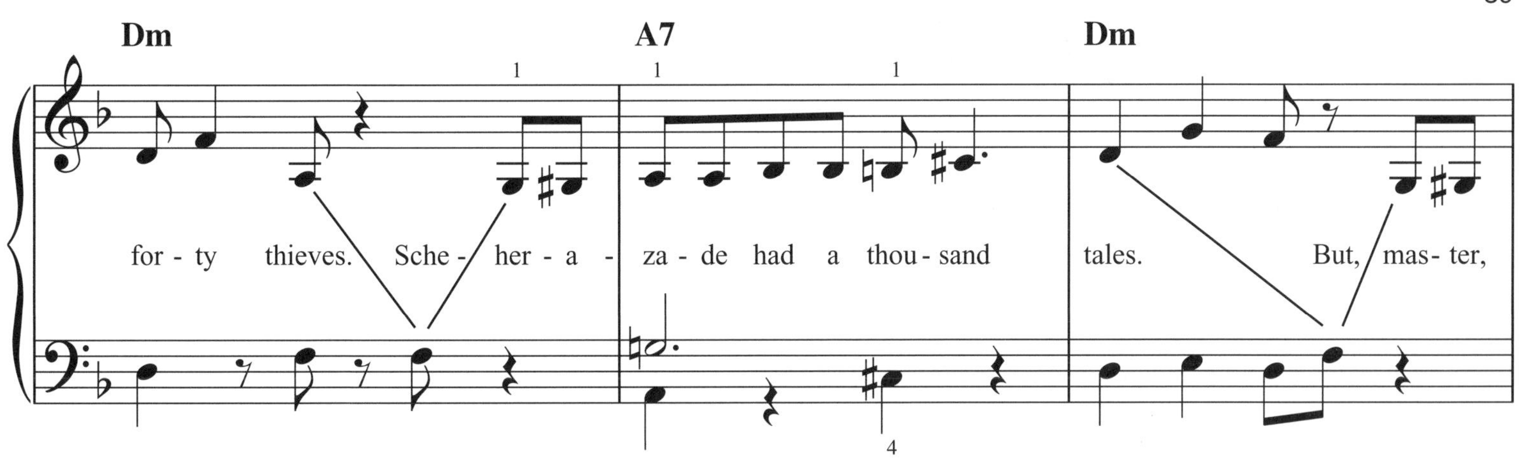
Dm
A7
Dm
for - ty thieves. Sche - her - a - za - de had a thou - sand tales. But, mas- ter,

A7
Dm
E7
you in luck 'cause up your sleeves you got a brand of mag - ic nev - er

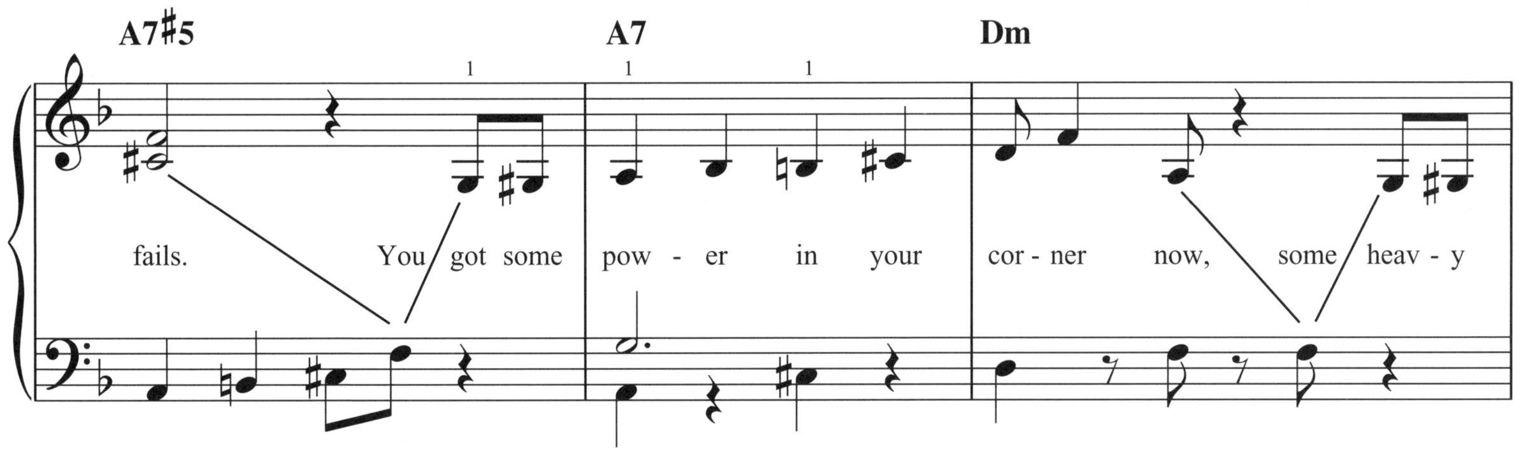
A7♯5
A7
Dm
fails. You got some pow - er in your cor - ner now, some heav - y

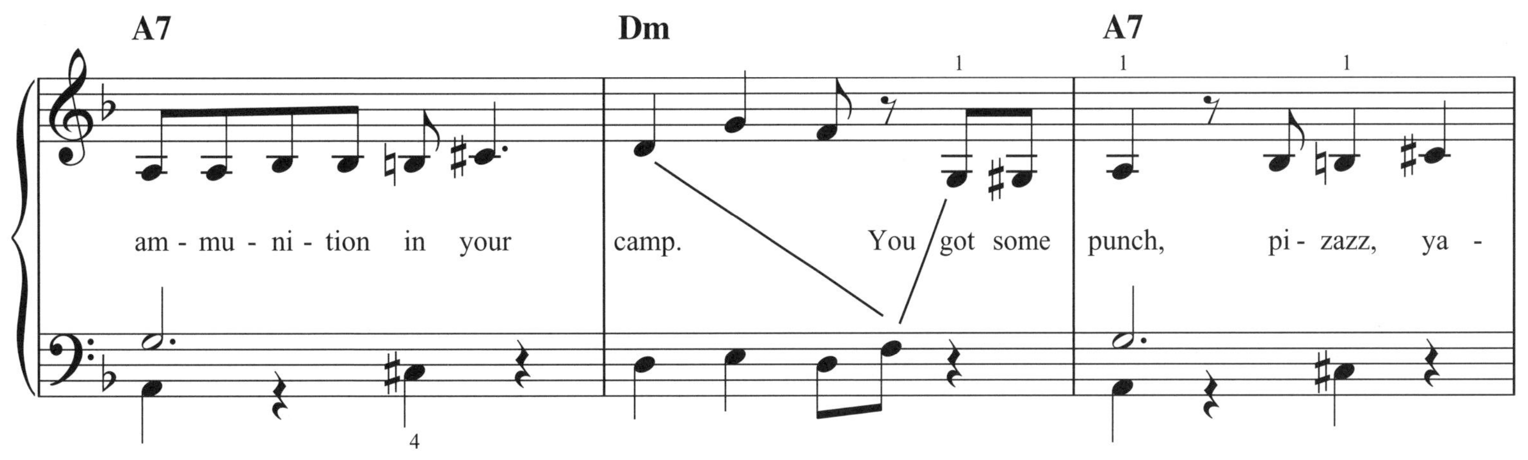
A7
Dm
A7
am - mu - ni - tion in your camp. You got some punch, pi - zazz, ya -

Dm
E7
A7♯5
hoo and how. See, all you
got - ta do is rub that
lamp. And I'll say

Dm
B♭7
A7
Dm
Mis - ter A - lad - din sir, what
will your pleas - ure

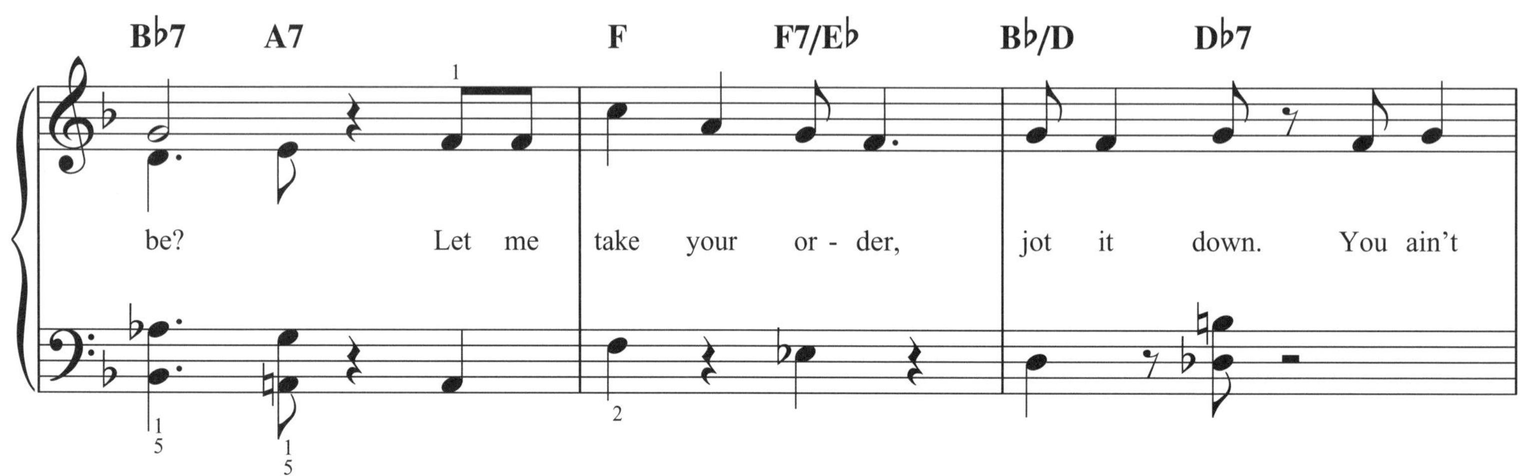
B♭7
A7
F
F7/E♭
B♭/D
D♭7
be? Let me
take your or - der,
jot it down. You ain't

F/C
A7♯5
D5
B♭7
A7
Dm
nev - er had a friend like
me. No no no.
Life is your

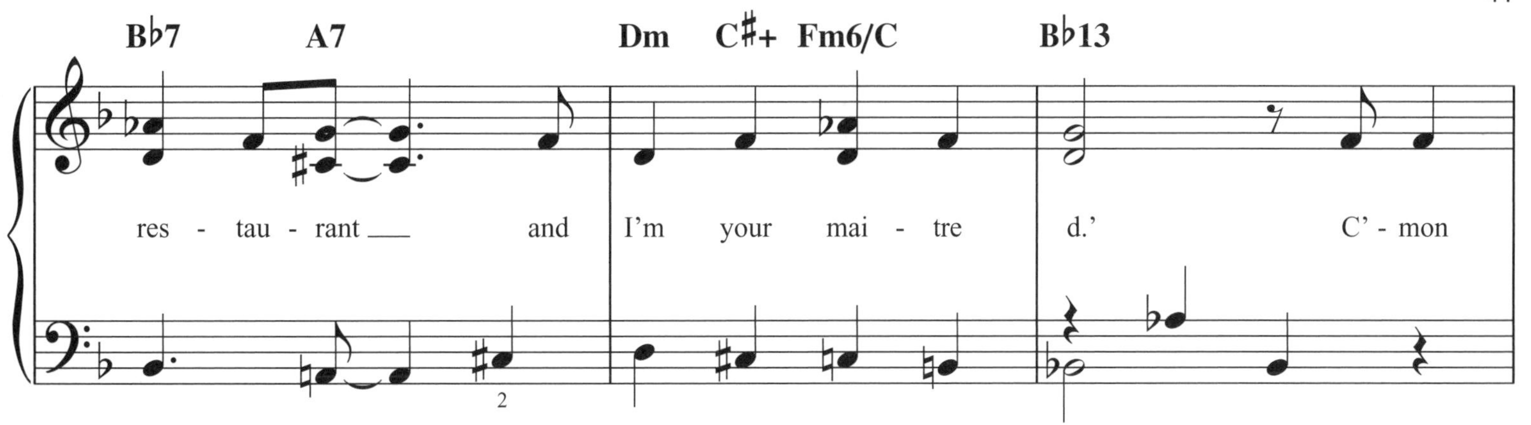
B♭7
A7
Dm
C♯+
Fm6/C
B♭13
res - tau - rant ___ and
I'm your mai - tre
d.' C' - mon
2

F
F/E♭
B♭/D
B♭/D♭
F/C
A7♯5
3
whis - per what it
is you want. You ain't
nev - er had a friend like
2

Dm
B♭7
4
4
3
me. Yes, sir, we
pride our - selves on
ser - vice. You're the

Dm
A7
Dm
B♭13
3
1
boss, the king, the
shah. Say
what you wish. ___ It's

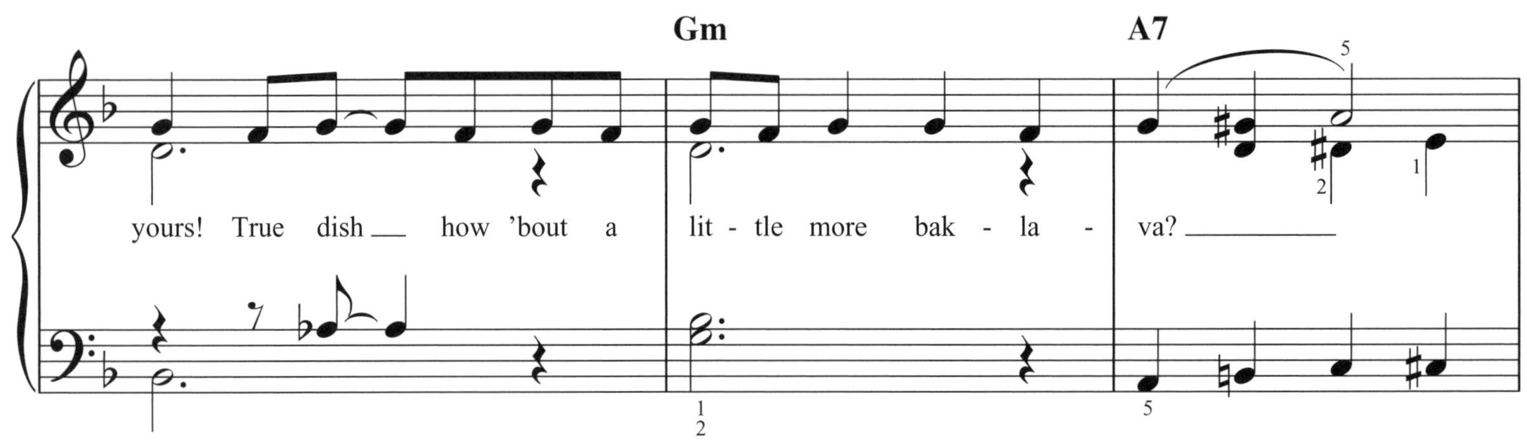
Gm
A7
yours! True dish __ how 'bout a
lit - tle more bak - la - va? ________

Dm
B♭7
A7
Dm
Have some of
col - umn "A." __ Try
all of col - umn

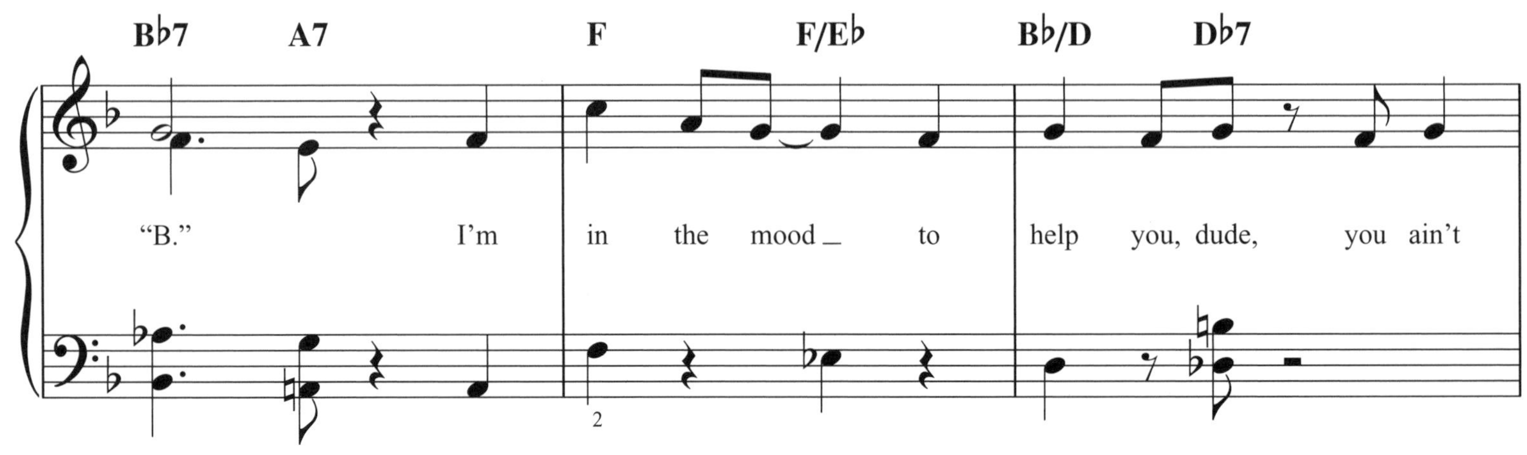
B♭7
A7
F
F/E♭
B♭/D
D♭7
"B." I'm
in the mood _ to
help you, dude, you ain't

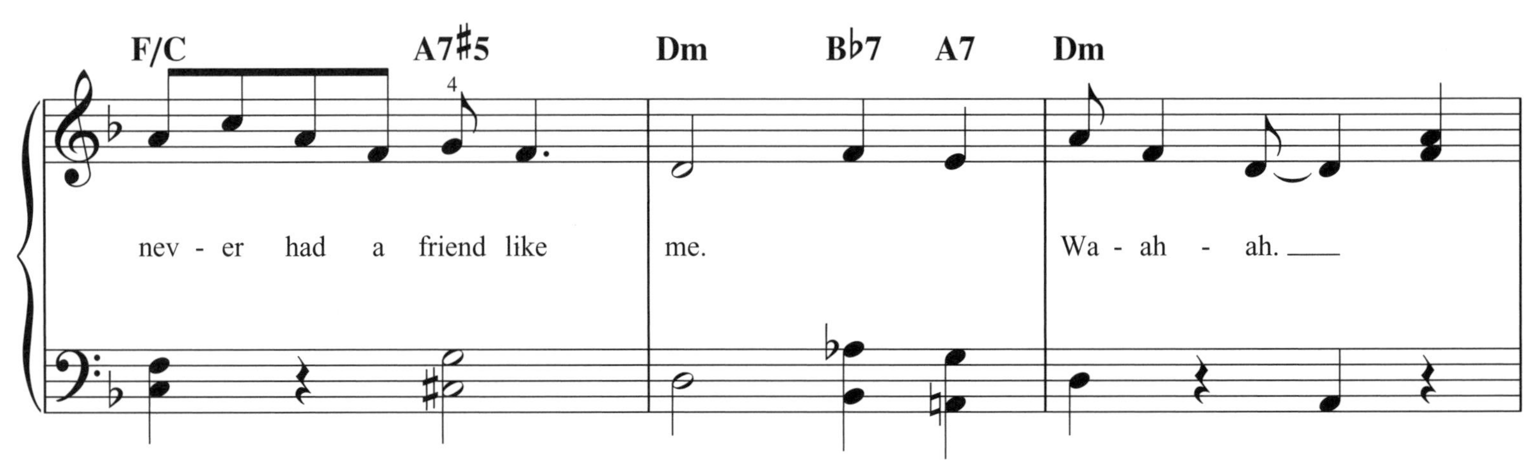
F/C
A7♯5
Dm
B♭7
A7
Dm
nev - er had a friend like
me.
Wa - ah - ah. ___

B♭7 A7
Dm
B♭7 A7
Oh my.
Wa - ah - ah.
No no.

Dm
B♭7 A7
B♭7 A7
Wa - ah - ah.
Na na na.

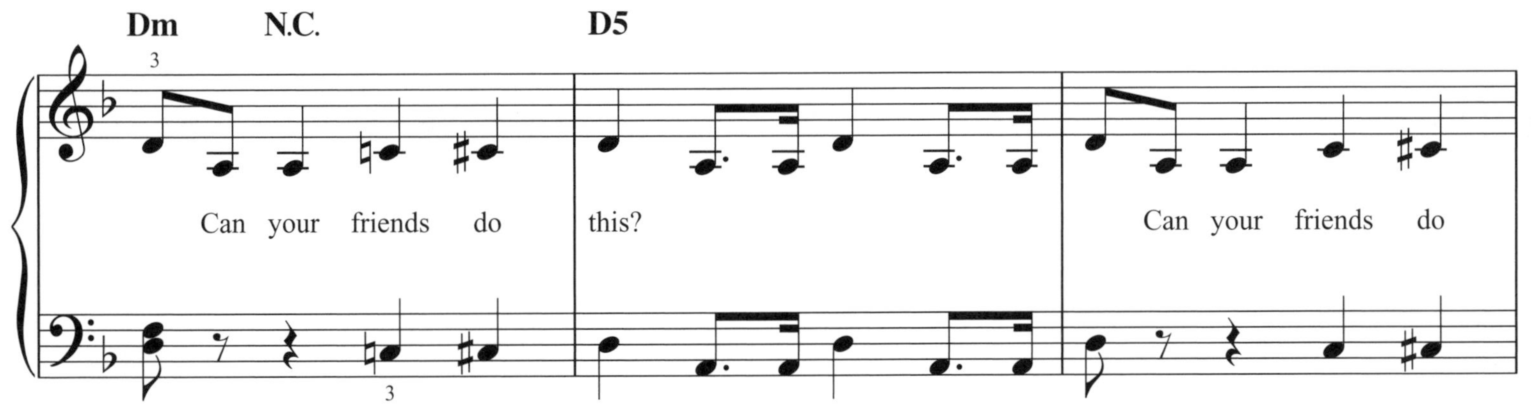
Dm N.C.
D5
Can your friends do
this?
Can your friends do

F5
that?
Can your friends pull
this

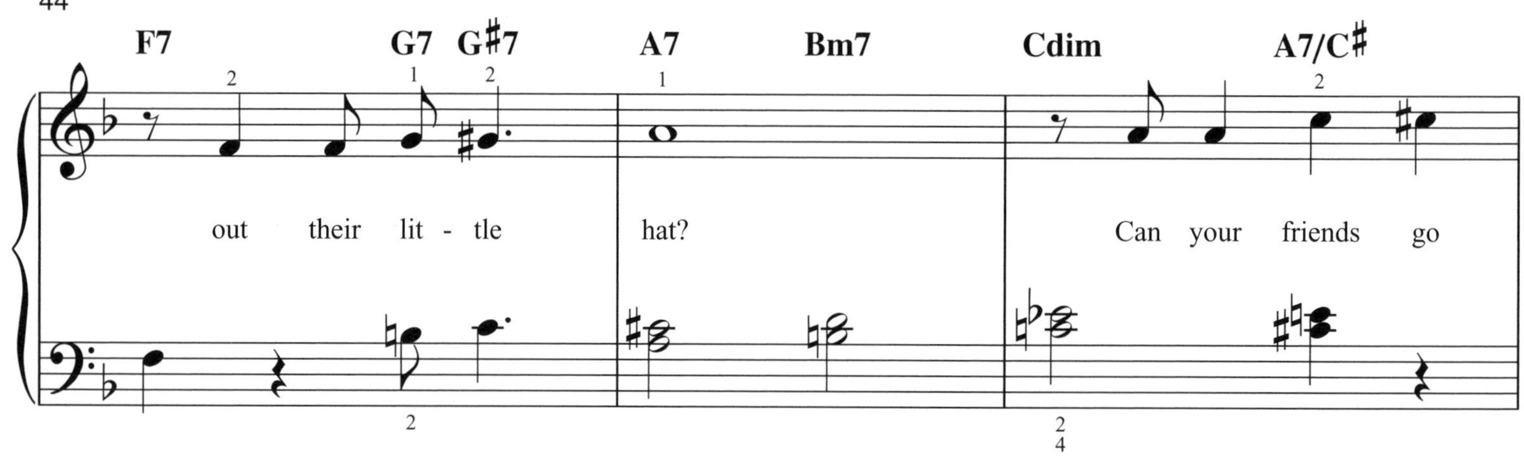
F7
G7
G♯7
A7
Bm7
Cdim
A7/C♯
out their lit - tle
hat?
Can your friends go

Dm
poof!
Well, look - y here.

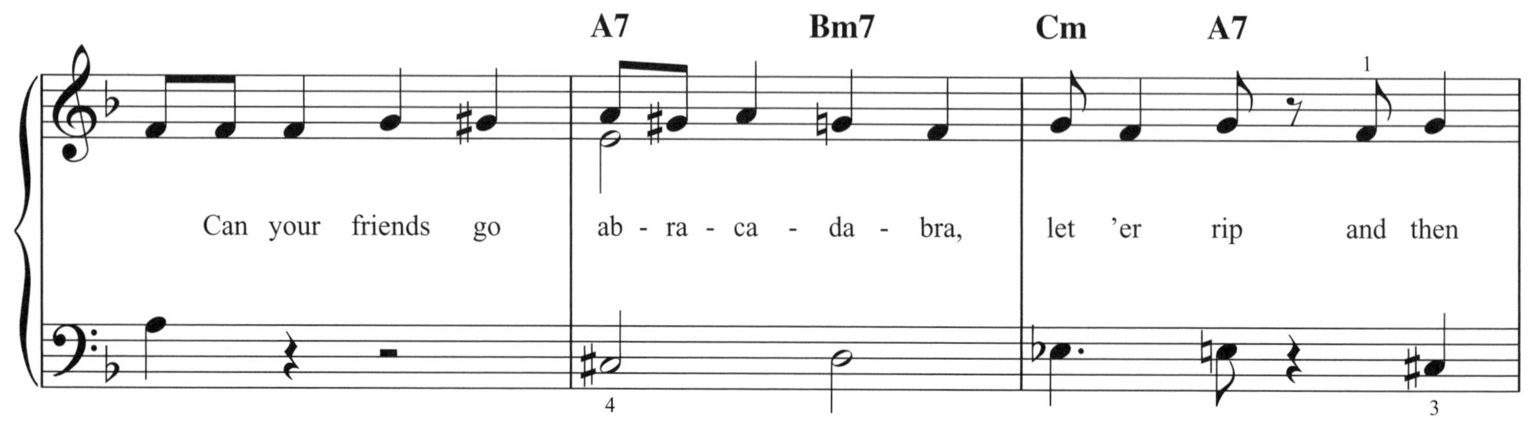
A7
Bm7
Cm
A7
Can your friends go
ab - ra - ca - da - bra,
let 'er rip and then

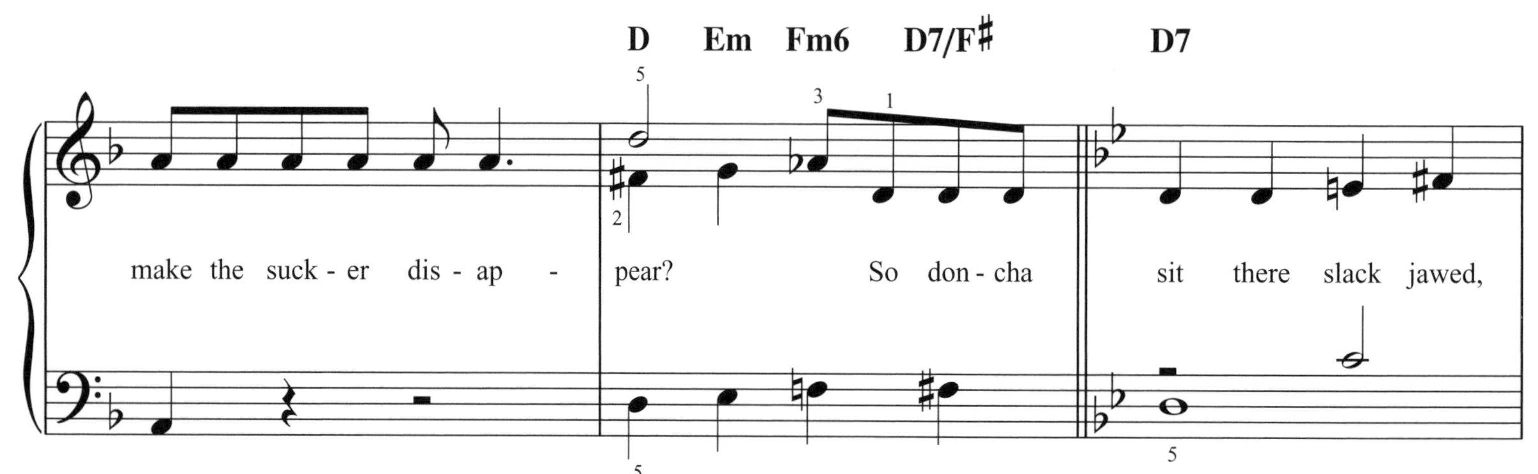
D
Em
Fm6
D7/F♯
D7
make the suck - er dis - ap - pear?
So don - cha
sit there slack jawed,

Gm
D7
Gm
bug - gy eyed. I'm here to
an- swer all your mid - day
prayers. You got me

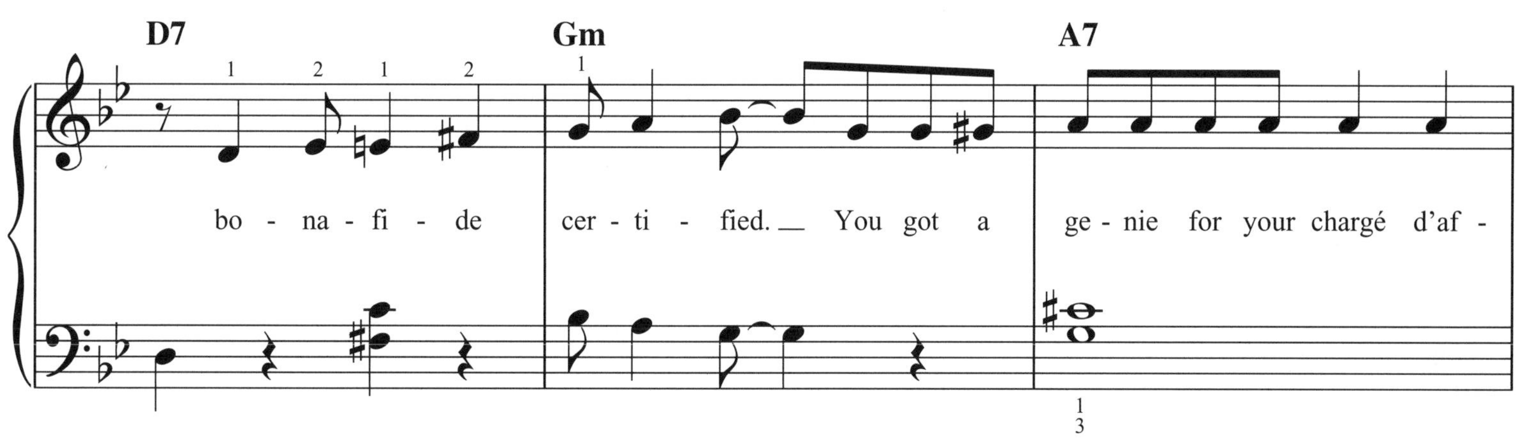
D7
Gm
A7
bo - na - fi - de
cer - ti - fied. You got a
ge - nie for your chargé d'af -

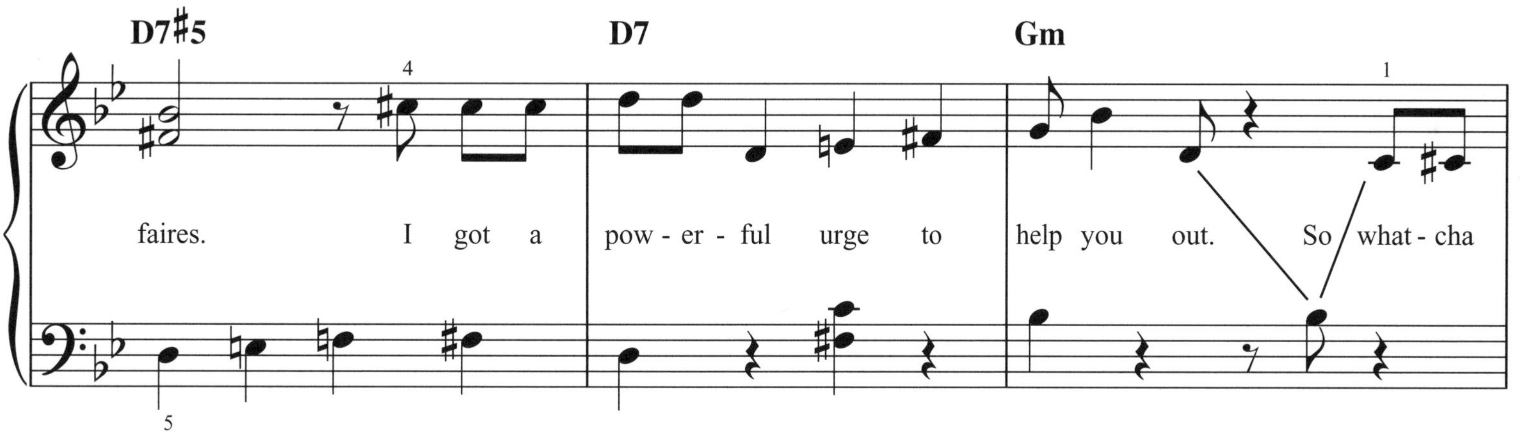
D7♯5
D7
Gm
faires. I got a
pow - er - ful urge to
help you out. So what - cha

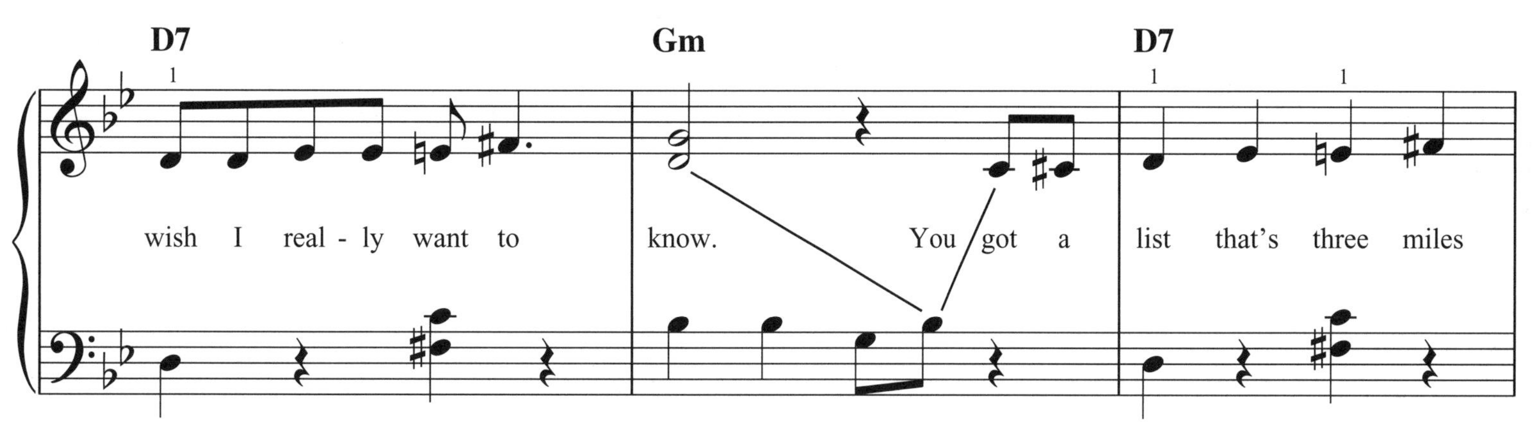
D7
Gm
D7
wish I real - ly want to
know. You got a
list that's three miles

Gm
A7
D7♯5
long no doubt. Well, all you
got - ta do is rub like
so. And oh.

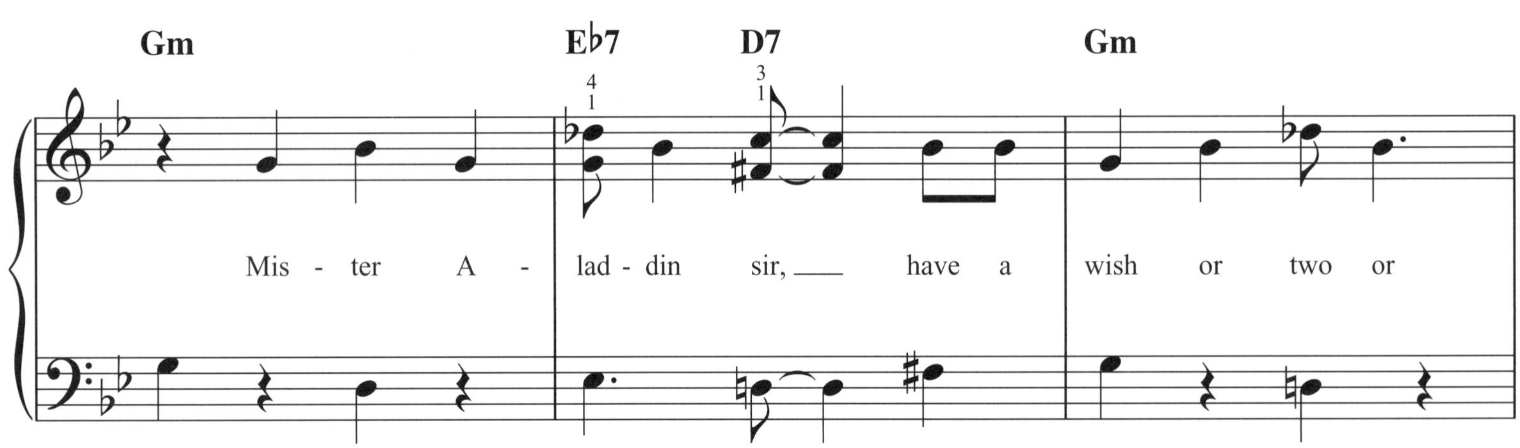
Gm
E♭7
D7
Gm
Mis - ter A - lad - din sir, have a
wish or two or

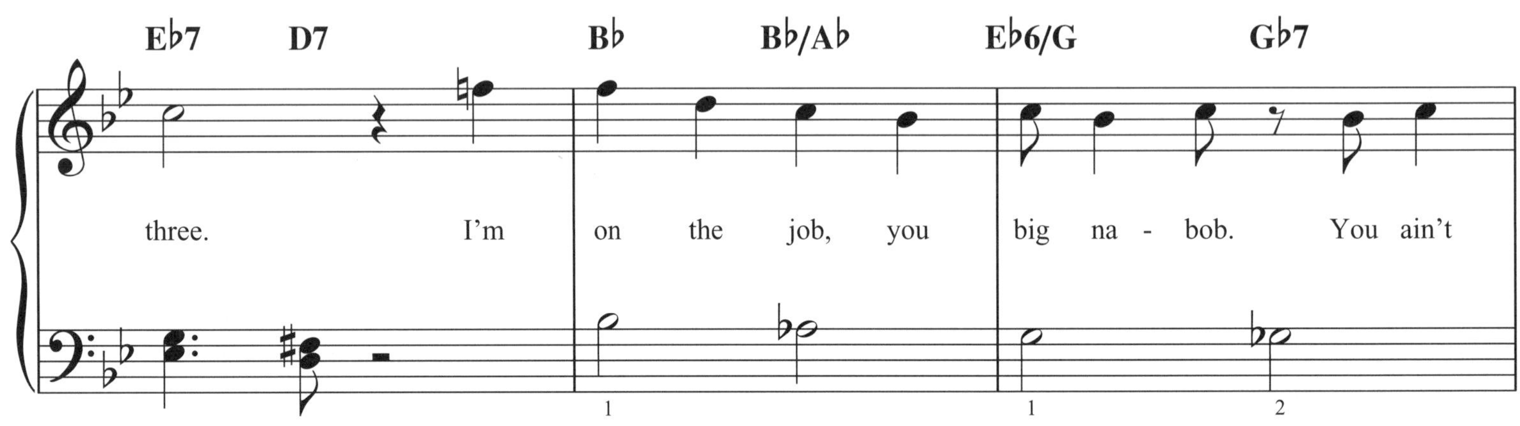
E♭7
D7
B♭
B♭/A♭
E♭6/G
G♭7
three. I'm
on the job, you
big na - bob. You ain't

B♭/F
G♭7
nev - er had a friend, nev - er
had a friend, you ain't
nev - er had a friend, nev - er

Eb7b5
had a friend. You ain't
nev - er
had a
D7sus
D7
Gm
Eb7 D7
friend
like
me.
Gm
Eb7 D7
Gm
Wa - ah ah.
Wa - ah ah.
Eb7 D7
Eb7
D7
Gm
You ain't
nev - er had a friend like
me. Ha!

GIVE A LITTLE WHISTLE

from PINOCCHIO

Words by NED WASHINGTON
Music by LEIGH HARLINE

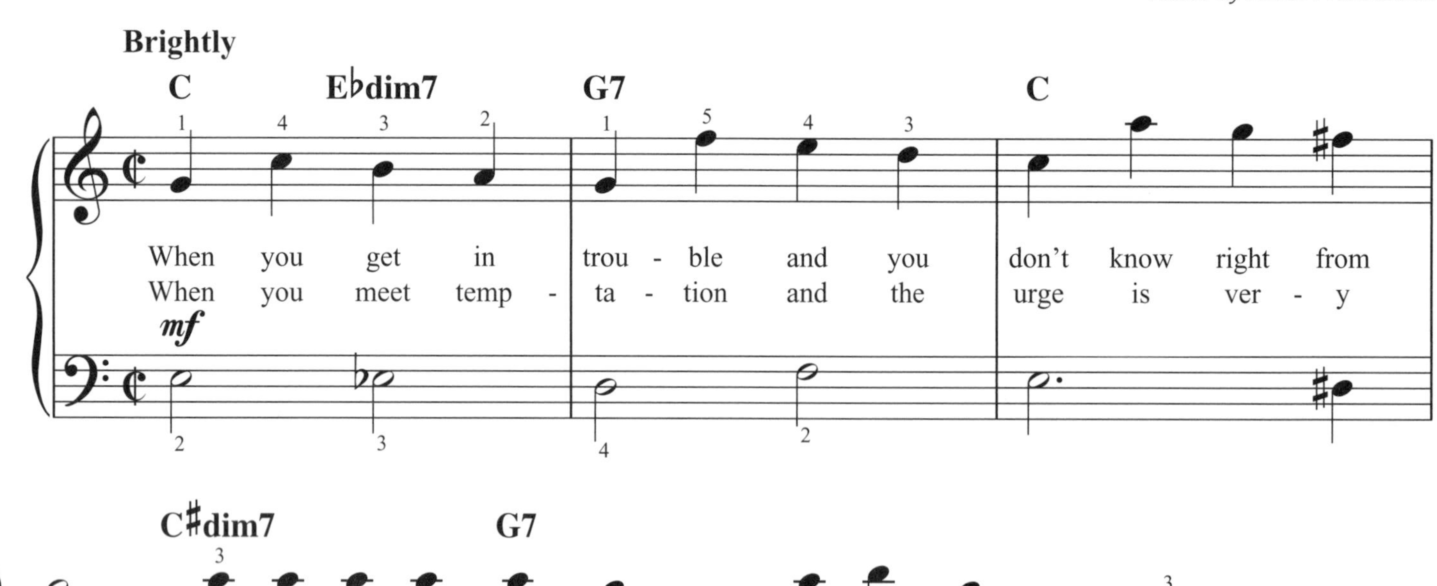

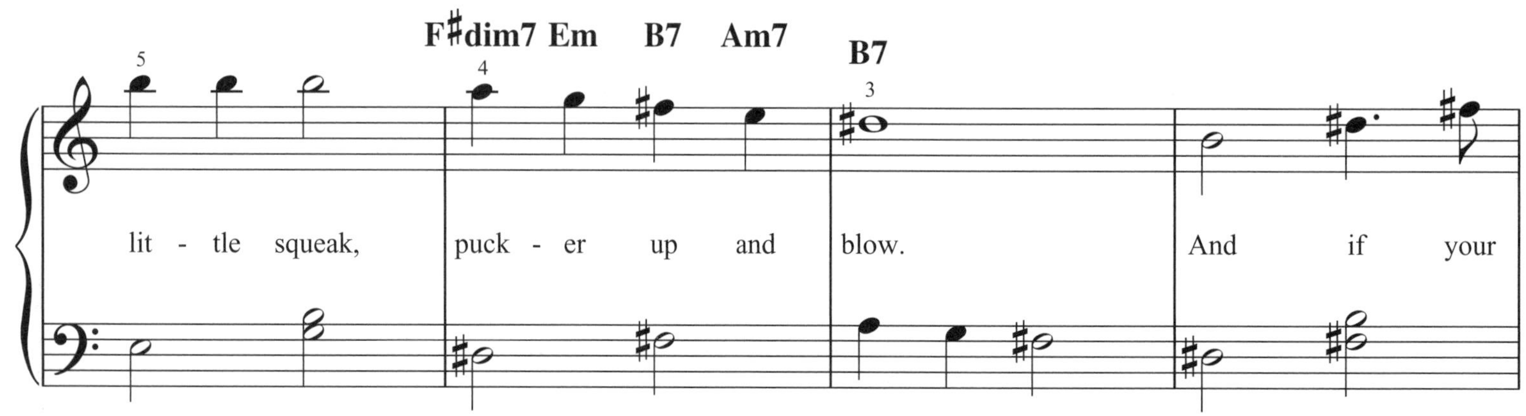

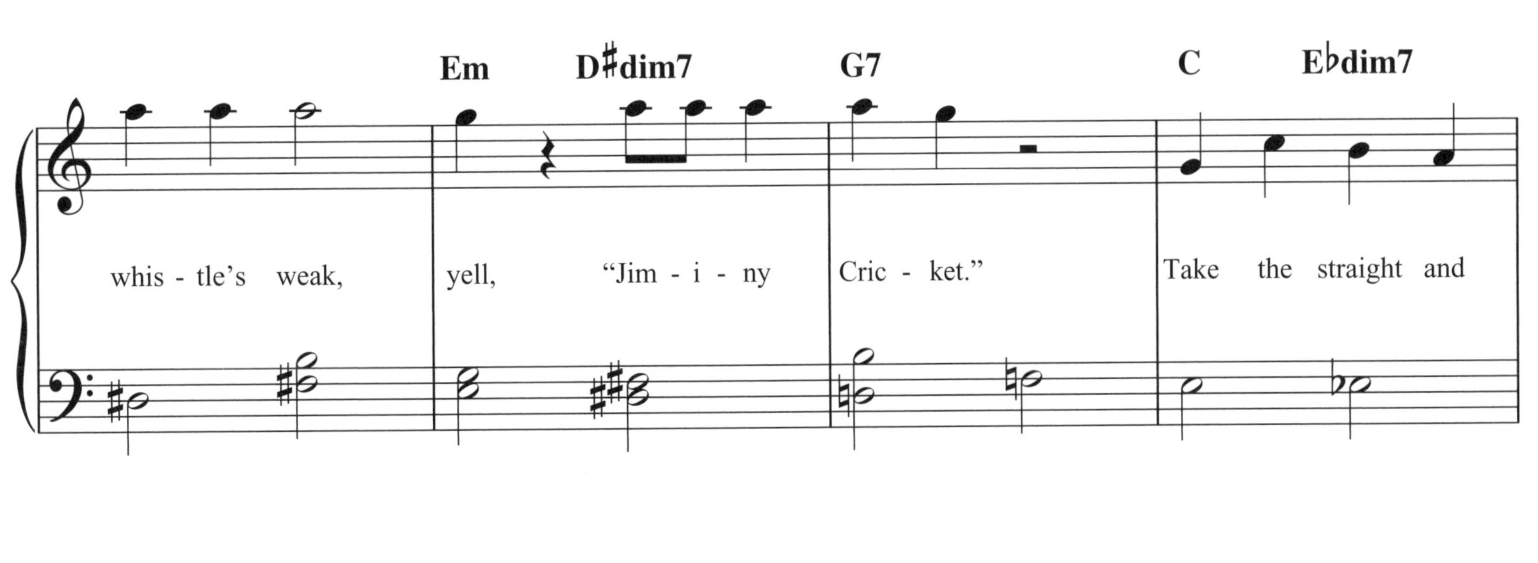
Em
D♯dim7
G7
C
E♭dim7
whis - tle's weak,
yell, "Jim - i - ny
Cric - ket."
Take the straight and

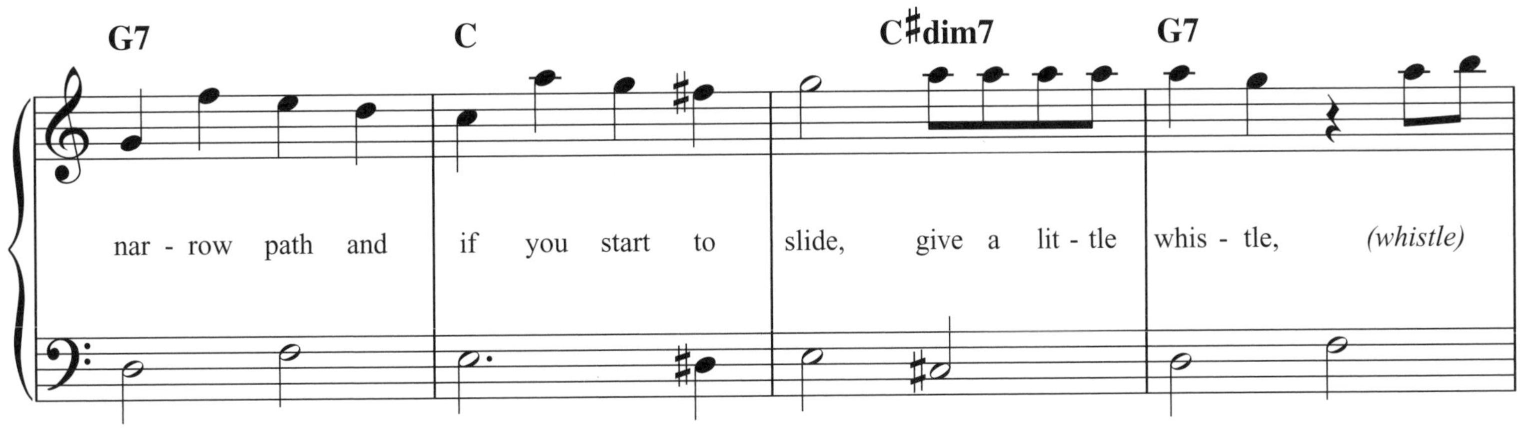
G7
C
C♯dim7
G7
nar - row path and
if you start to
slide, give a lit - tle
whis - tle, (whistle)

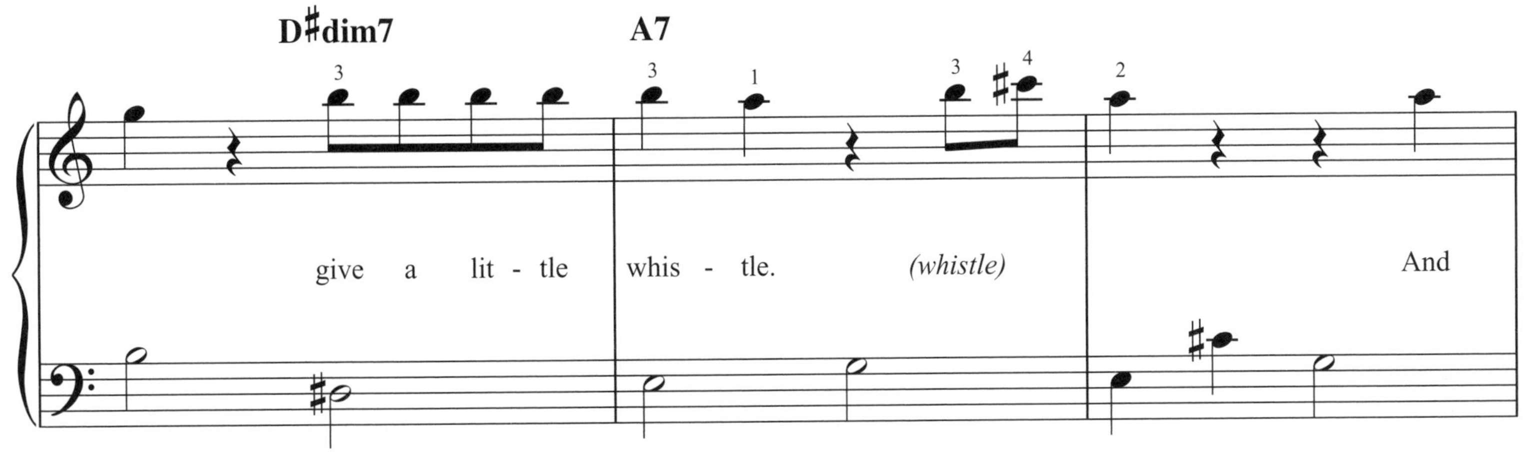
D♯dim7
A7
give a lit - tle
whis - tle. (whistle)
And

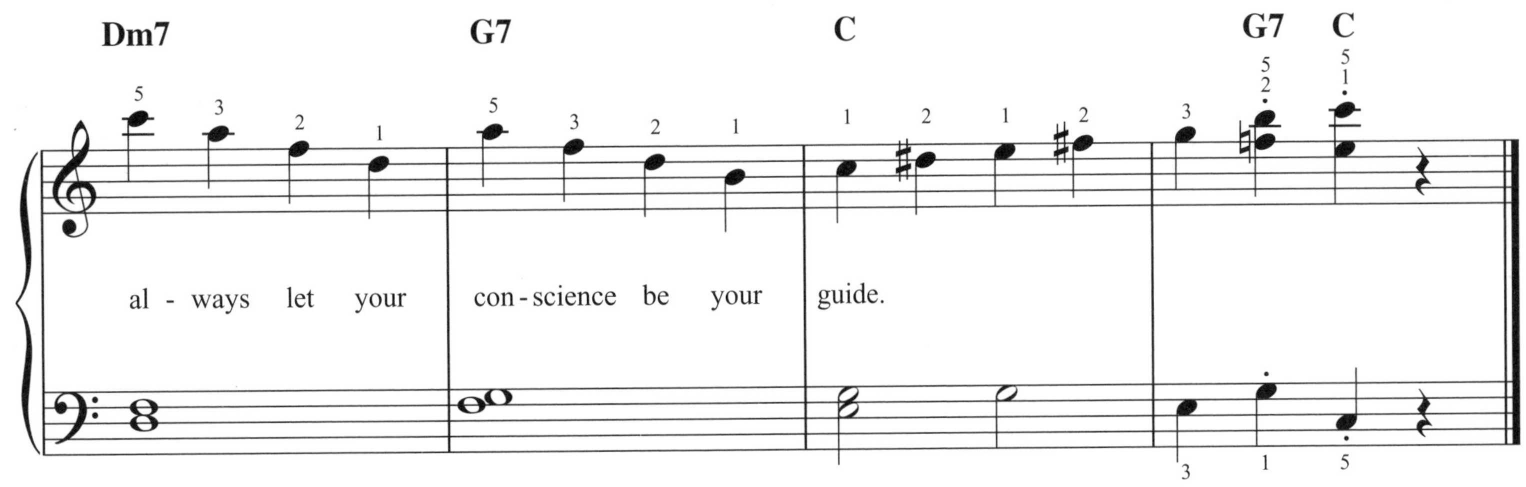
Dm7
G7
C
G7
C
al - ways let your
con - science be your
guide.

I JUST CAN'T WAIT TO BE KING

from THE LION KING

Music by ELTON JOHN
Lyrics by TIM RICE

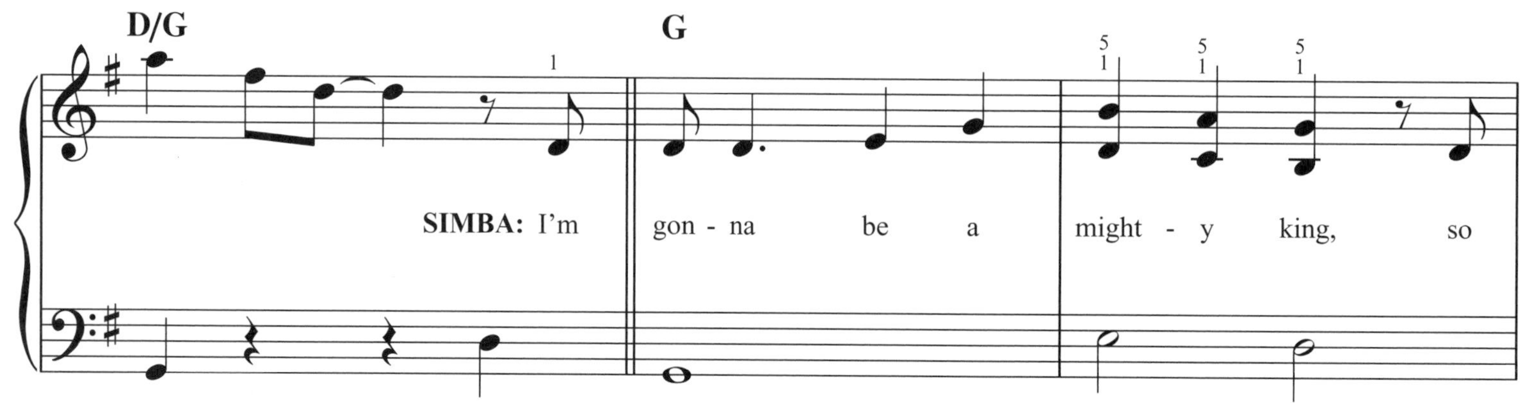

C
2
1
en - e - mies be - ware! ZAZU: Well, I've nev - er seen a
3
3

G
5
1
5
1
1
king of beasts with quite so lit - tle hair. SIMBA: I'm
1

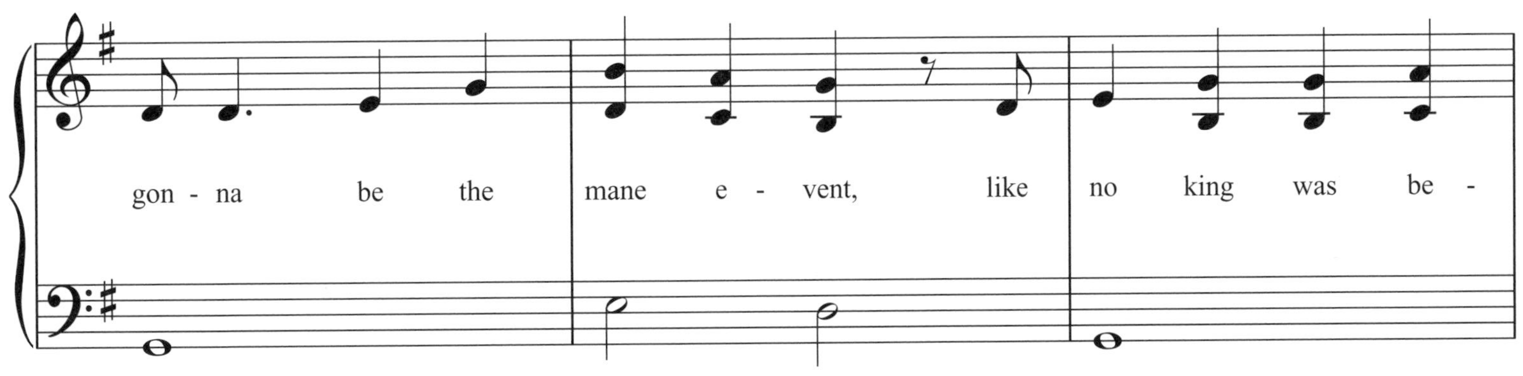
gon - na be the mane e - vent, like no king was be -

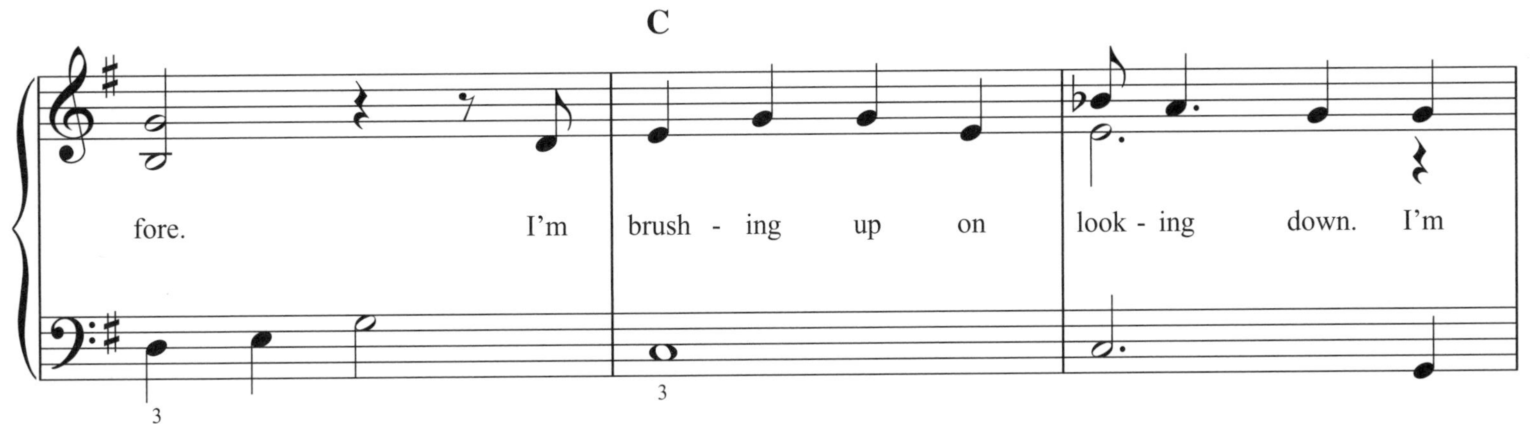
C
fore. I'm brush - ing up on look - ing down. I'm
3
3

G
Am
1
work - ing on my roar! ZAZU: Thus far, a rath - er
2

G
D
3
un - in - spir - ing thing. SIMBA: Oh, I

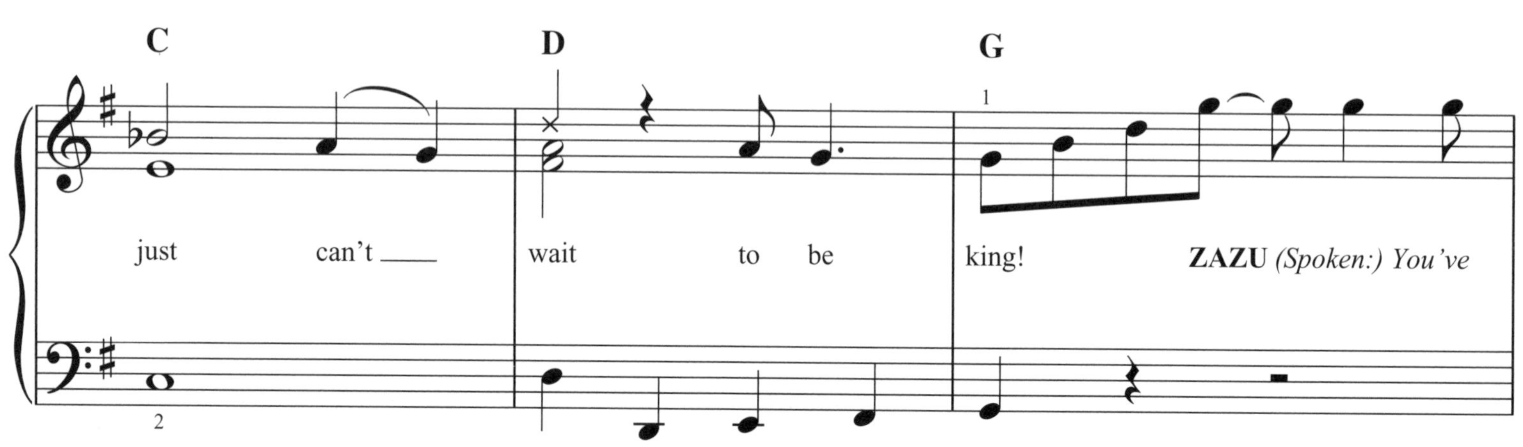
C
D
G
1
just can't ___ wait to be king! ZAZU (Spoken:) You've
2

C/G
G
1
rather a long way to go, young master! If you think... SIMBA: No one say - ing
5

C
Am
ZAZU (Spoken:) Now, when I said that, I...
What I
"do this,"
no one say - ing
"be there,"

D/F♯
D7
meant was that the...
But what you don't re - al - ize...
no one say - ing
"stop that,"
no one say - ing

G
C
G/B
Am
C
Now see here!
"see here."
Free to run a - round all

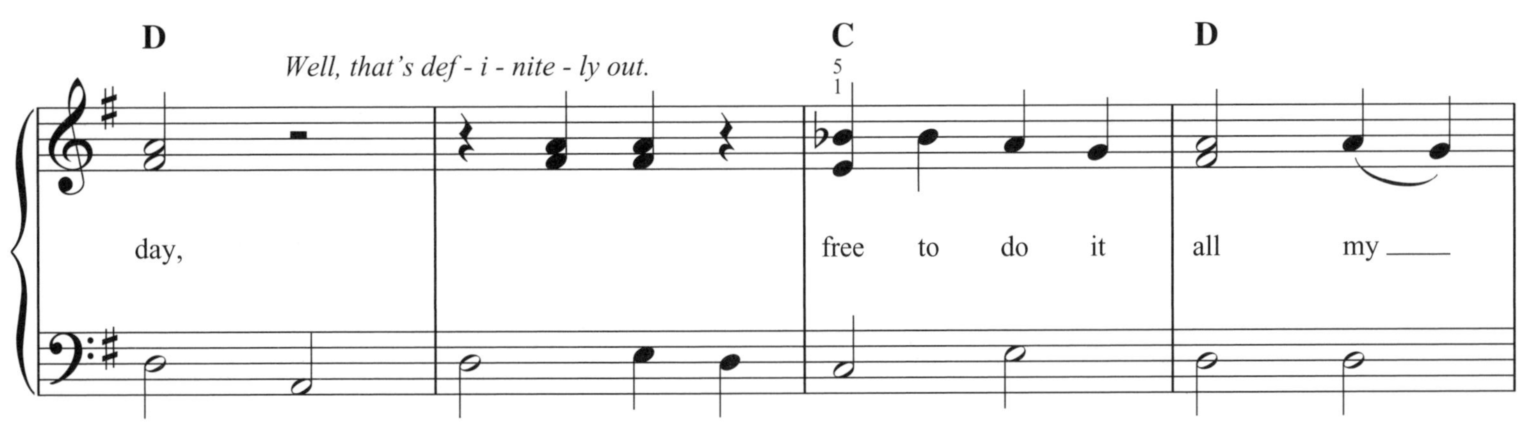
D
C
D
Well, that's def - i - nite - ly out.
day,
free to do it all my

G
(Quasi spoken:)
way!
ZAZU: I

think it's time that you and I ar - ranged a heart to

C
(Sung:)
heart.
SIMBA: Kings don't need ad - vice from lit - tle

G
(Quasi spoken:)
horn - bills, for a start.
ZAZU: If this is where the

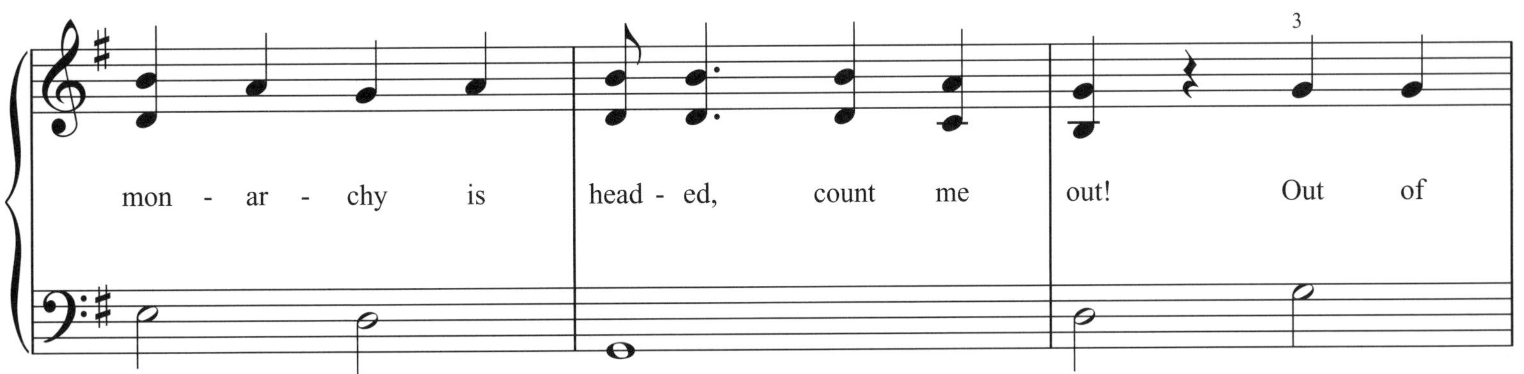
3
mon - ar - chy is head - ed, count me out! Out of

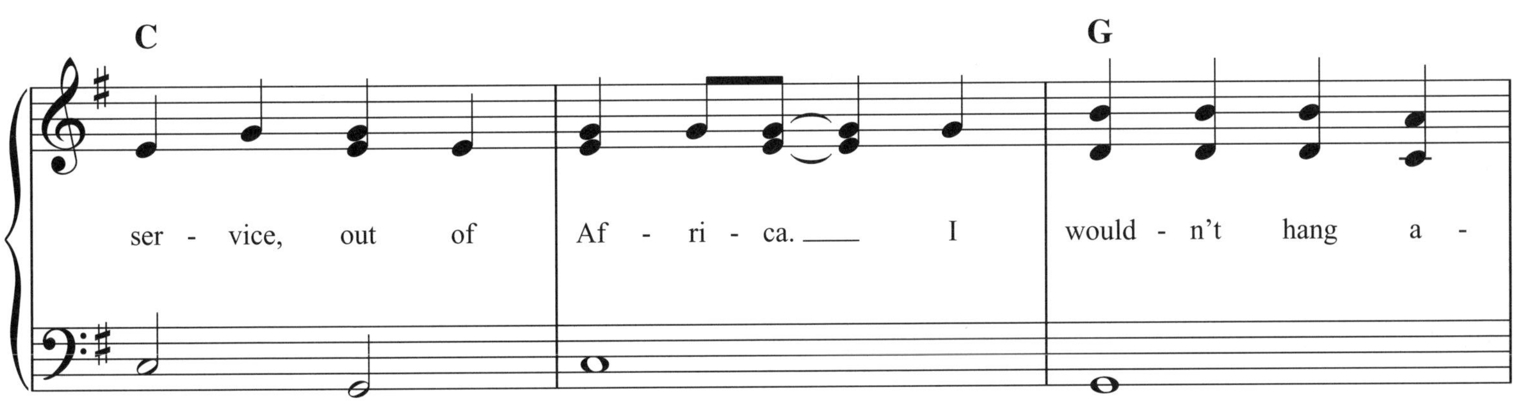
C
G
ser - vice, out of Af - ri - ca. I would - n't hang a -

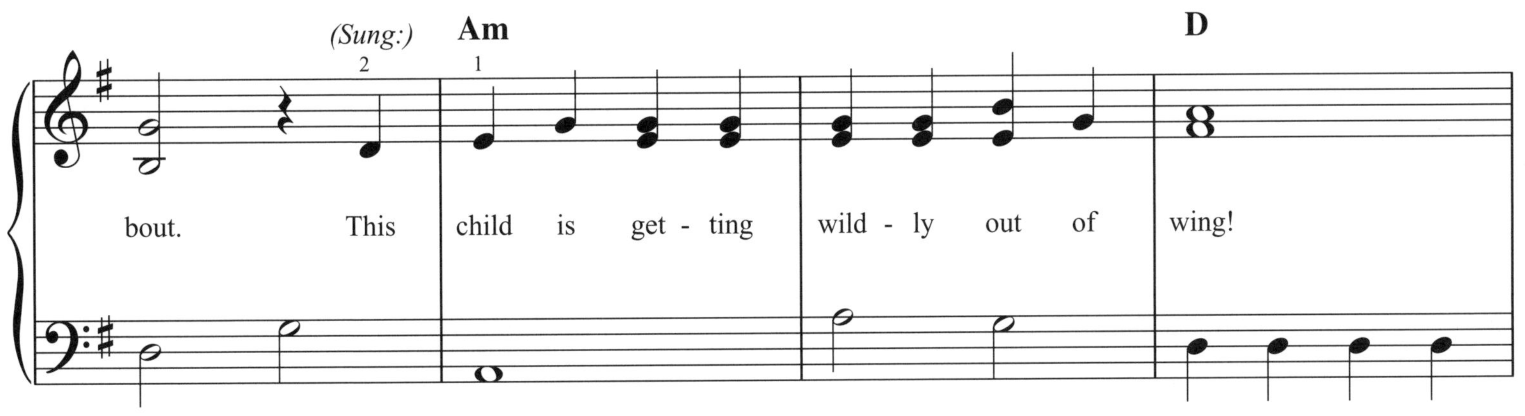
(Sung:)
Am
D
2
1
bout. This child is get - ting wild - ly out of wing!

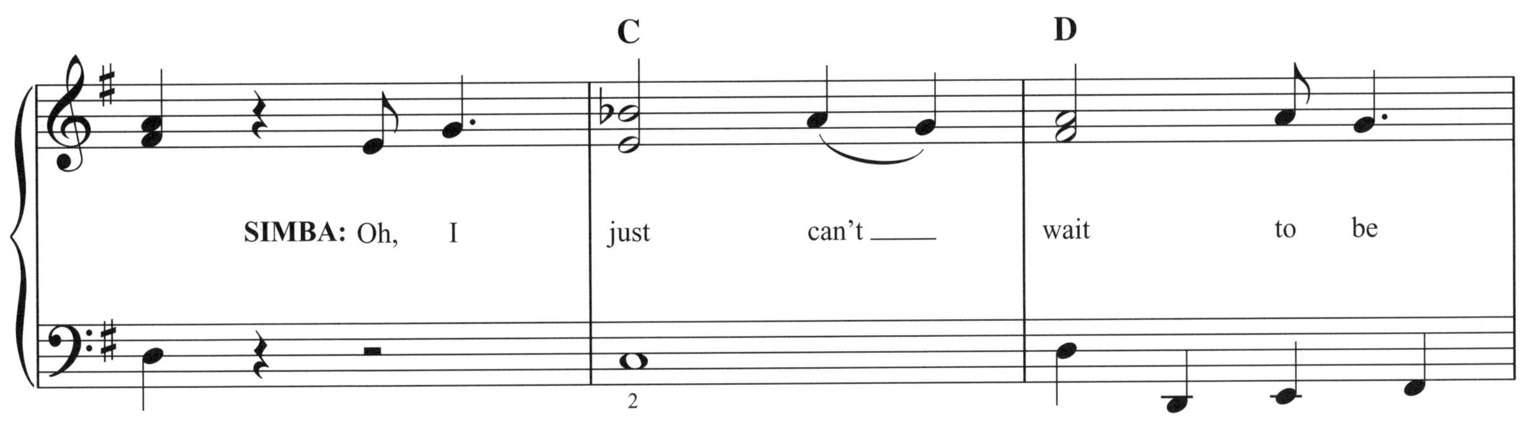
C
D
SIMBA: Oh, I just can't wait to be
2

G
king!
5

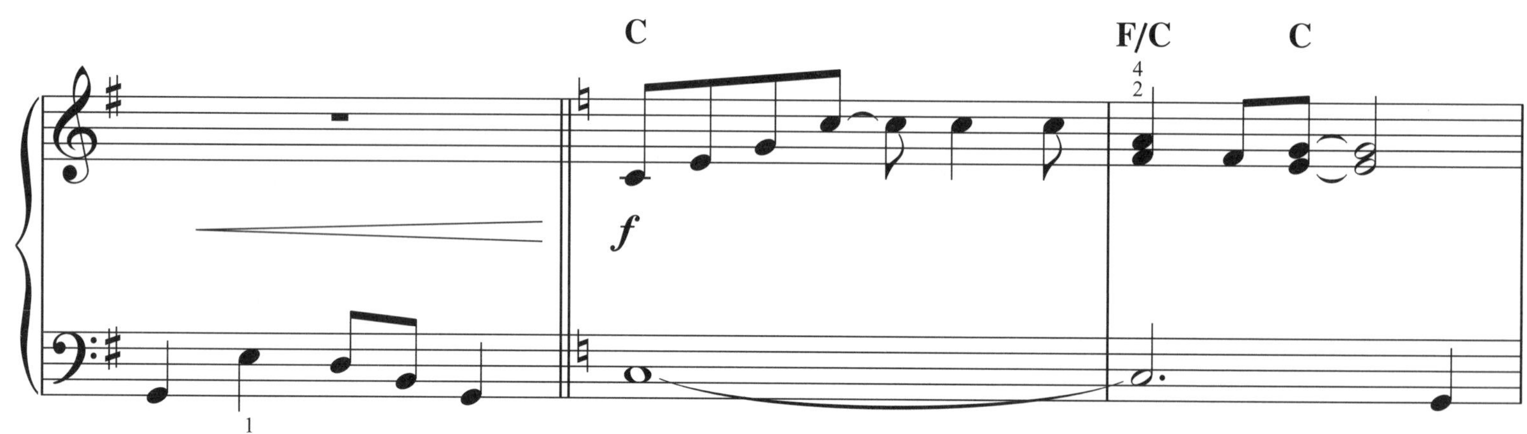
C
F/C
C
4
2
f
1

G/C
C
4

F/C
C
2
SIMBA: Ev - 'ry - bod - y
2

F
Dm
look left,
ev - 'ry - bod - y
look right.

G/B
G
1
2
Ev - 'ry - where you
look, I'm
stand - ing in the

C
ZAZU (Spoken:)
Not yet!
F
C/E
1
spot - light.
SIMBA & CHORUS: Let
ev - 'ry crea - ture

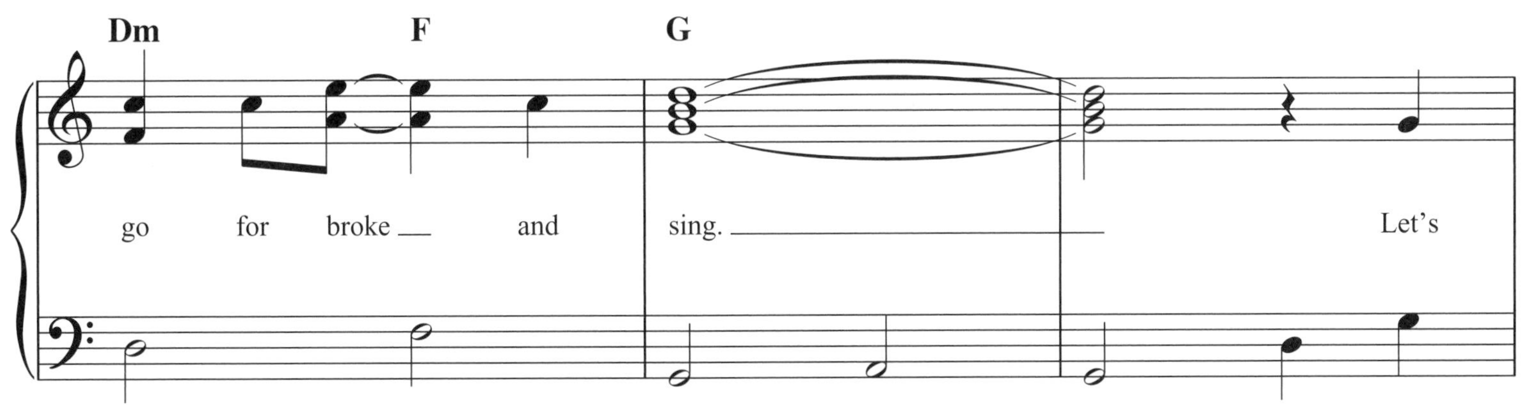
Dm
F
G
go for broke and
sing.
Let's

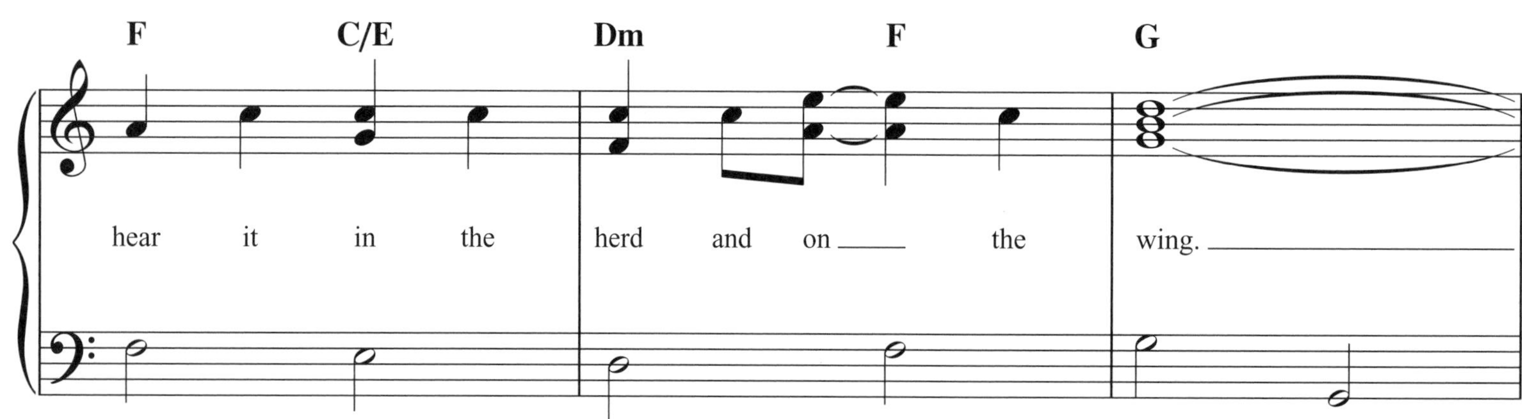
F
C/E
Dm
F
G
hear it in the herd and on ___ the wing. ___

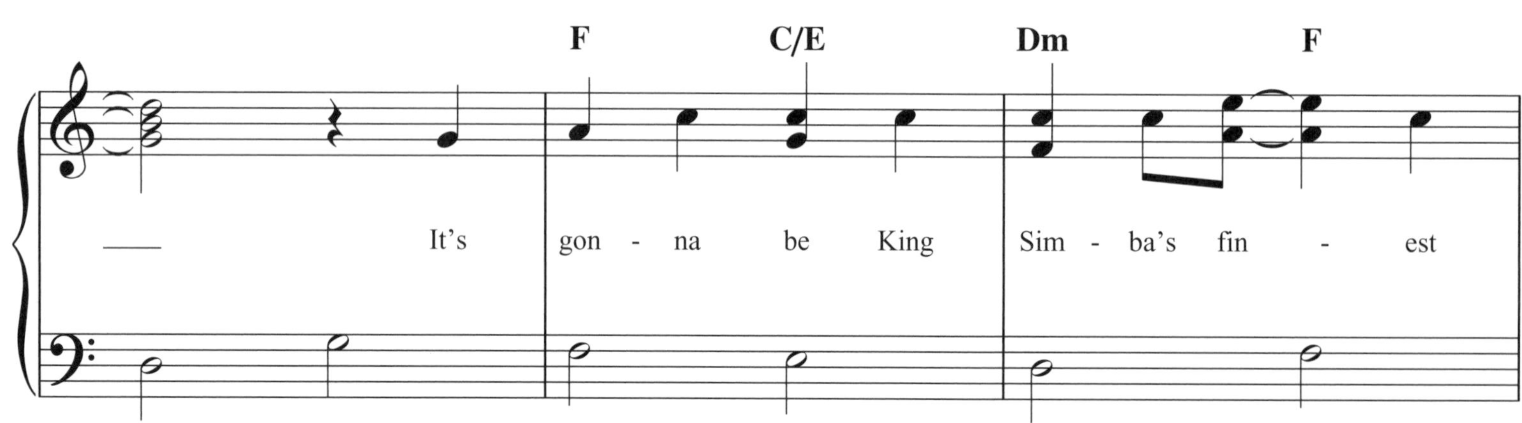
F
C/E
Dm
F
___ It's gon - na be King Sim - ba's fin - est

G
1
3
F
fling.
SIMBA: Oh, I just can't ___

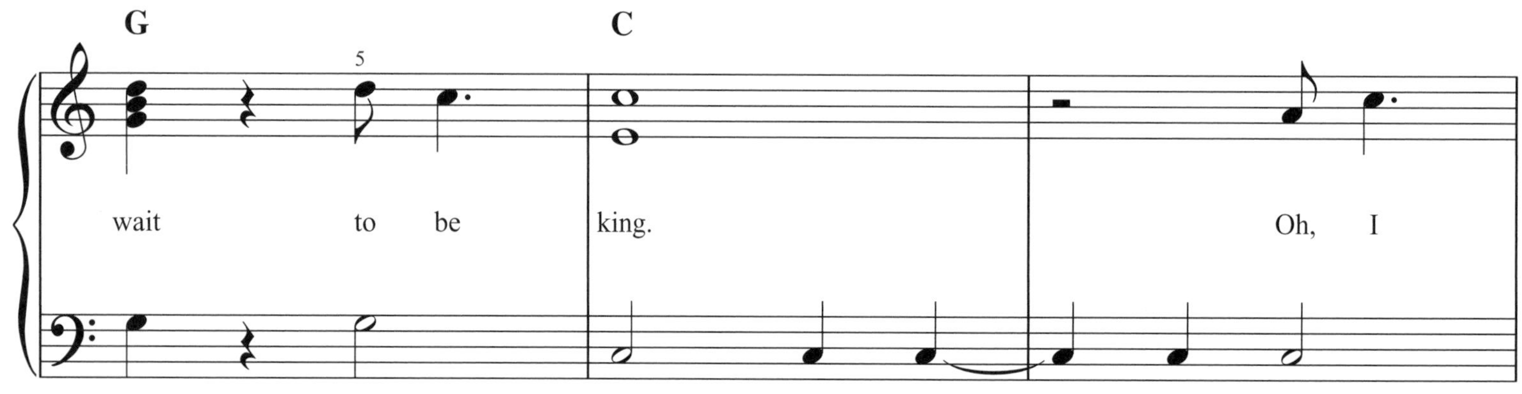
G
5
C
wait to be king. Oh, I

F
G
C
just can't
wait to be
king.

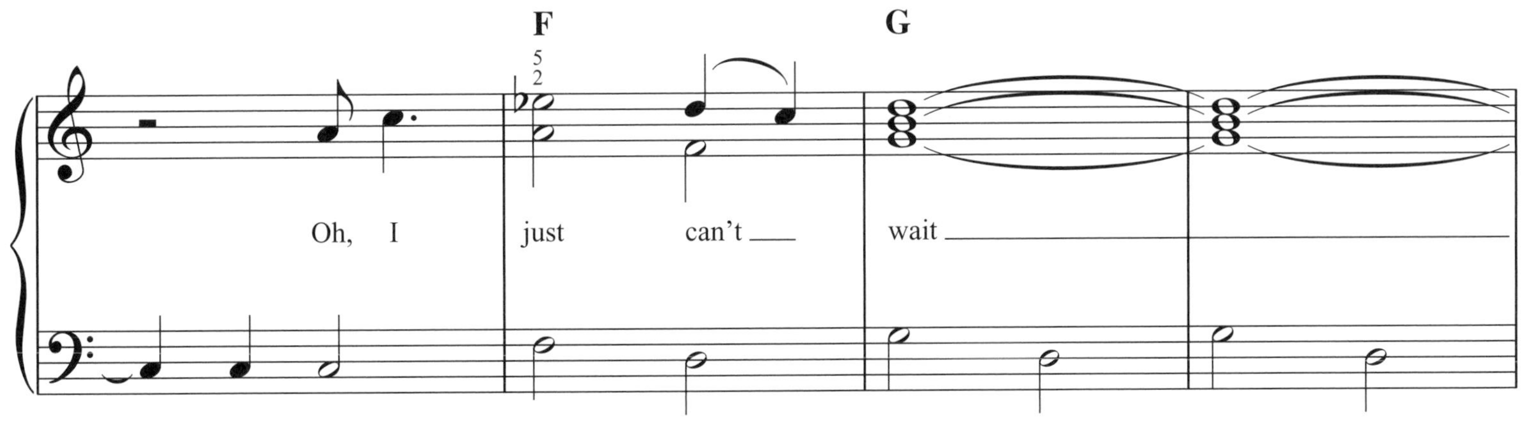
F
G
5
2
Oh, I
just can't
wait

C
5
to be
king!
1

F/C
C

HEIGH-HO

The Dwarfs' Marching Song
from SNOW WHITE AND THE SEVEN DWARFS

Words by LARRY MOREY
Music by FRANK CHURCHILL

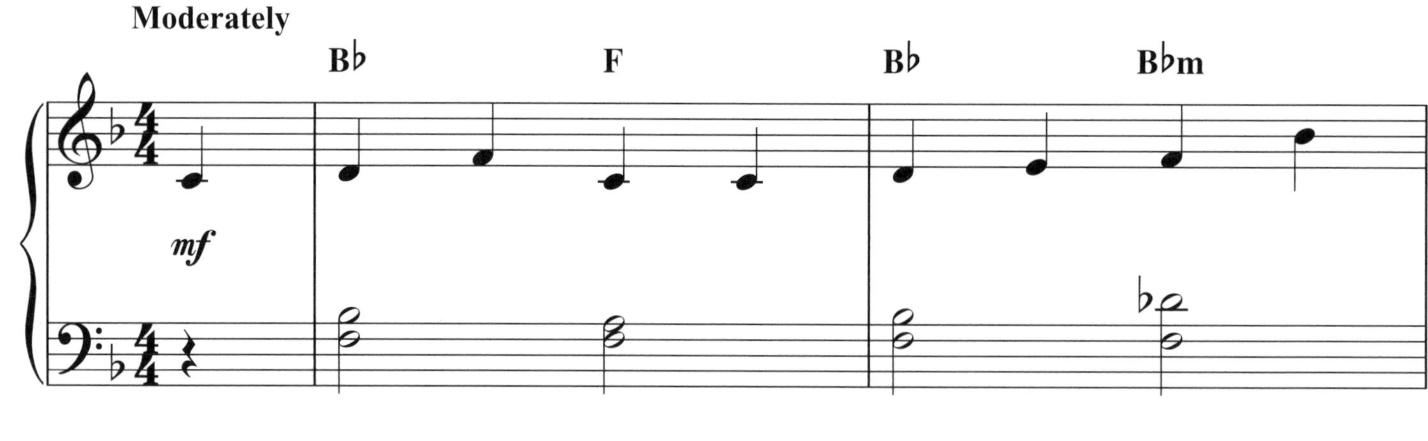

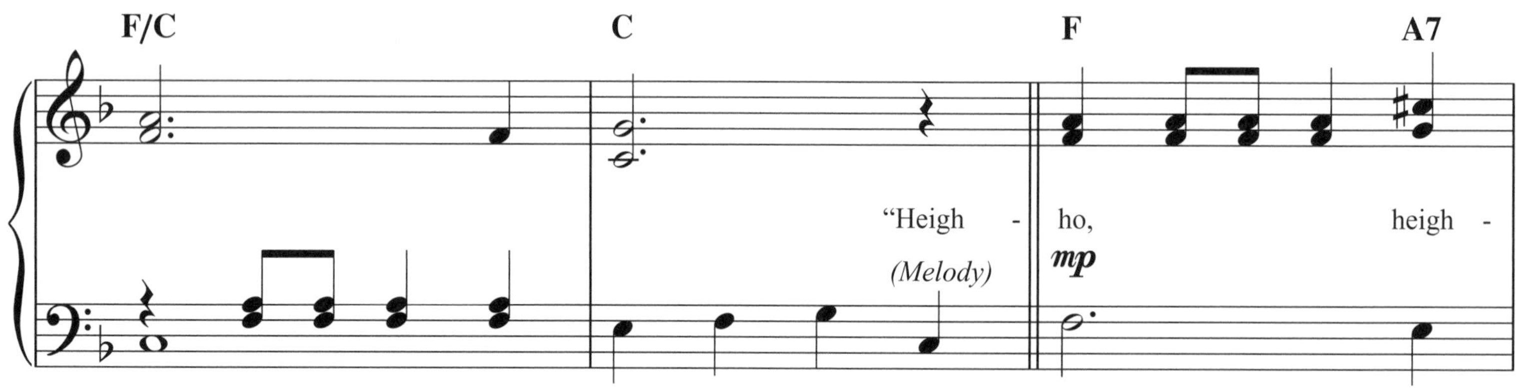

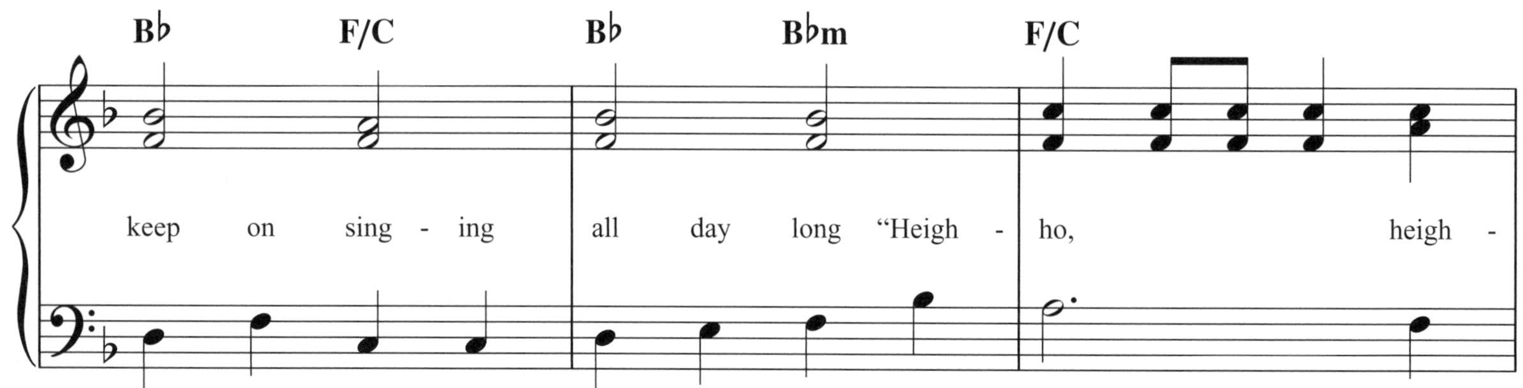

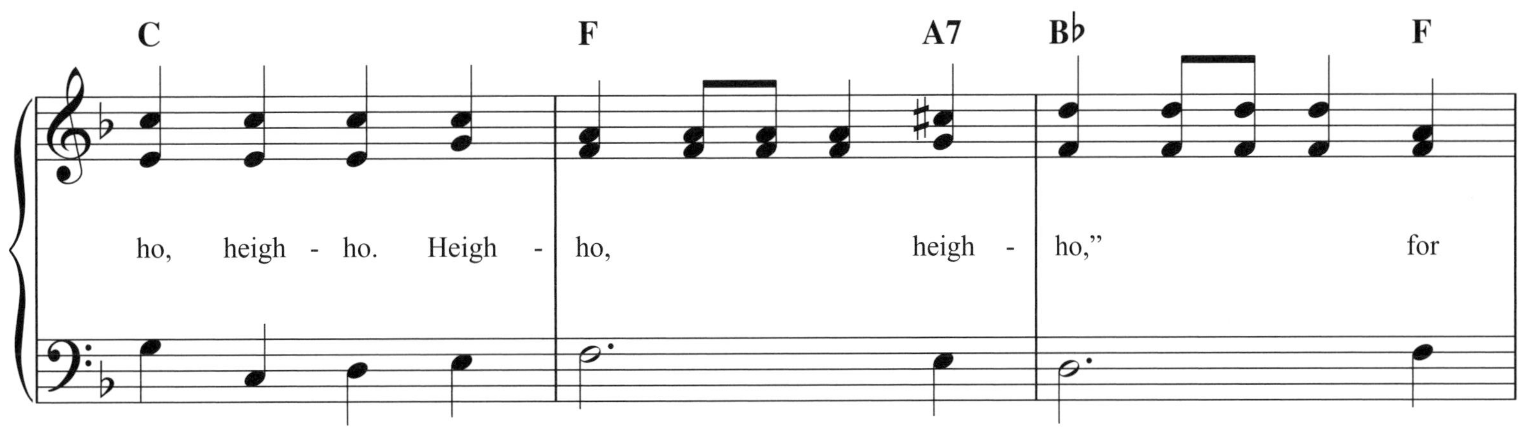
C
F
A7
B♭
F
ho, heigh - ho. Heigh - ho, heigh - ho," for

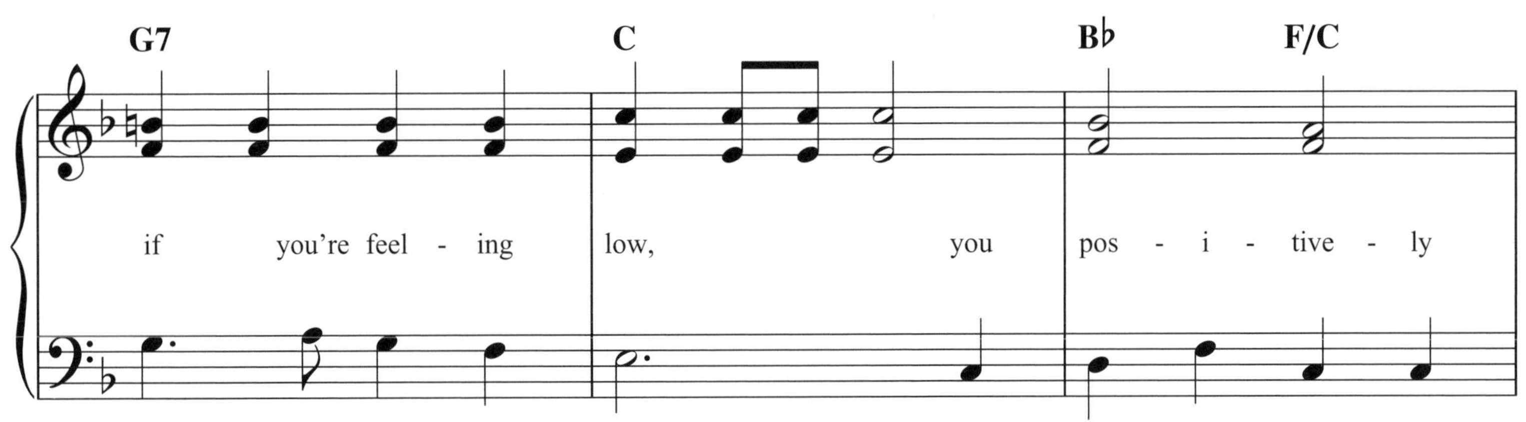
G7
C
B♭
F/C
if you're feel - ing low, you pos - i - tive - ly

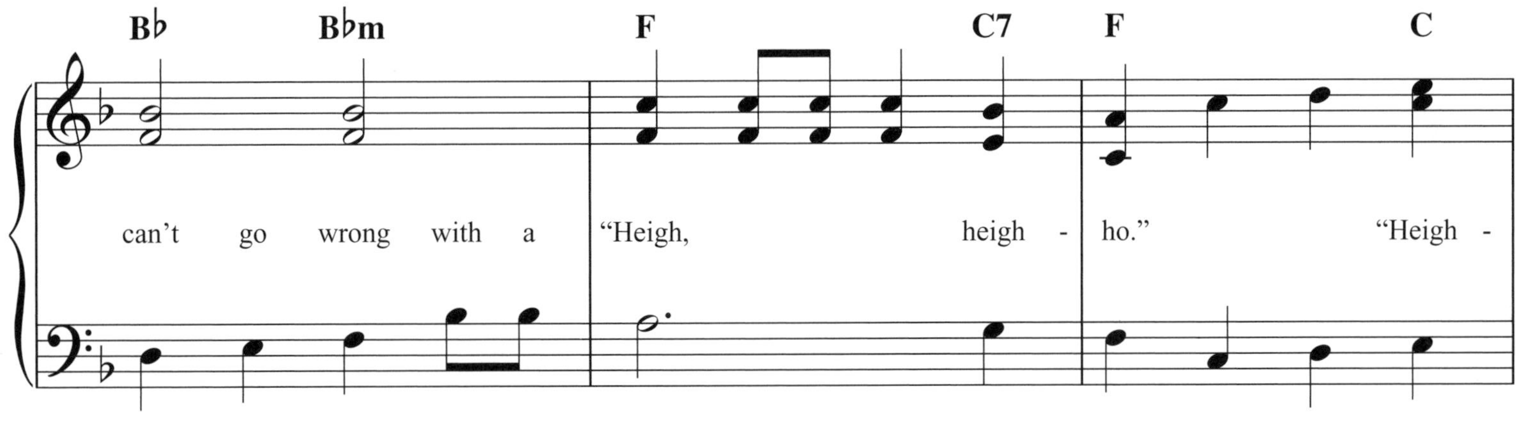
B♭
B♭m
F
C7
F
C
can't go wrong with a "Heigh, heigh - ho." "Heigh -

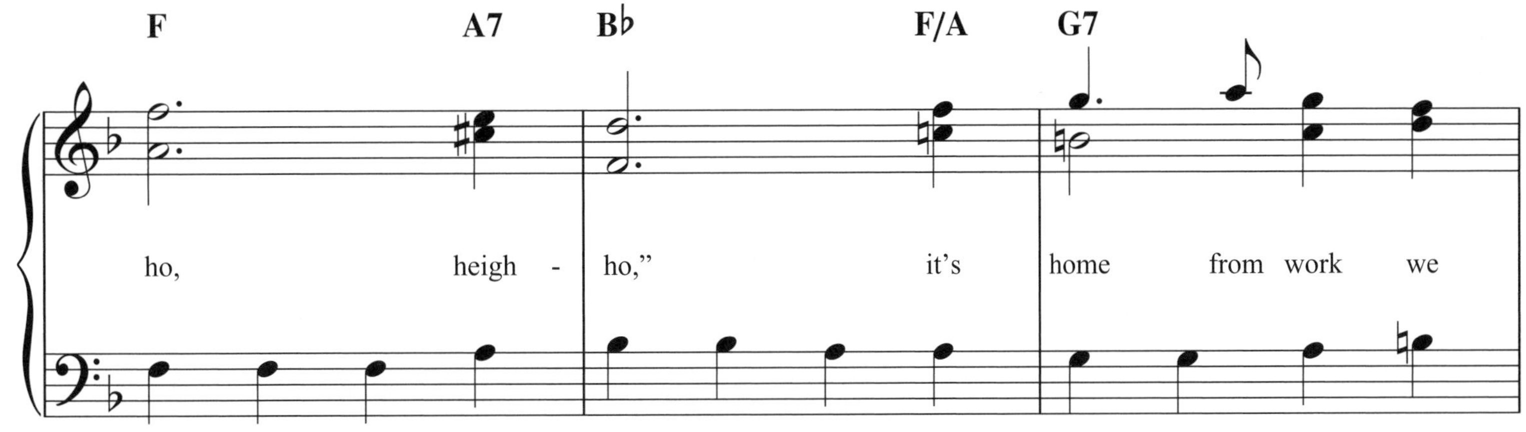
F
A7
B♭
F/A
G7
ho, heigh - ho," it's home from work we

C
C7
B♭
F
B♭
B♭m
go. (whistle)
"Heigh -

F/C
C7
F
ho, heigh - ho, heigh - ho. Heigh - ho, heigh -

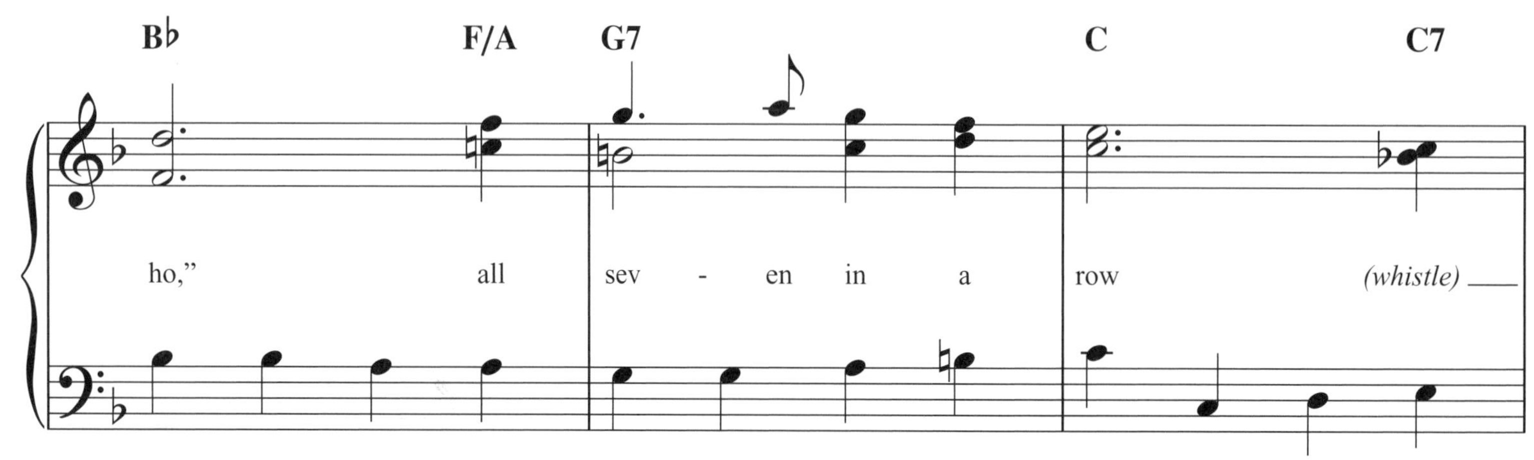
B♭
F/A
G7
C
C7
ho," all sev - en in a row (whistle)

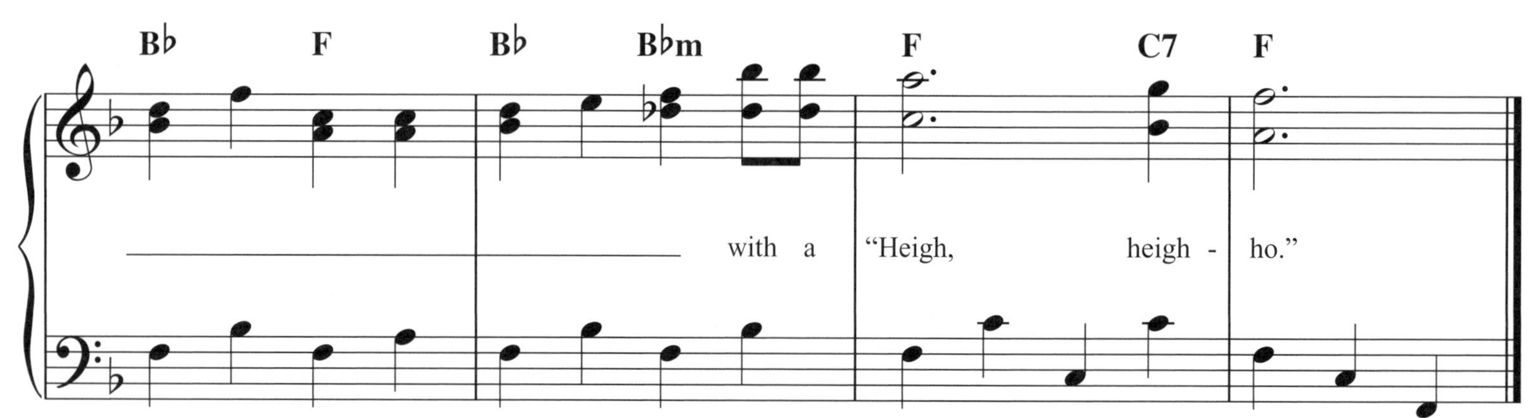
B♭
F
B♭
B♭m
F
C7
F
with a "Heigh, heigh - ho."

IF I DIDN'T HAVE YOU

from MONSTERS, INC.

Music and Lyrics by
RANDY NEWMAN

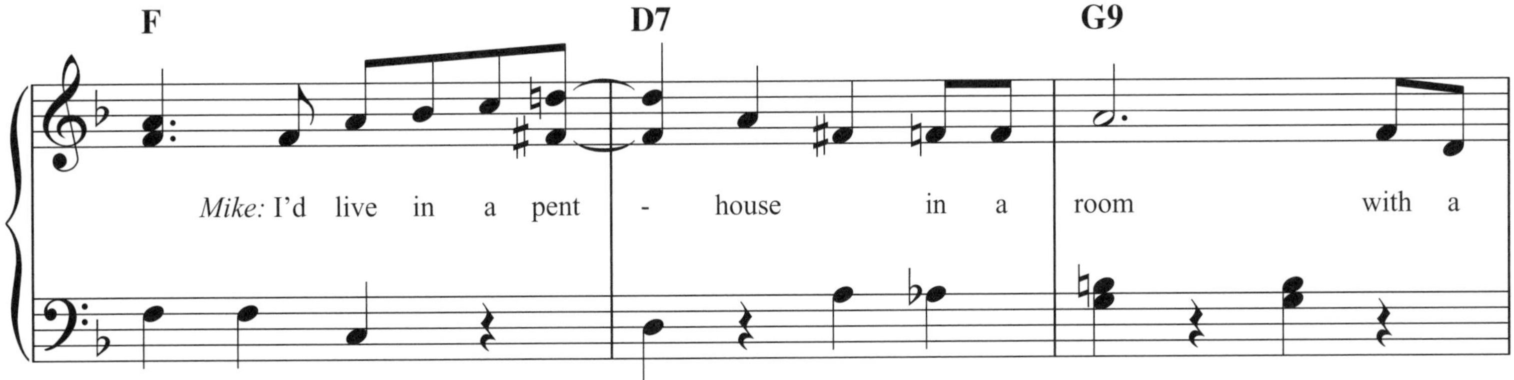

B♭6
B♭m6
F
D7
Sulley: 'cause dreams do come true, I would - n't have

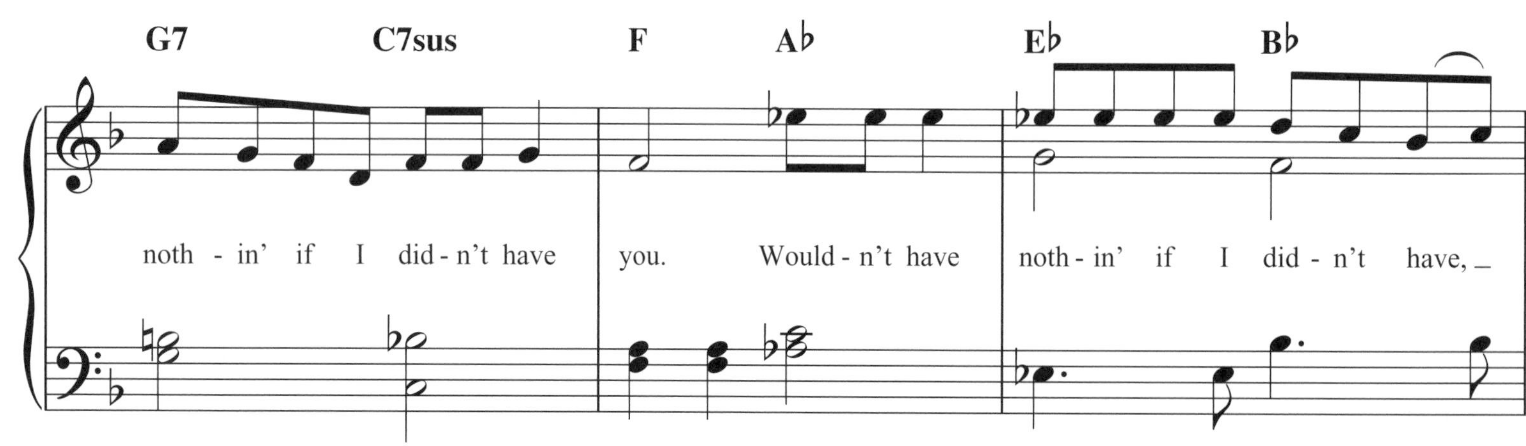
G7
C7sus
F
A♭
E♭
B♭
noth - in' if I did - n't have you. Would - n't have noth - in' if I did - n't have,

A♭
E♭
B♭sus
B♭
A♭
E♭
would - n't have noth - in' if I did - n't have, would - n't have

C
C7♯5
F
F9
noth - in'. Mike: For years I have en - vied
Mike: (spoken) Can I tell you something? Sulley (spoken): (You're green with it.)

B♭6
B♭m6
F6
Mike: your grace and your charm.
Ev - 'ry - one loves

D
G7
C7
you, you know.
Sulley: Yes, I know, I know, I know.

F
F9
B♭6
Mike: But I must ad - mit it,
big guy, you al - ways come

B♭m6
F
D7
G9
C7sus
through.
I would - n't have noth - ing if I did - n't have you.

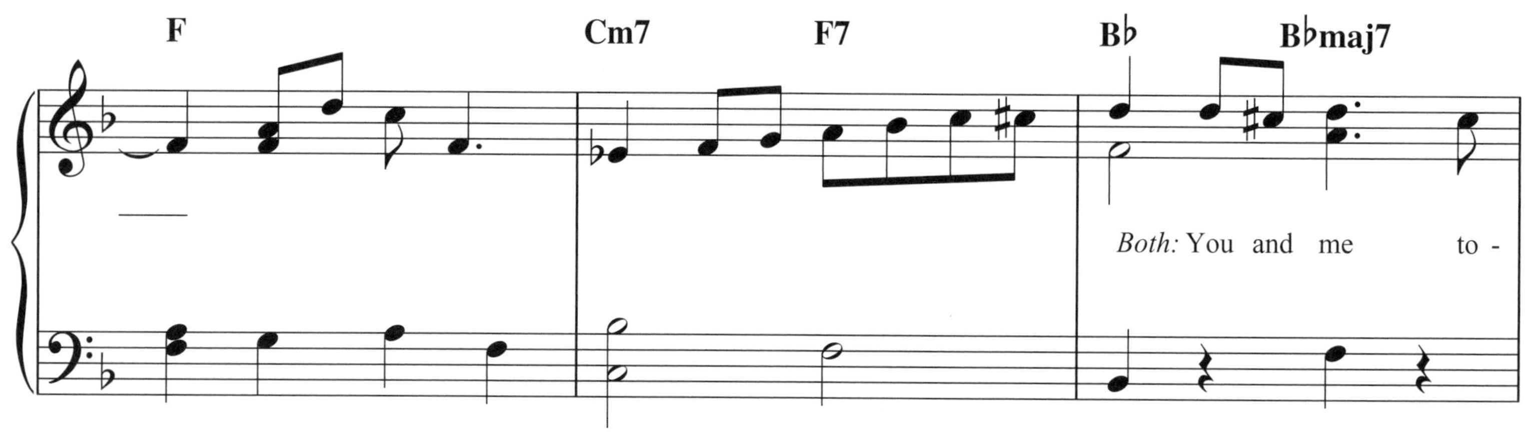
F
Cm7
F7
B♭
B♭maj7
Both: You and me to -

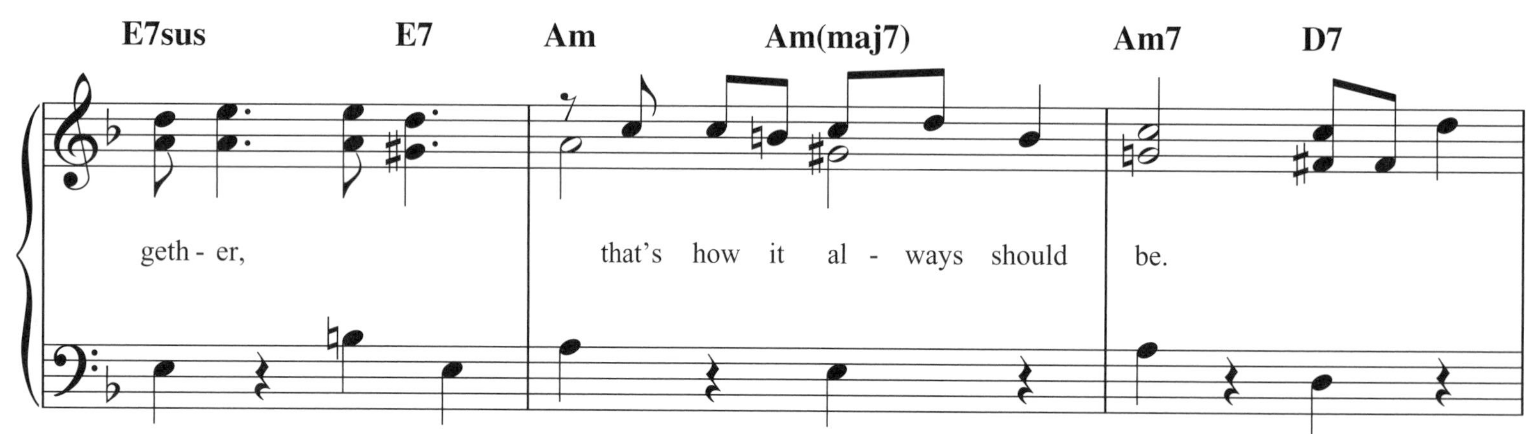
E7sus
E7
Am
Am(maj7)
Am7
D7
geth - er,
that's how it al - ways should
be.

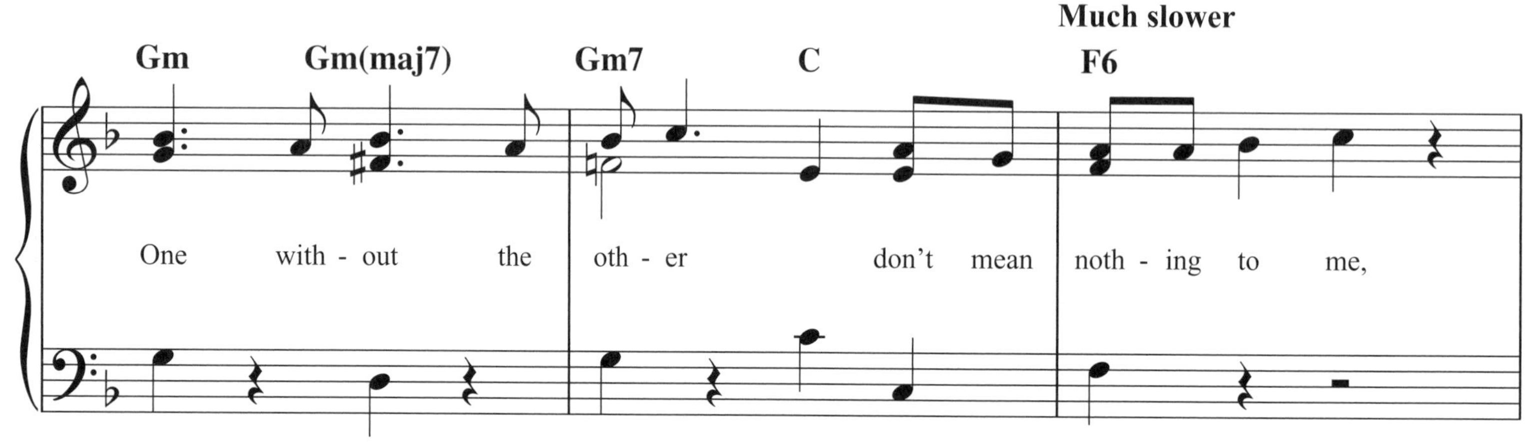
Much slower
Gm
Gm(maj7)
Gm7
C
F6
One with - out the
oth - er don't mean
noth - ing to me,

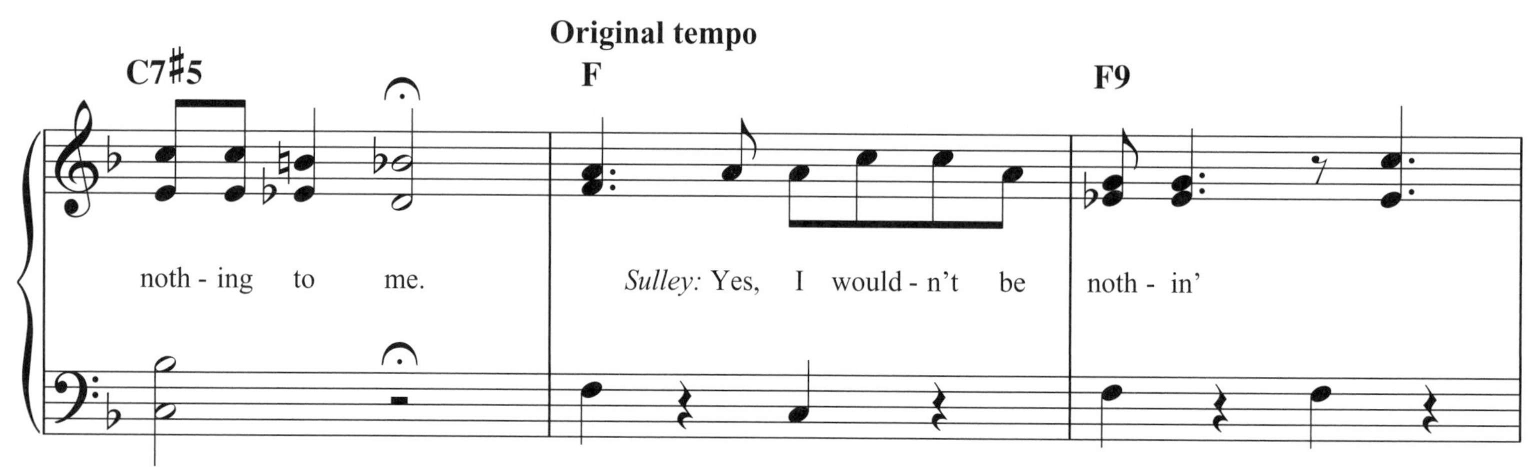
Original tempo
C7♯5
F
F9
noth - ing to me.
Sulley: Yes, I would - n't be
noth - in'

B♭6
B♭m6
F
if I did - n't have you
Mike: I know what you mean,
Sulley:
I would - n't know where to
Sulley, because...

D7
G9
C7sus
go would - n't
Mike: Me too, because I...
know what to
Mike:
do.
Why do you keep singing my part?

F
F9
B♭6
Both: I don't have to
say it
Sulley: I'll say it anyway.
Mike: 'Cause we
Both: both know it's true.

B♭m6
F
D7
G9
C7sus
I would - n't have
noth - in' if I did - n't have,

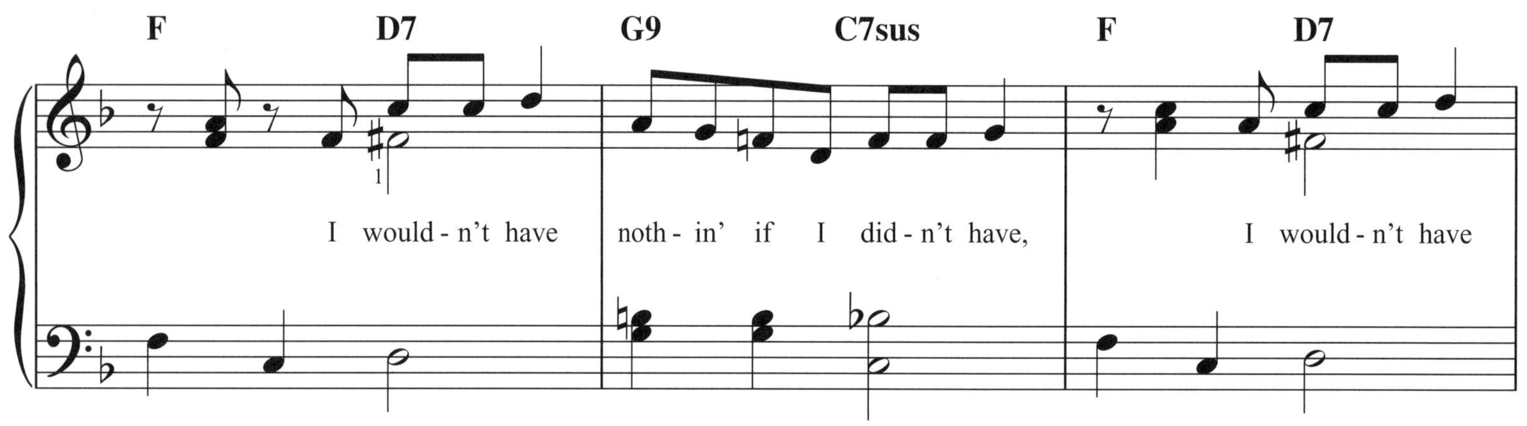
F
D7
G9
C7sus
F
D7
I would - n't have
noth - in' if I did - n't have,
I would - n't have

Much slower
G9
C7sus
F6
A♭
E♭
noth - in' if I did - n't have
you. Would - n't have
noth - in' if I did - n't have

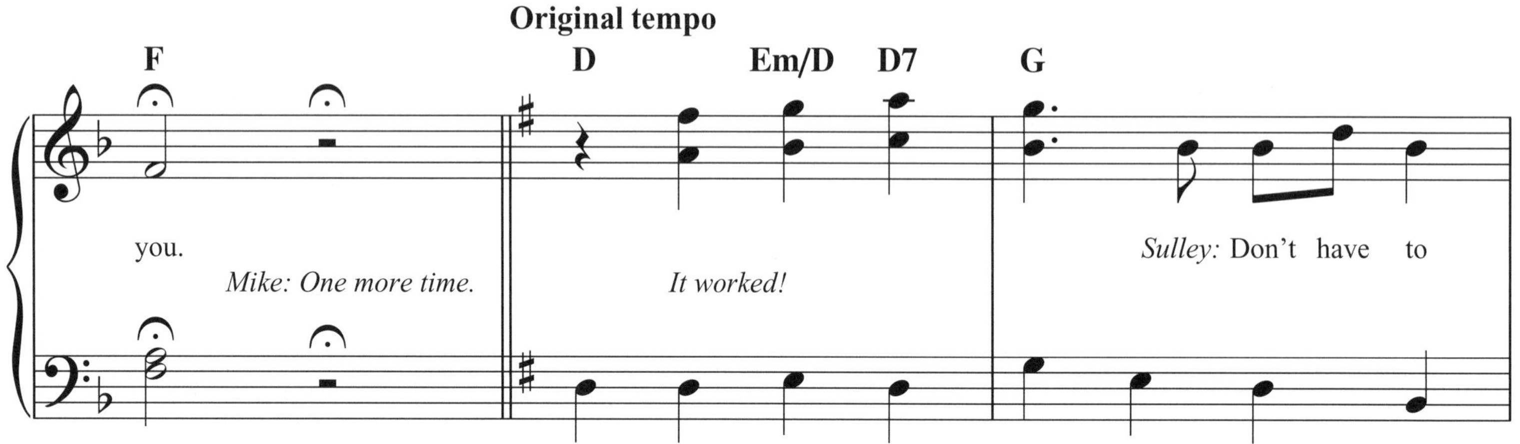
Original tempo
F
D
Em/D
D7
G
you.
Mike: One more time.
It worked!
Sulley: Don't have to

G9
C6
Cm6
say it
Mike: Where'd everybody come from?
Sulley: 'cause we both know it's true.
Mike: Let's take it home, big guy!

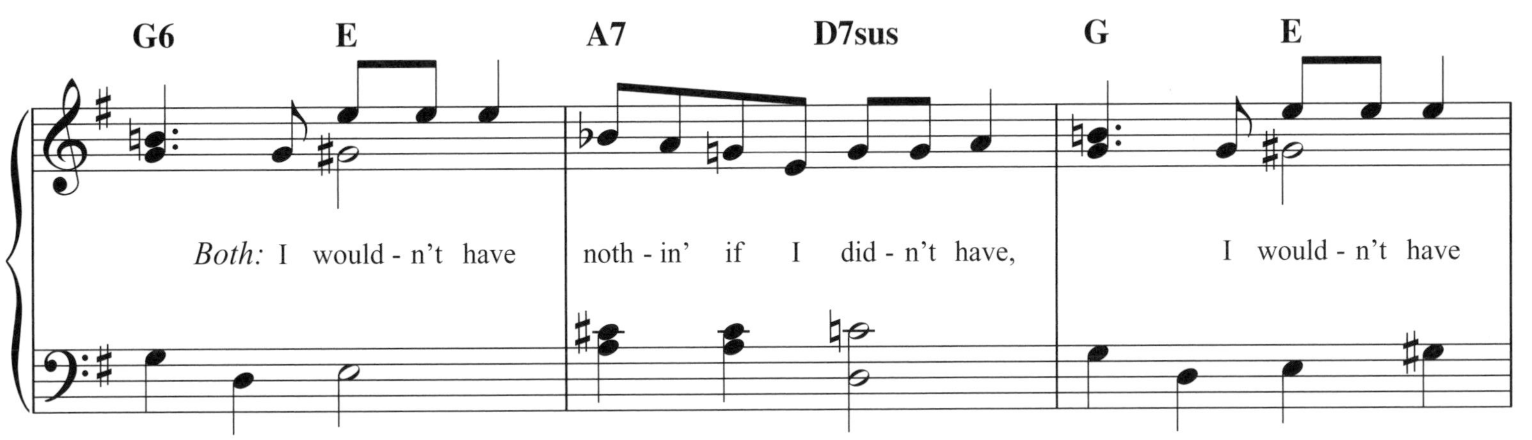
G6
E
A7
D7sus
G
E
Both: I would - n't have
noth - in' if I did - n't have,
I would - n't have

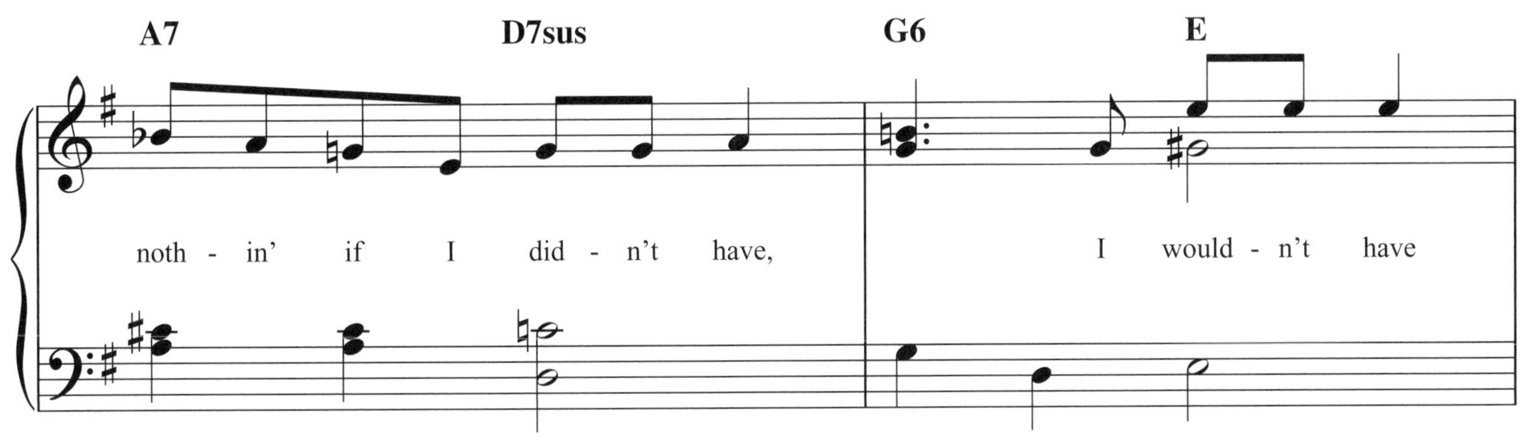
A7
D7sus
G6
E
noth - in' if I did - n't have,
I would - n't have

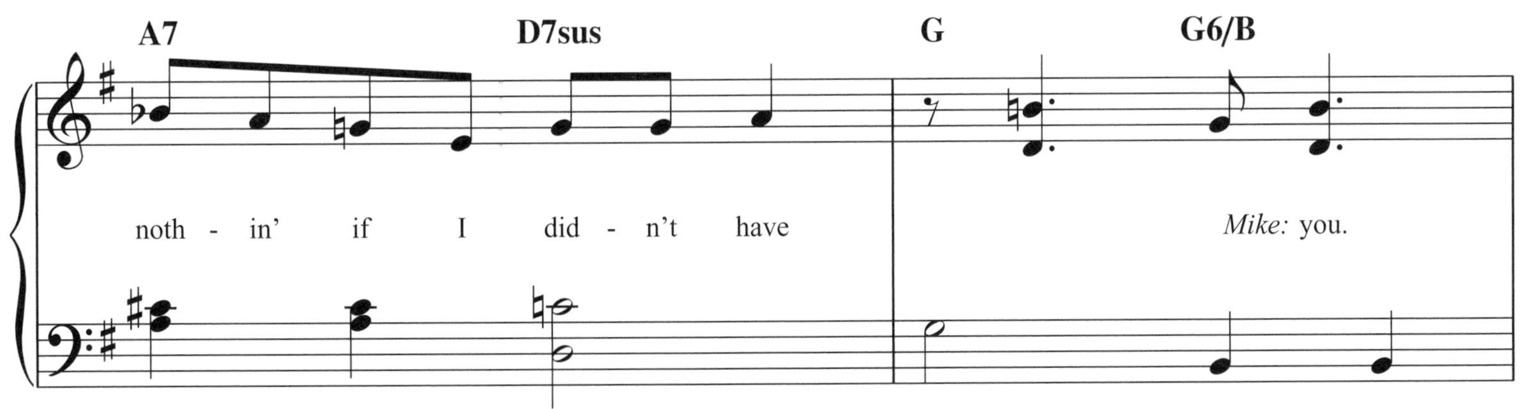
A7
D7sus
G
G6/B
noth - in' if I did - n't have
Mike: you.

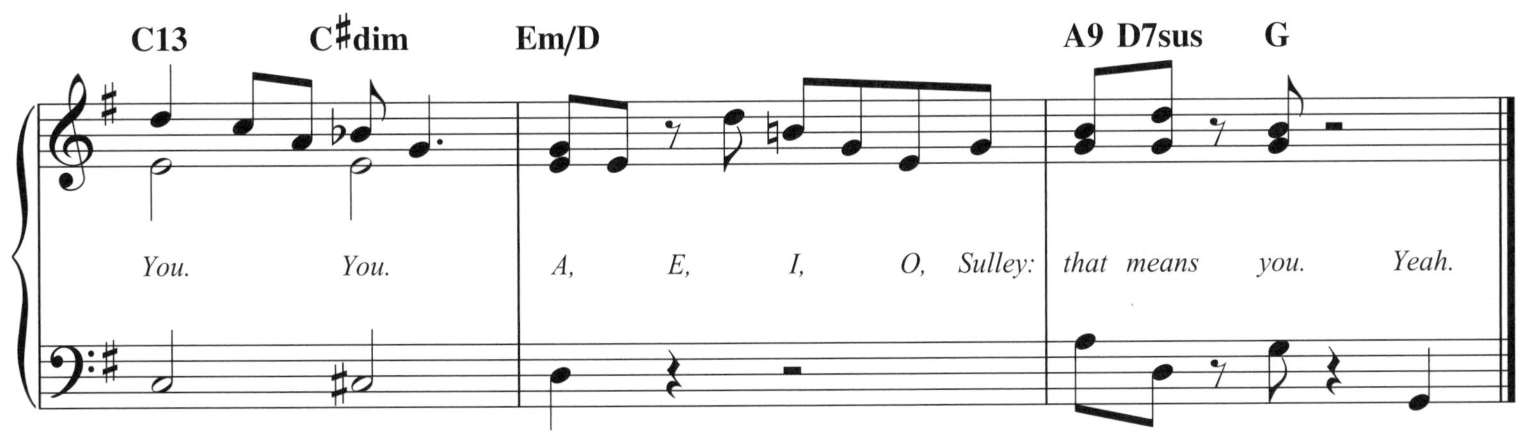
C13
C♯dim
Em/D
A9 D7sus
G
You. You.
A, E, I, O, Sulley: that means you. Yeah.

I'VE GOT NO STRINGS

from PINOCCHIO

Words by NED WASHINGTON
Music by LEIGH HARLINE

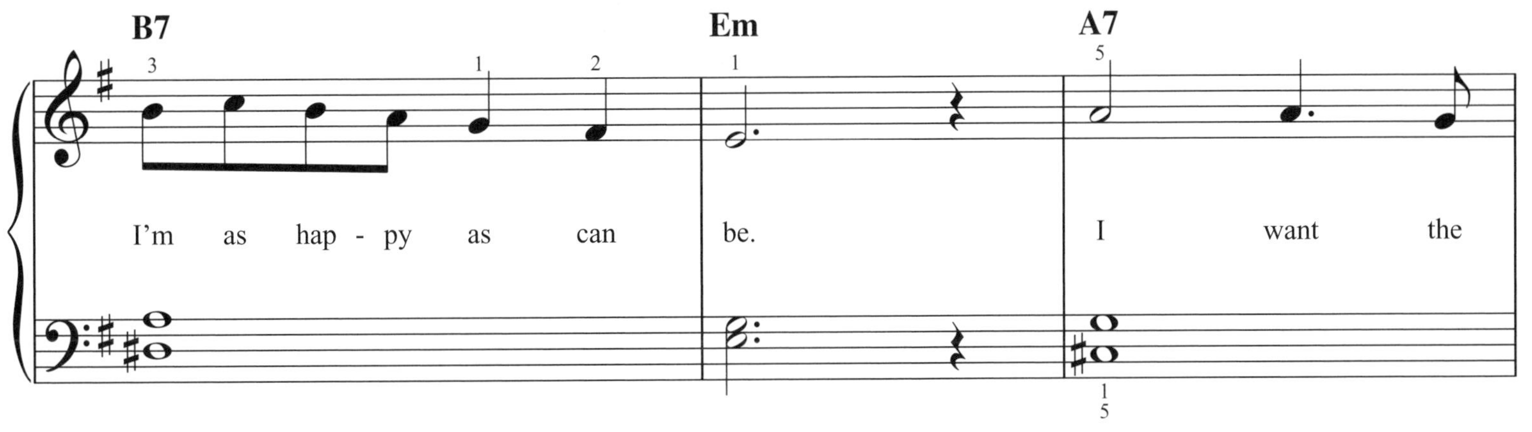
B7
Em
A7
I'm as hap - py as can be. I want the

D
A7
D
D7
world to know noth - ing ev - er wor - ries me. I've

G
Am7
D7
Am7
D7
G
got no strings so I have fun, I'm not tied up to an - y - one.

Am7
D7
Am7
D7
G
How I love my li - ber - ty, there are no strings on me.

IN SUMMER
from FROZEN

Music and Lyrics by KRISTEN ANDERSON-LOPEZ
and ROBERT LOPEZ

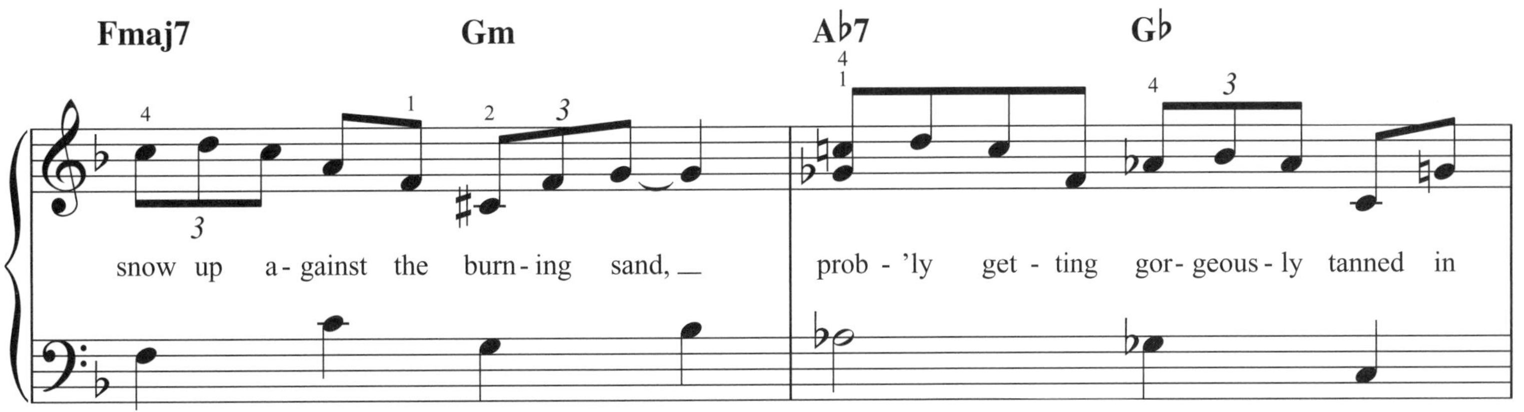
Fmaj7
Gm
A♭7
G♭
snow up a - gainst the burn - ing sand, __ prob - 'ly get - ting gor - geous - ly tanned in

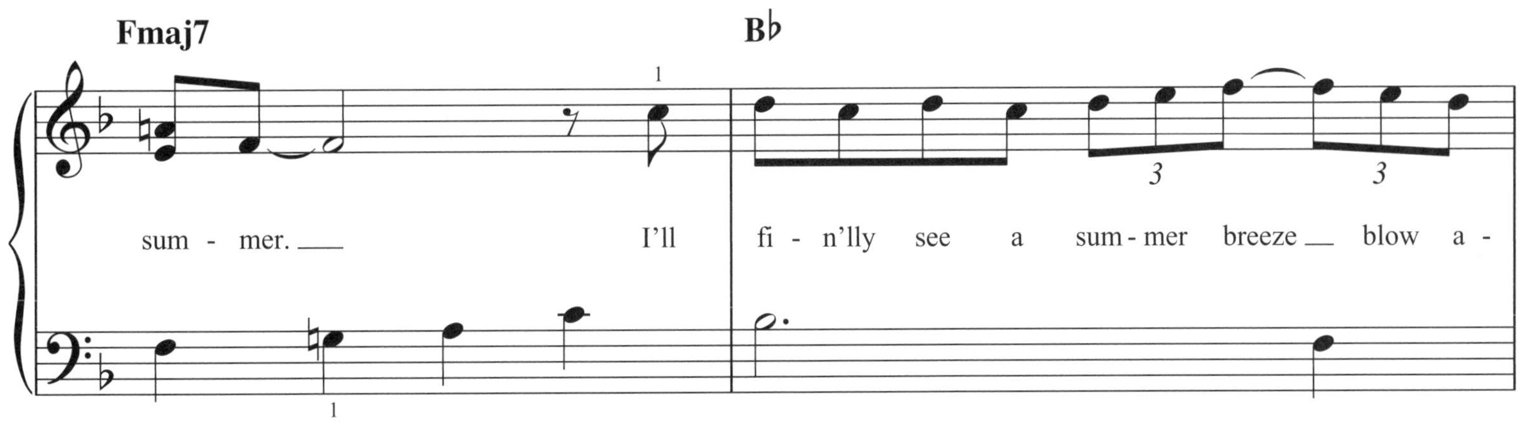
Fmaj7
B♭
sum - mer. __ I'll fi - n'lly see a sum - mer breeze __ blow a -

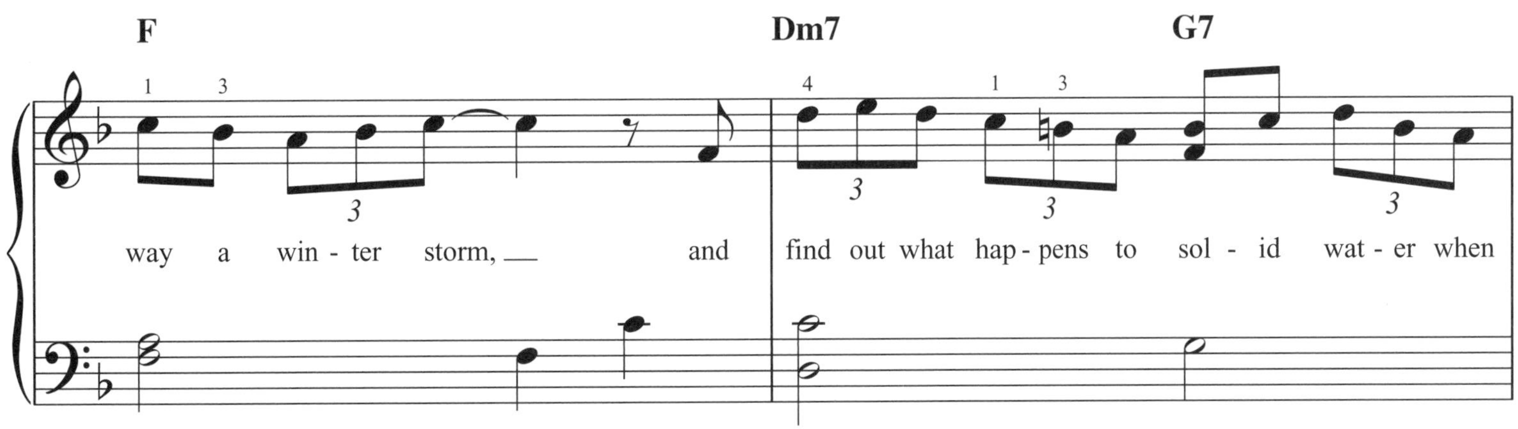
F
Dm7
G7
way a win - ter storm, __ and find out what hap - pens to sol - id wat - er when

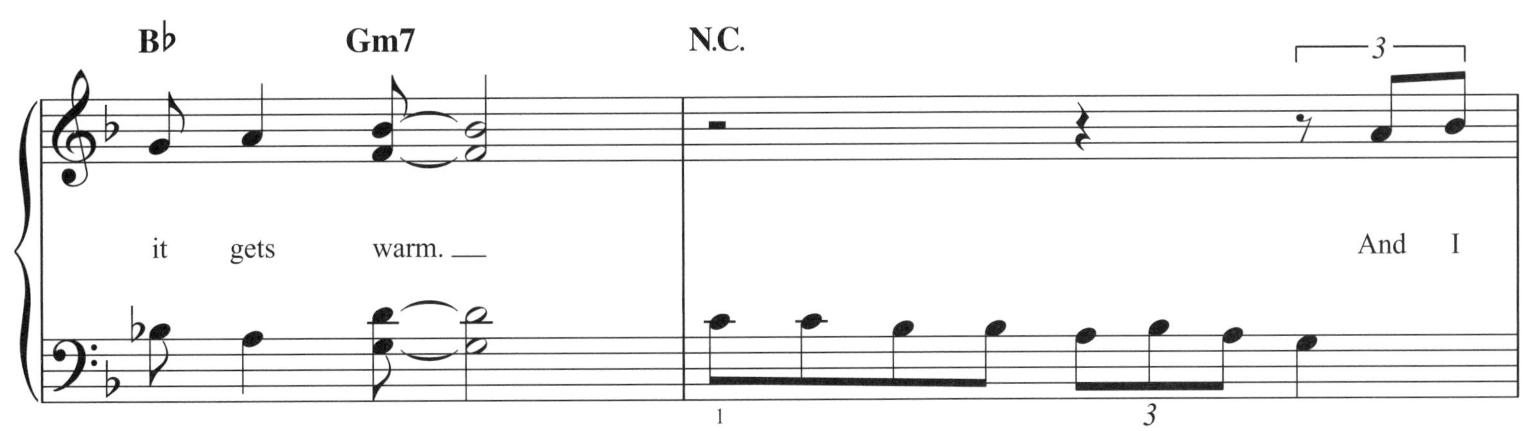
B♭
Gm7
N.C.
it gets warm. __ And I

F6
Gm
Fmaj7
B♭m6
can't wait to see what my bud - dies all think of me. Just im -

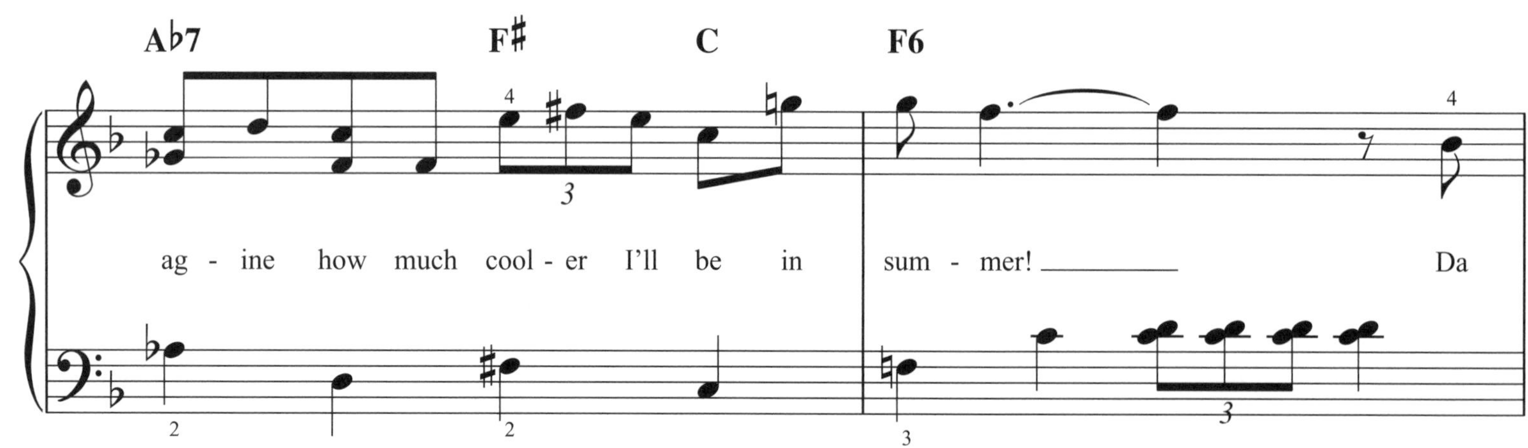
A♭7
F♯
C
F6
ag - ine how much cool - er I'll be in sum - mer! Da

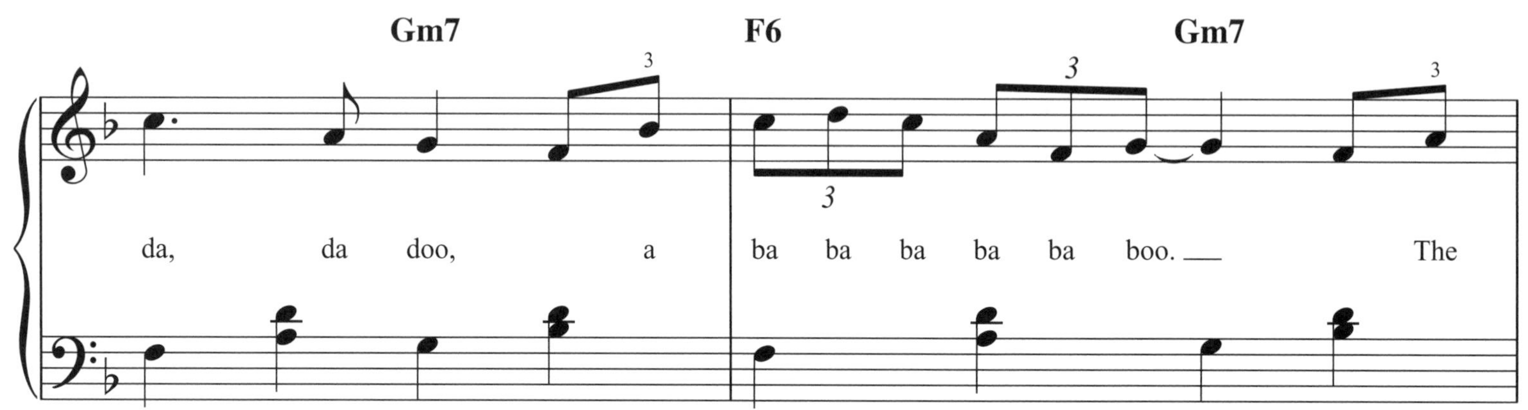
Gm7
F6
Gm7
da, da doo, a ba ba ba ba ba boo. The

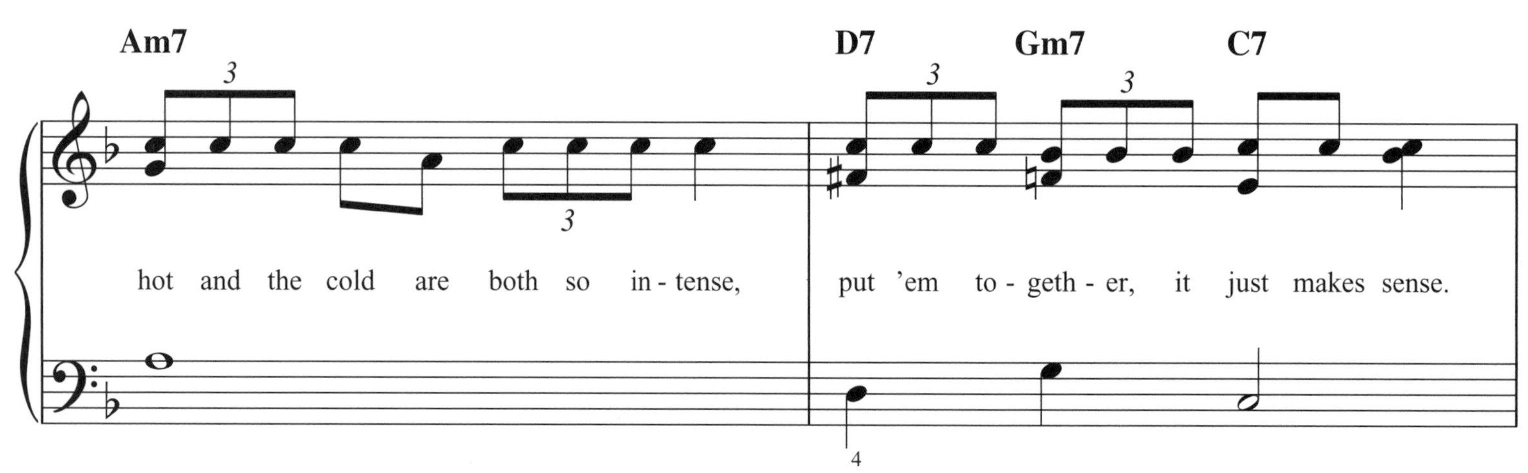
Am7
D7
Gm7
C7
hot and the cold are both so in - tense, put 'em to - geth - er, it just makes sense.

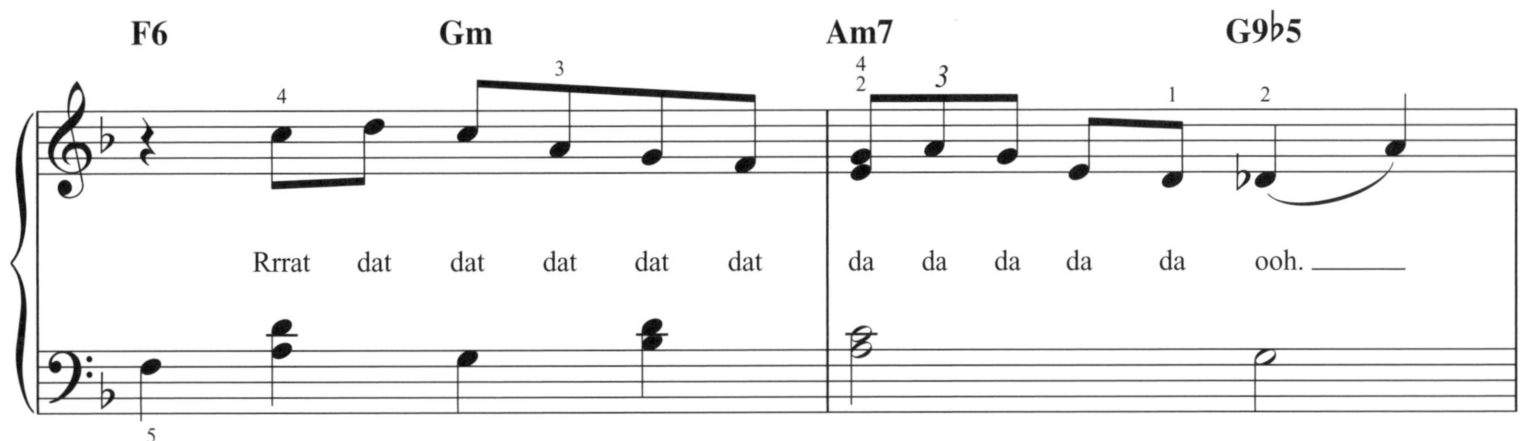
F6
Gm
Am7
G9♭5
Rrrat dat dat dat dat dat
da da da da da ooh.

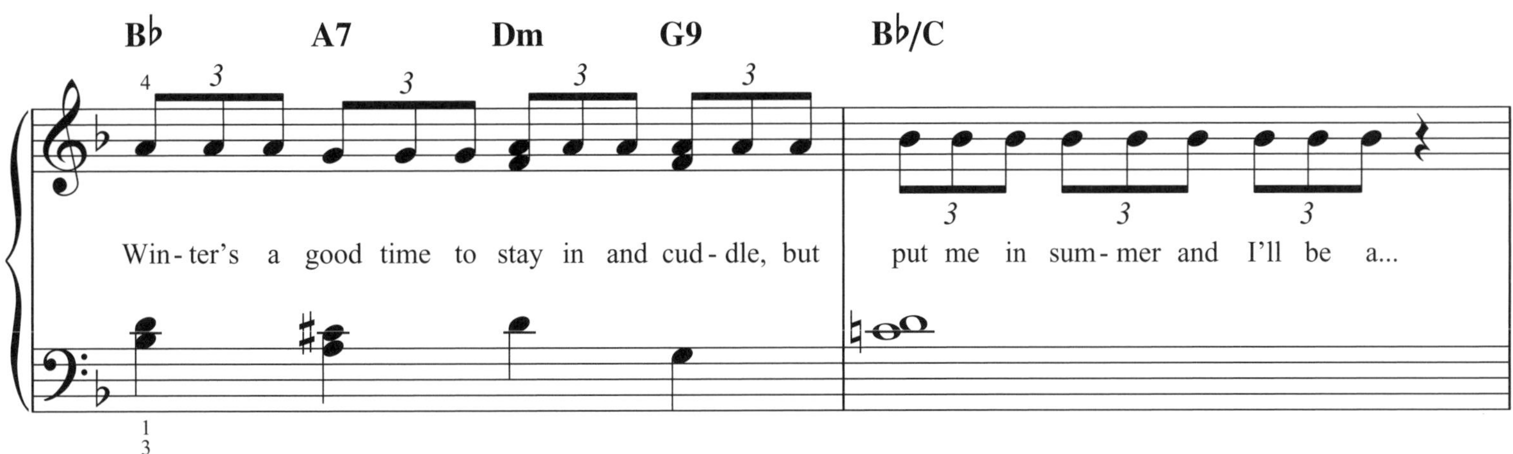
B♭
A7
Dm
G9
B♭/C
Win-ter's a good time to stay in and cud-dle, but
put me in sum-mer and I'll be a...

N.C.
B♭6
(Spoken:) happy snowman!
(Sung:) When life gets rough, I like to

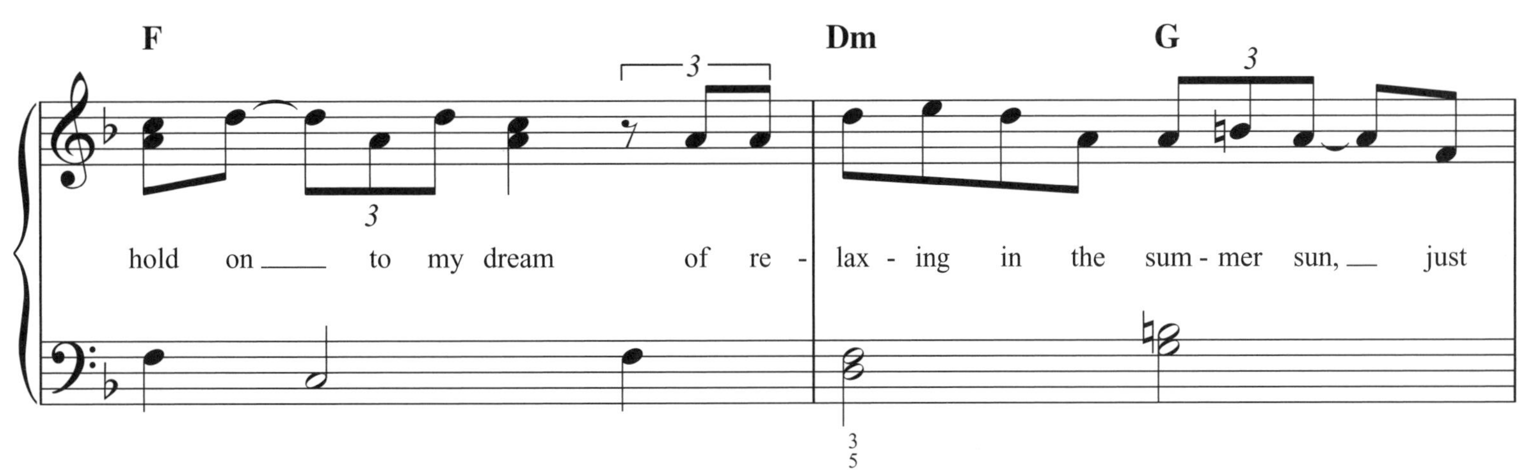
F
Dm
G
hold on to my dream of re-
lax-ing in the sum-mer sun, just

B♭6
Gm7
B♭/C
F
Gm7
let - tin' off steam. ___
Oh, the
sky will be blue, and

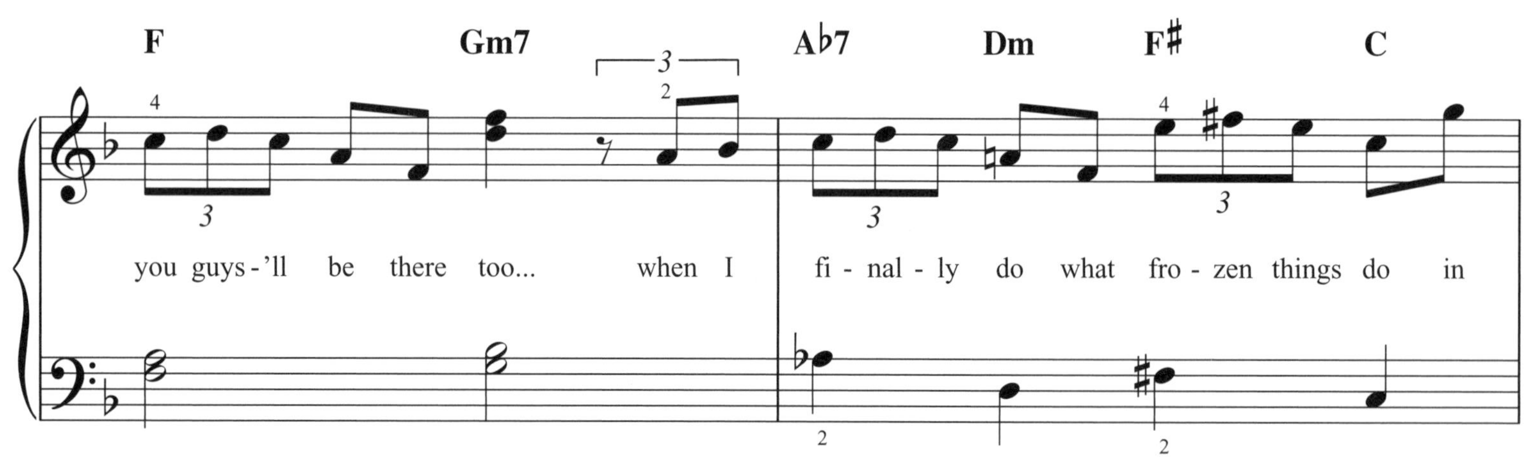
F
Gm7
A♭7
Dm
F♯
C
you guys-'ll be there too... when I
fi - nal - ly do what fro - zen things do in

F
N.C.
sum - mer.
KRISTOFF: (Spoken:) I'm gonna tell him.

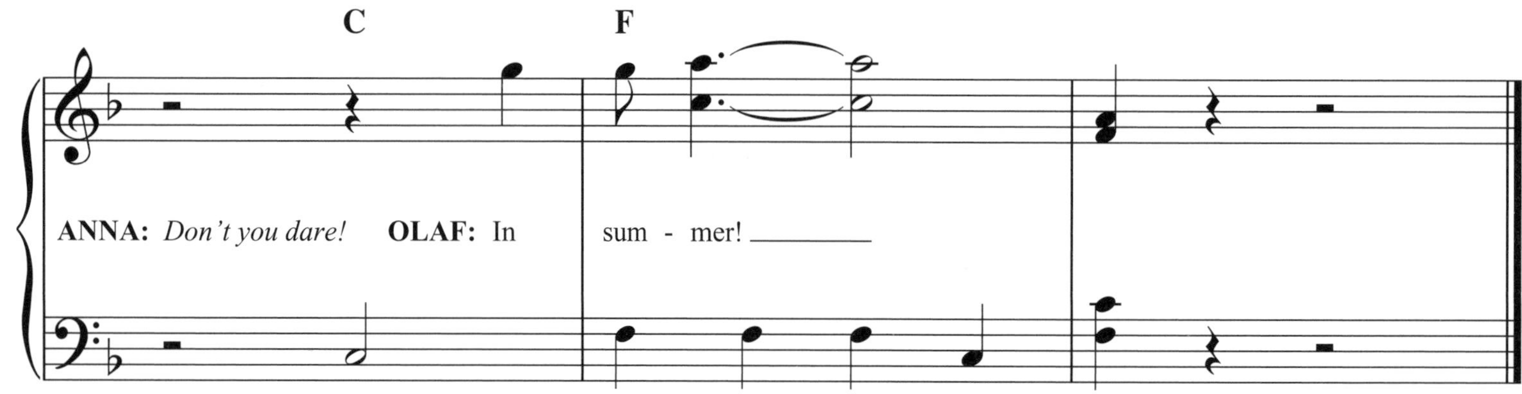
C
F
ANNA: Don't you dare!
OLAF: In
sum - mer! ______

REINDEER(S) ARE BETTER THAN PEOPLE

from FROZEN

Music and Lyrics by KRISTEN ANDERSON-LOPEZ
and ROBERT LOPEZ

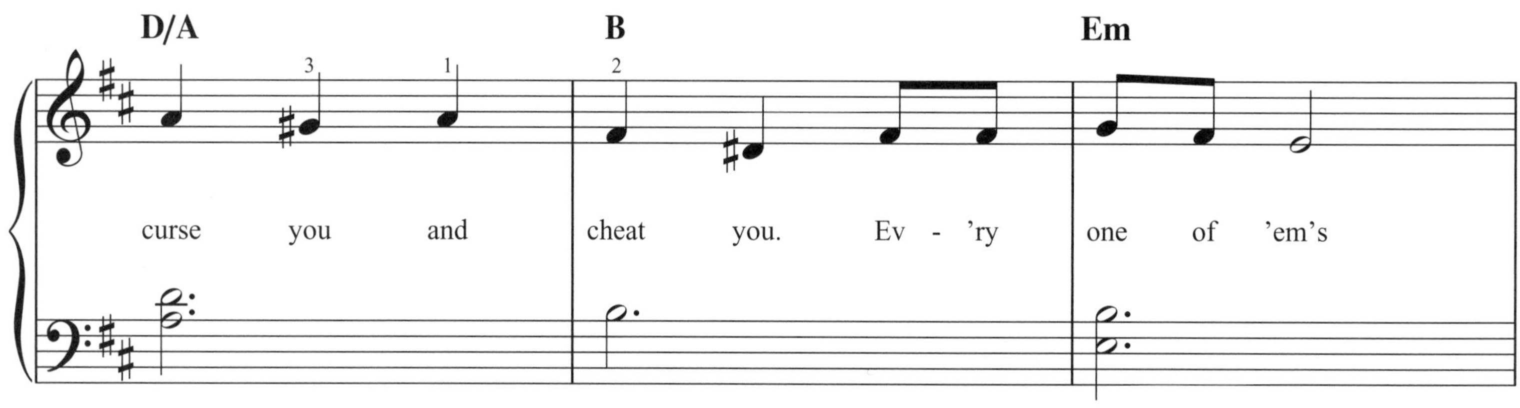
D/A
B
Em
3
1
2
curse you and
cheat you. Ev - 'ry
one of 'em's

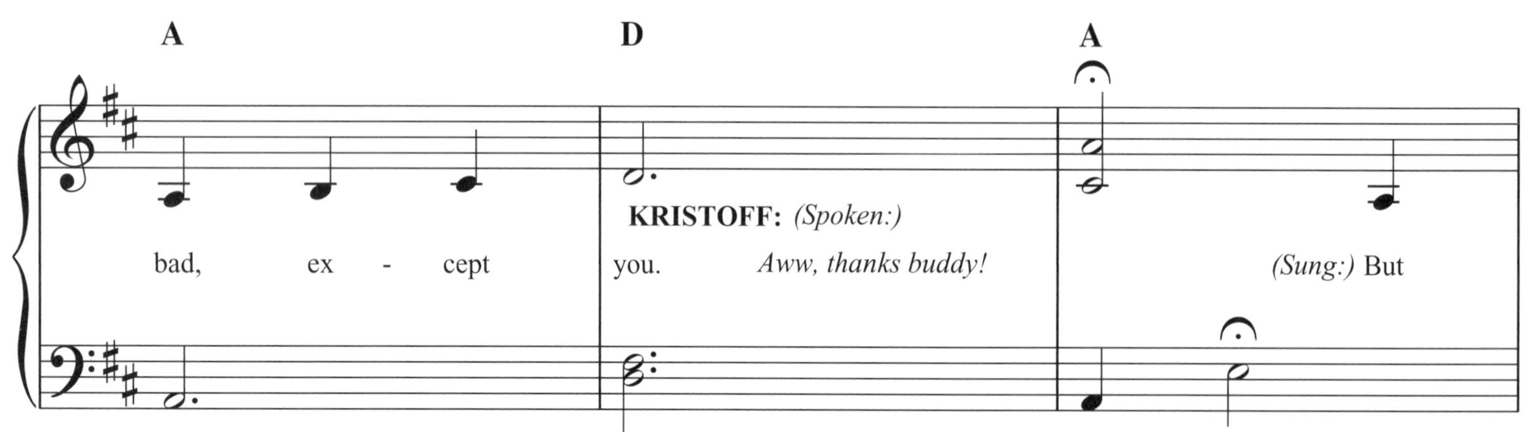
A
D
A
bad, ex - cept
KRISTOFF: (Spoken:)
you. Aww, thanks buddy!
(Sung:) But

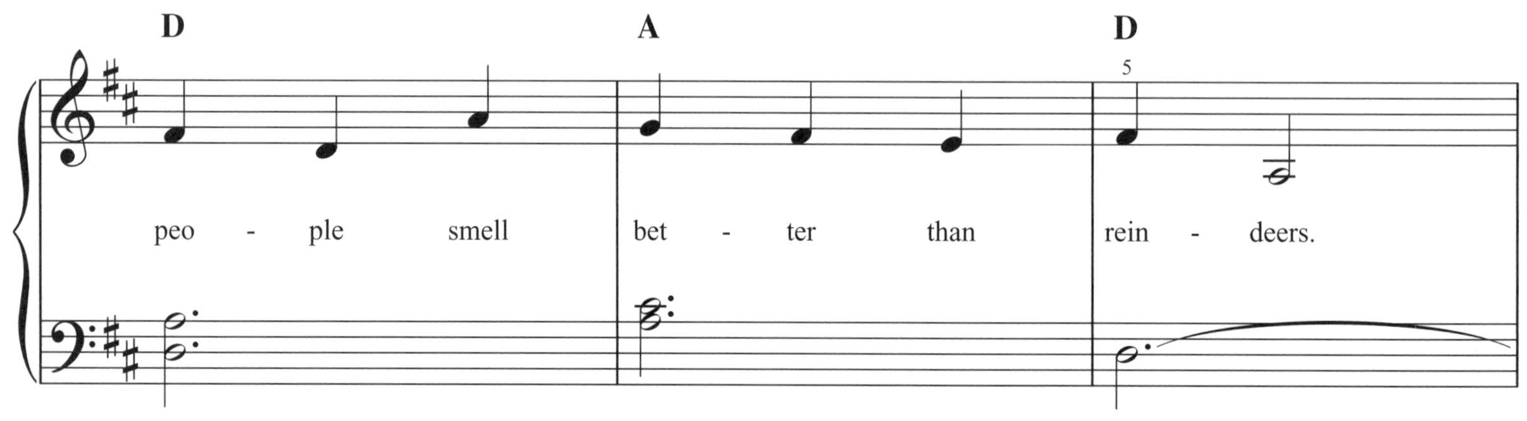
D
A
D
5
peo - ple smell
bet - ter than
rein - deers.

D7
G
A
F♯m
Sven, don't you
think I'm
right?
2

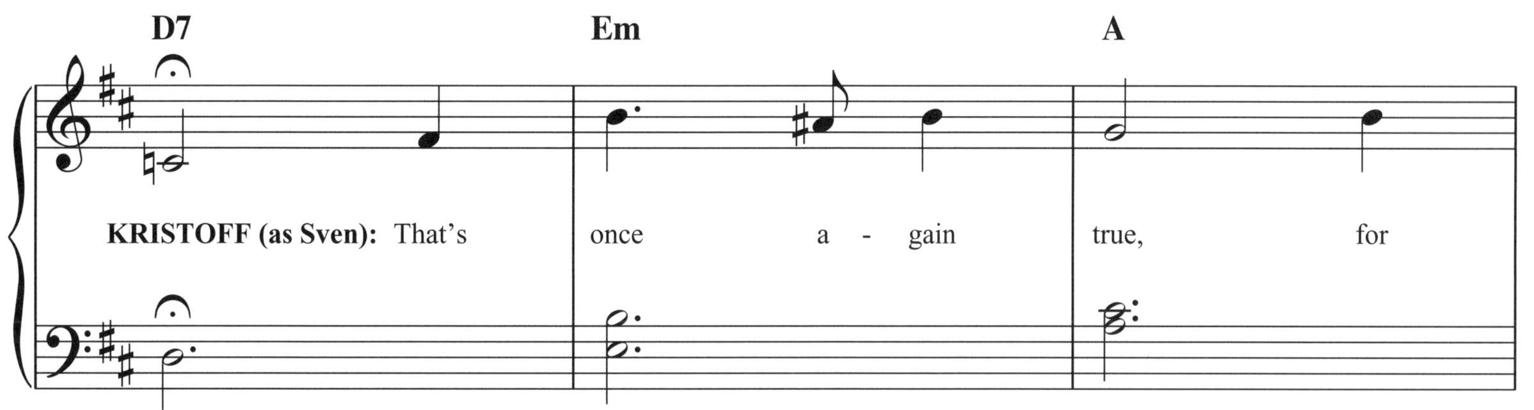
D7
Em
A
KRISTOFF (as Sven): That's
once a - gain
true, for

D
B
Em
all ex - cept
you. KRISTOFF: You
got me! Let's

A
Bm
E(♭5)
call it a
KRISTOFF (as Sven):
night. Good -
night!

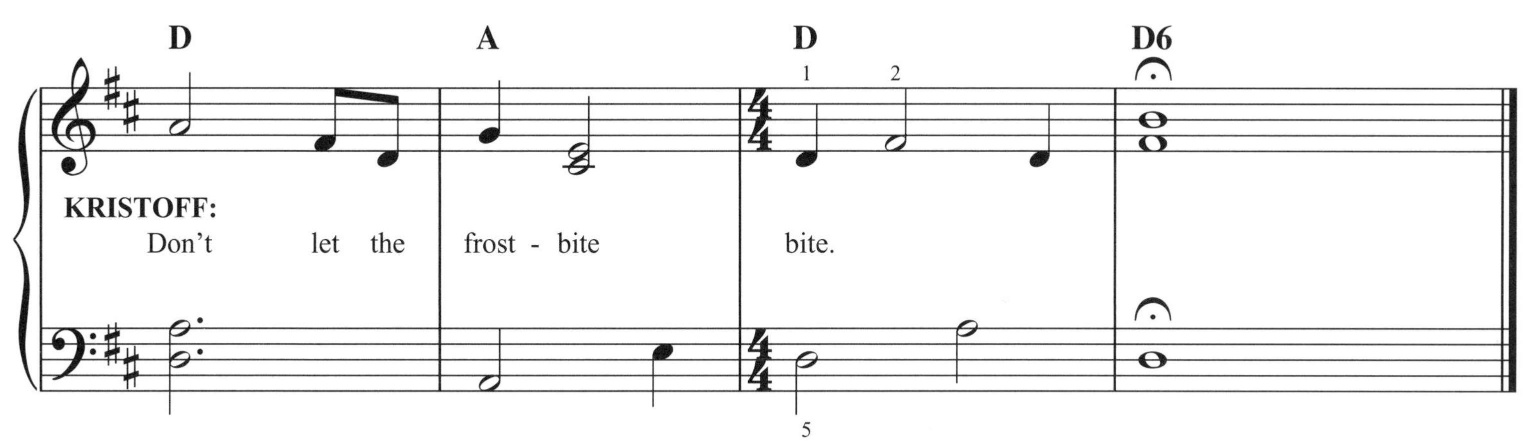
D
A
D
D6
KRISTOFF:
Don't let the
frost - bite
bite.

IT'S A SMALL WORLD

from IT'S A SMALL WORLD® ATTRACTION AT DISNEYLAND® PARK AND MAGIC KINGDOM® PARK

Words and Music by RICHARD M. SHERMAN
and ROBERT B. SHERMAN

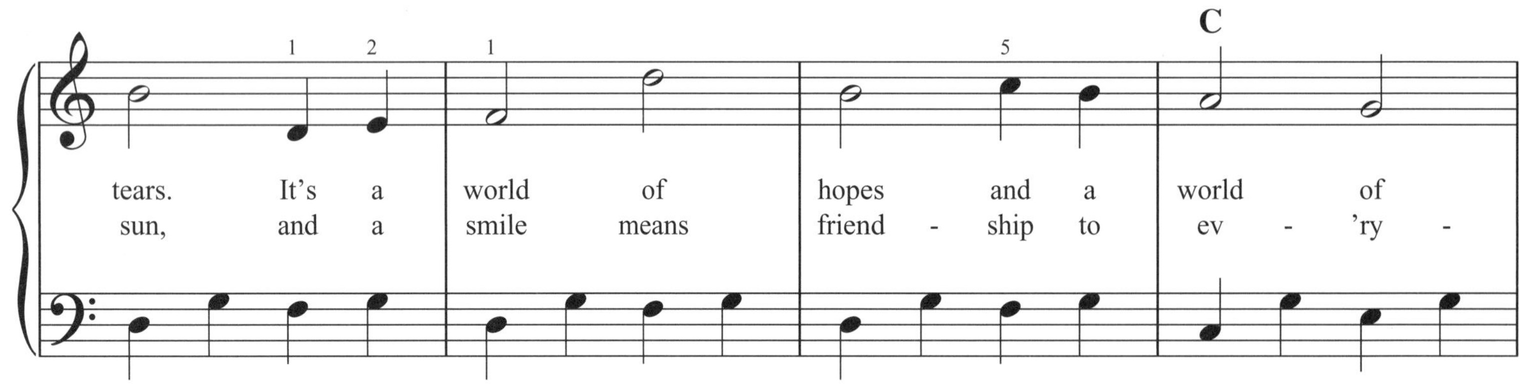

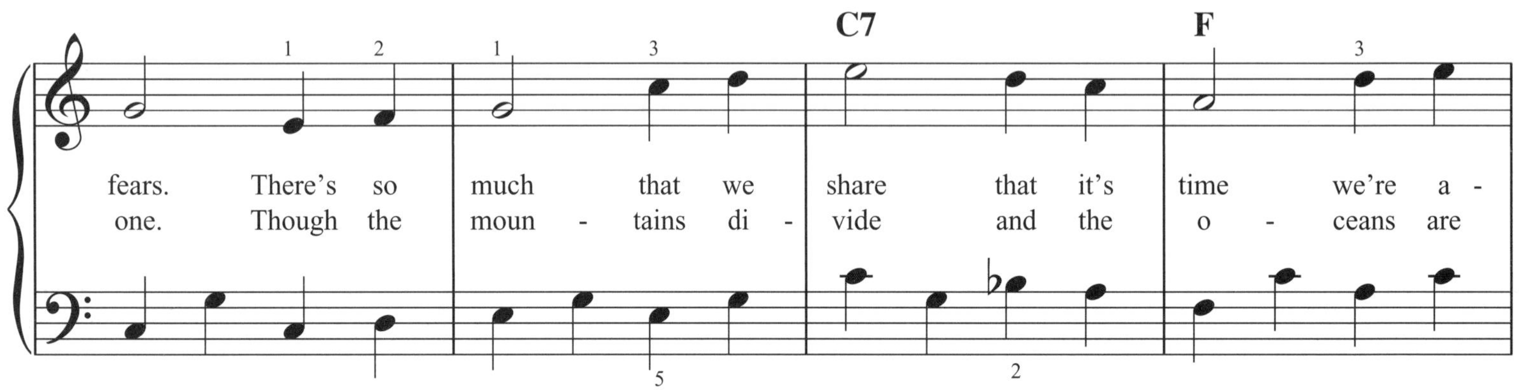

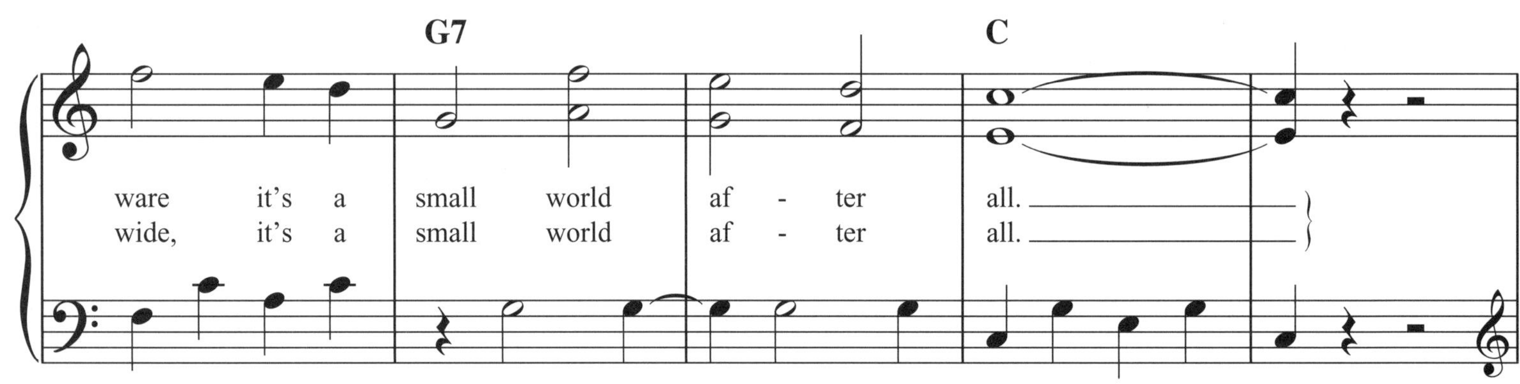

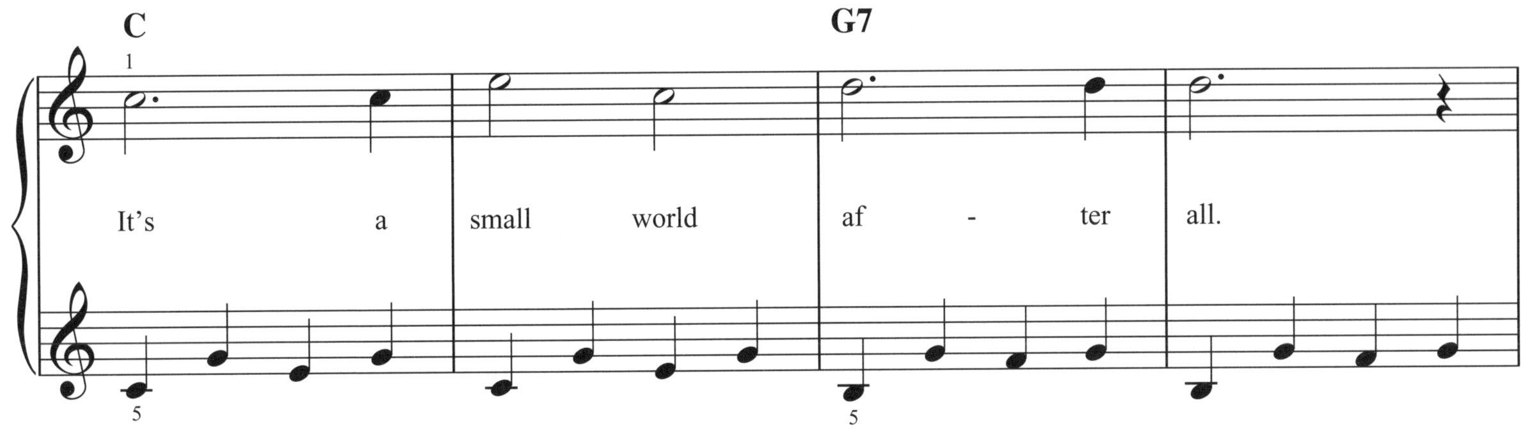
C
G7
It's a small world af - ter all.

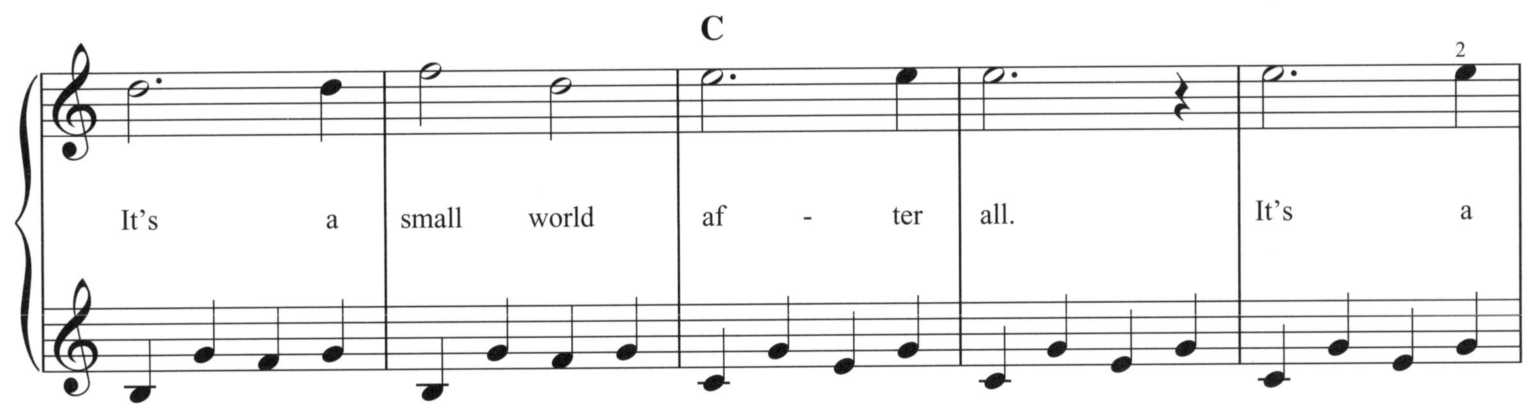
C
It's a small world af - ter all. It's a

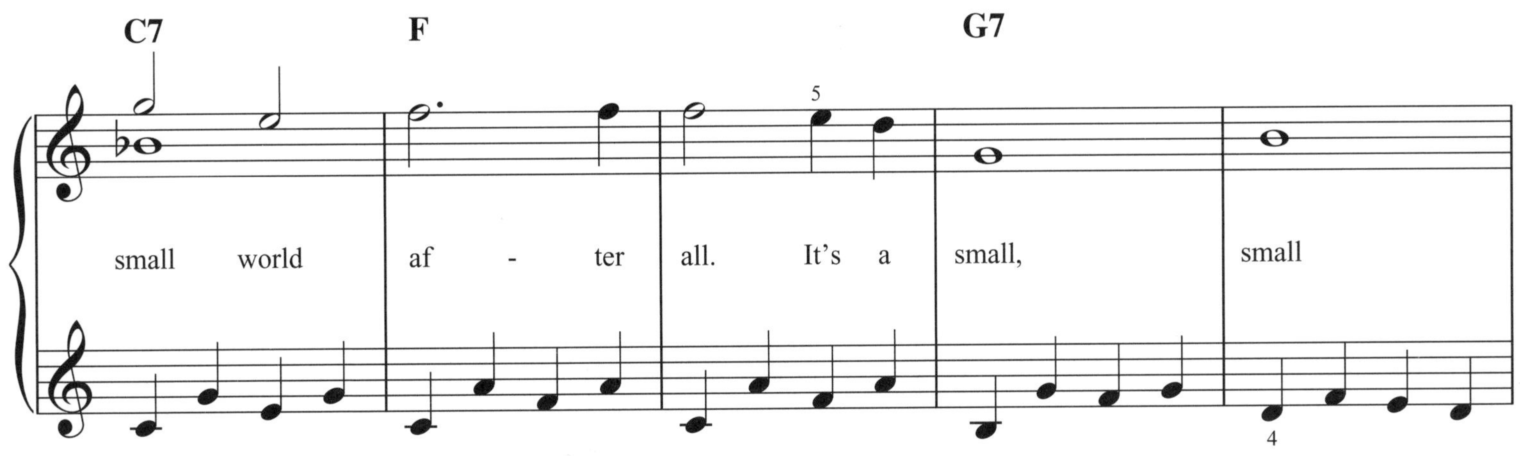
C7
F
G7
small world af - ter all. It's a small, small

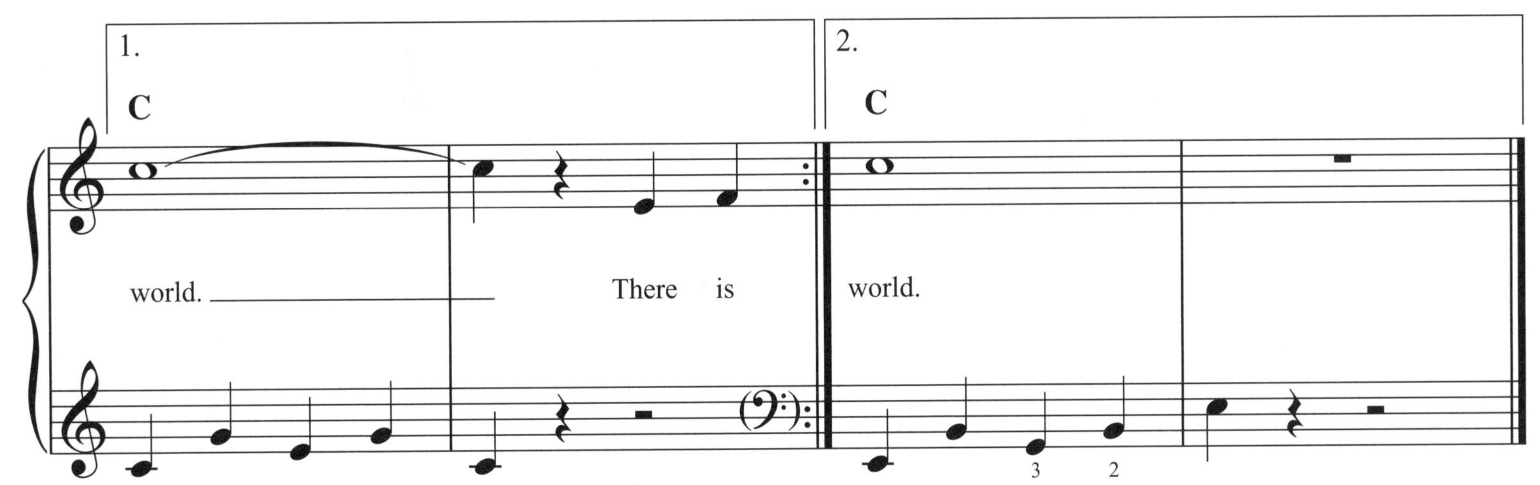
1.
C
2.
C
world. There is world.

from LAVA

Music and Lyrics by
JAMES FORD MURPHY

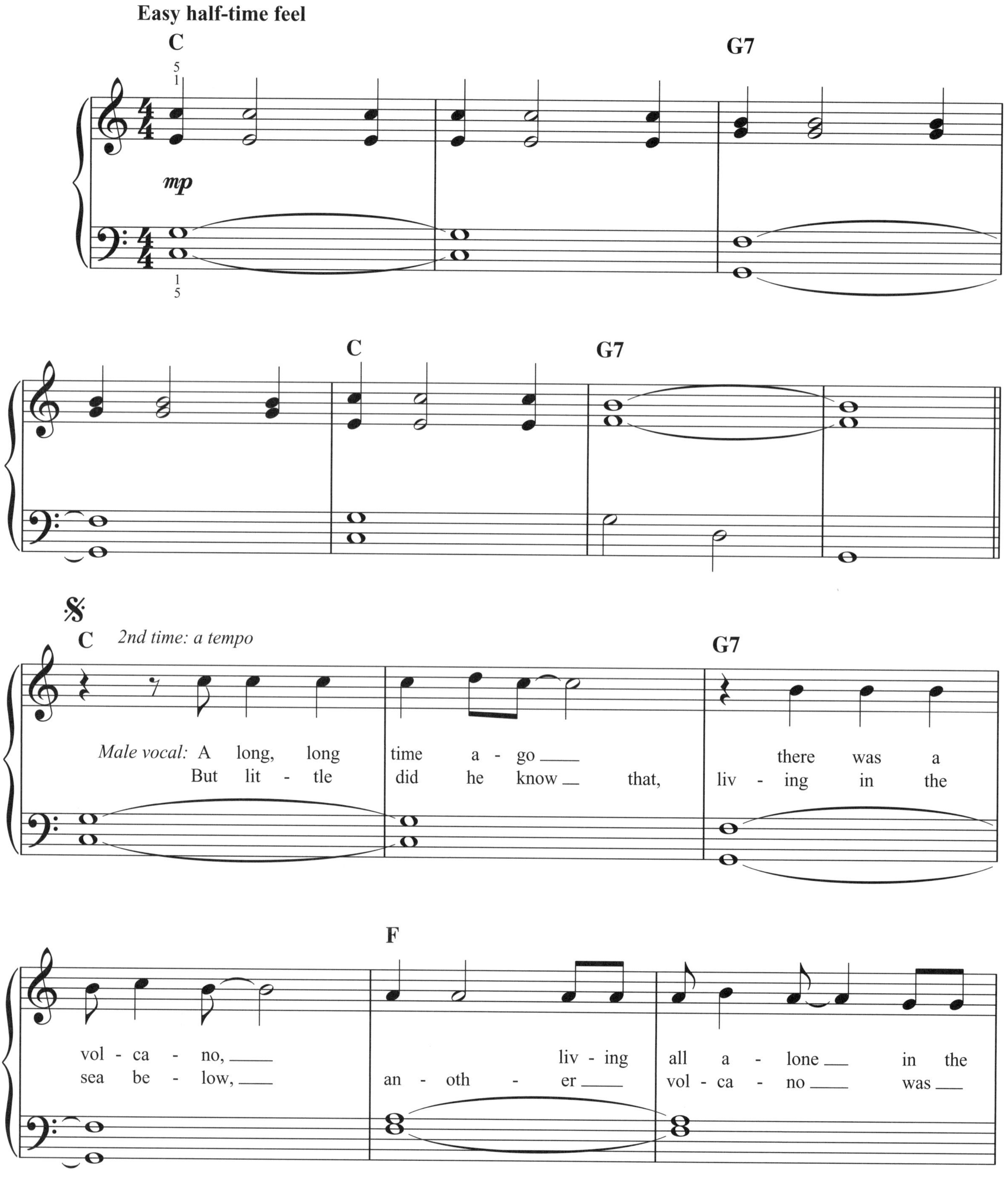

Easy half-time feel

C G7 C G7

mp

𝄋

C *2nd time: a tempo* G7

Male vocal: A long, long time a - go ___ there was a
But lit - tle did he know ___ that, liv - ing in the

F

vol - ca - no, ___ liv - ing all a - lone ___ in the
sea be - low, ___ an - oth - er ___ vol - ca - no ___ was ___

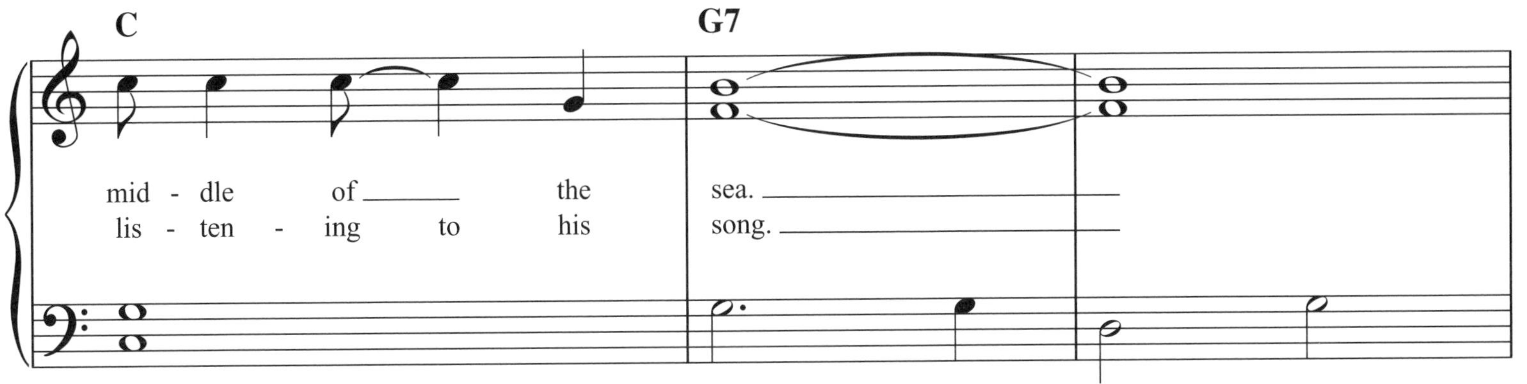
C
G7
mid - dle of the sea.
lis - ten - ing to his song.

C
G7
He sat high a - bove his bay, watch - ing all the
Ev - 'ry day she heard his tune, her la - va

F
cou - ples play, and wish - ing that
grew and grew, be - cause she be - lieved his

C
G7
he had some - one too.
song was meant for her.

C
G7
And from his la - va came this song of hope
Now she was so read - y to meet him a -

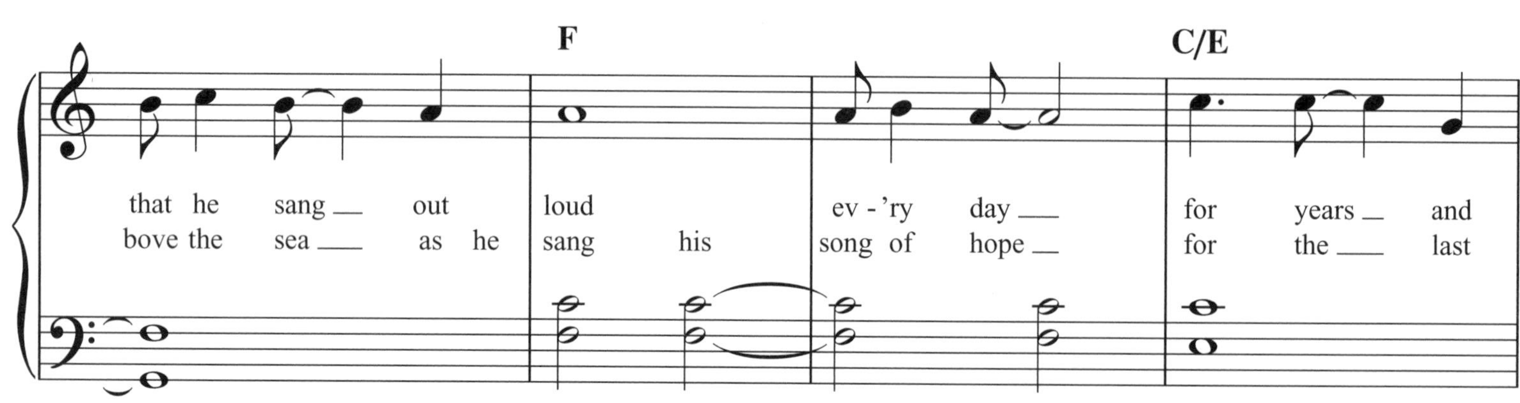
F
C/E
that he sang out loud every day for years and
bove the sea as he sang his song of hope for the last

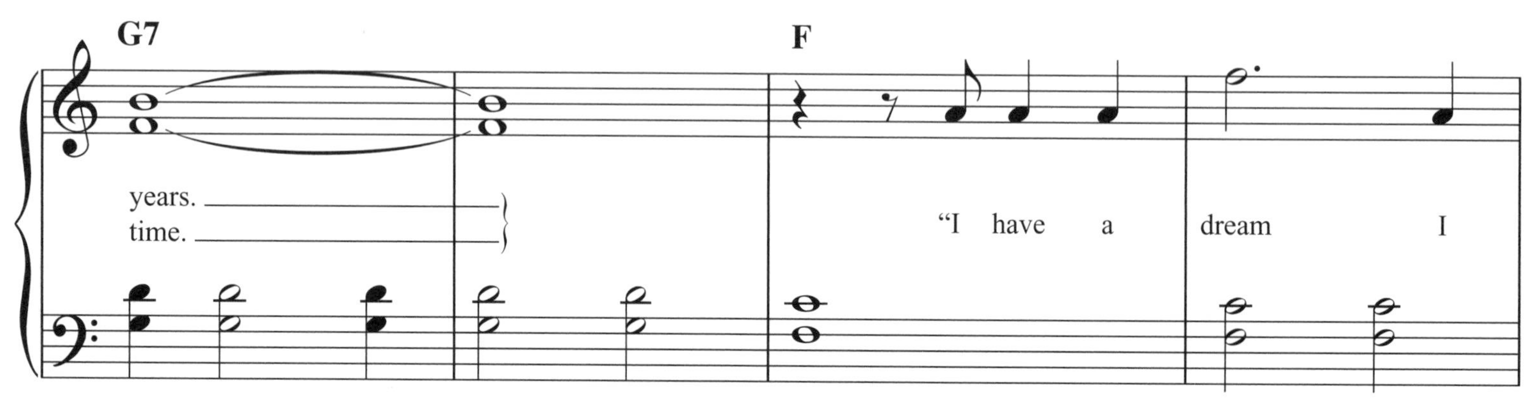
G7
F
years.
time.
"I have a dream I

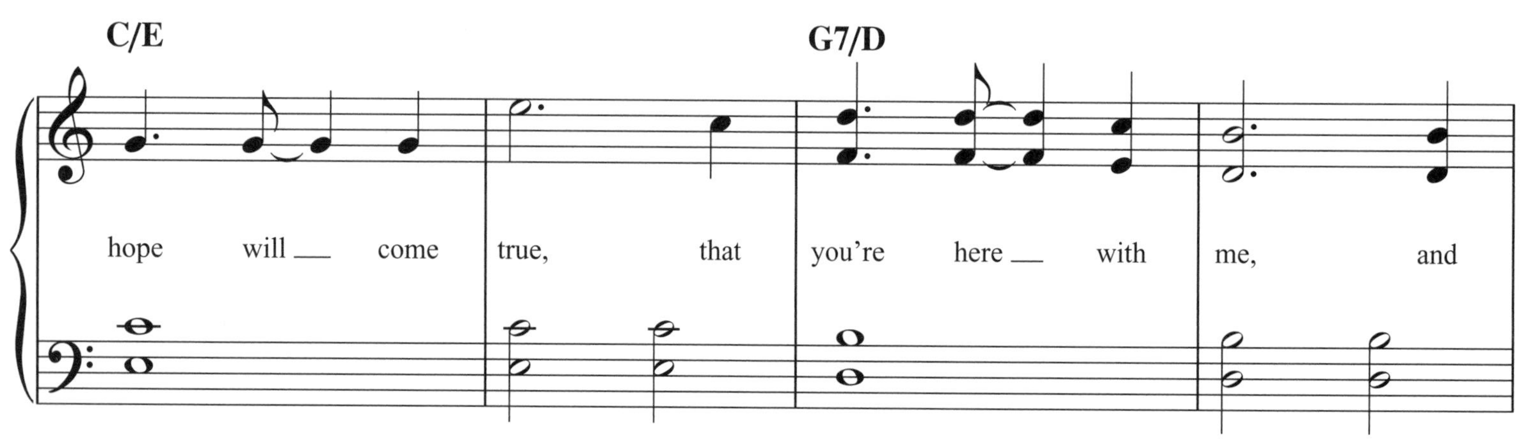
C/E
G7/D
hope will come true, that you're here with me, and

C
F
I'm here with you. I wish that the earth, sea, and the

C/E
F
G
To Coda
sky up a - bove - a will send me some - one to

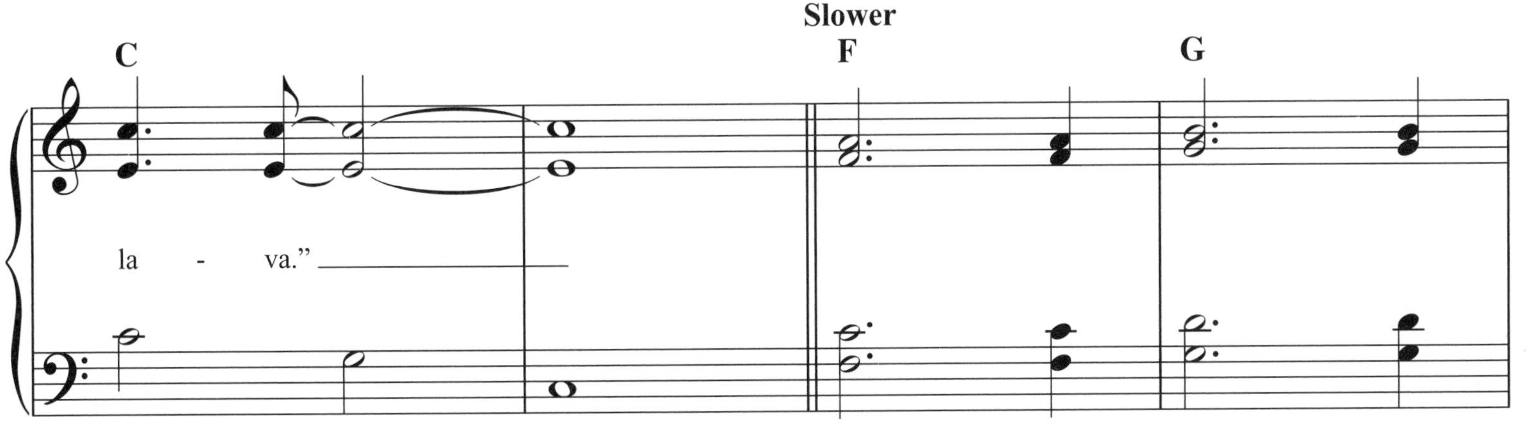
C
Slower
F
G
la - va."

C
Years of sing - ing all a - lone

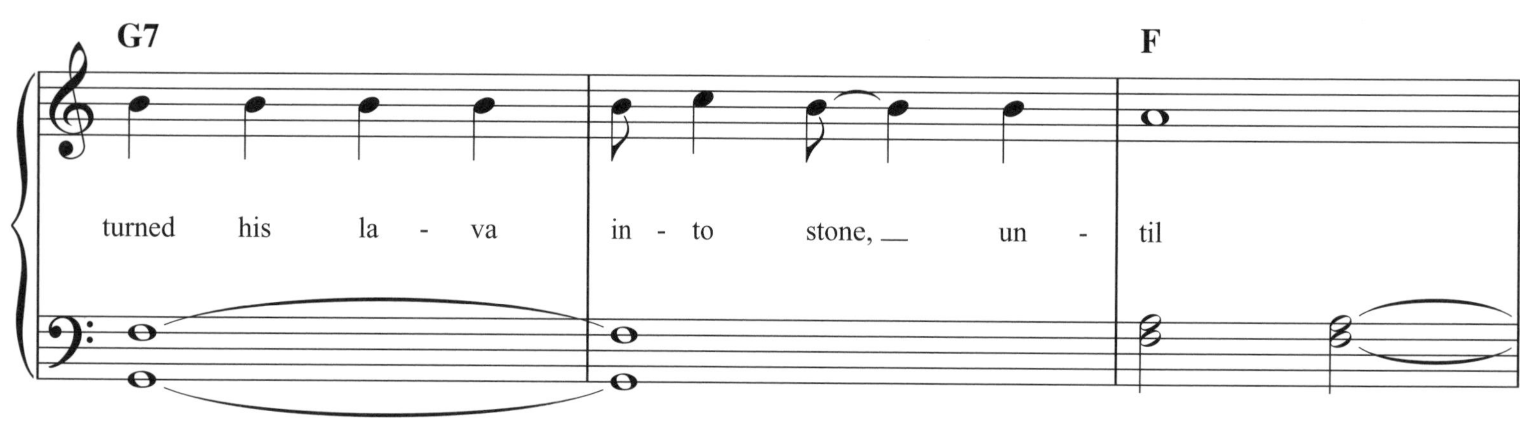
G7
F
turned his la - va in - to stone, un - til

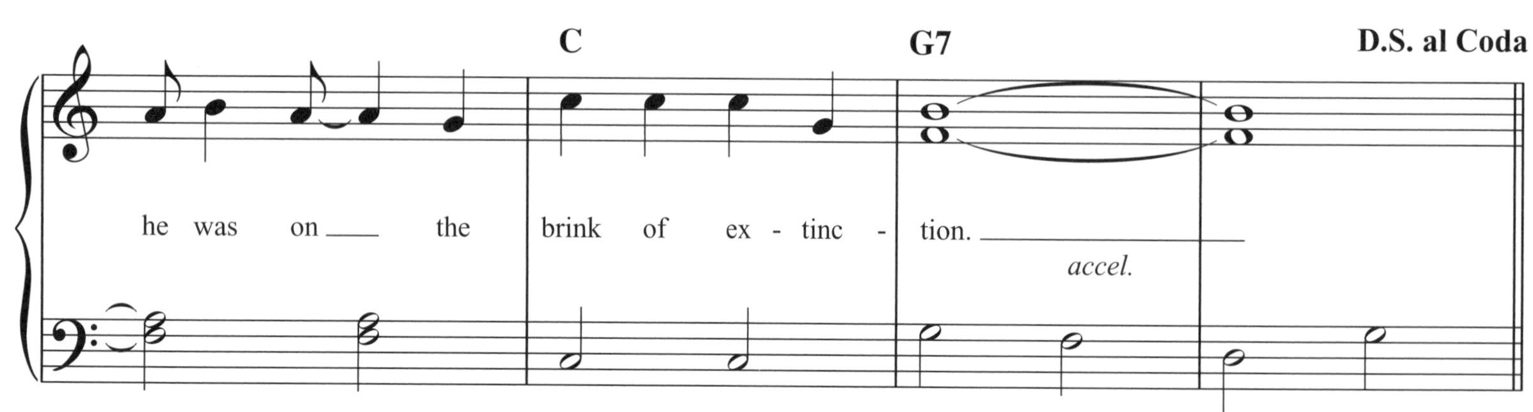
C
G7
D.S. al Coda
he was on the brink of ex - tinc - tion.
accel.

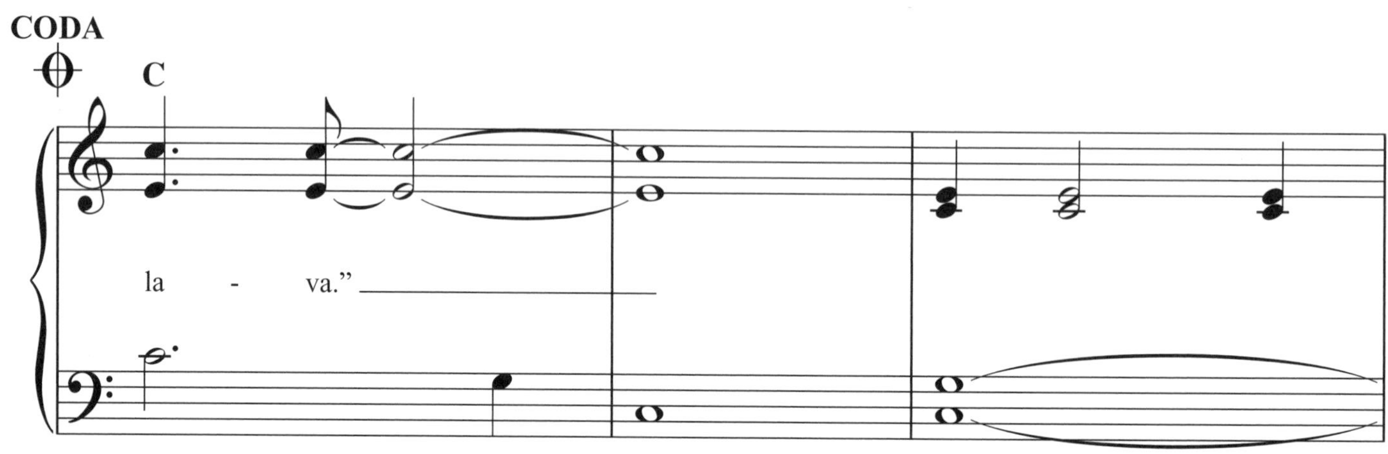
CODA
C
la - va."

G7
Ris - ing from the sea be - low stood a love - ly

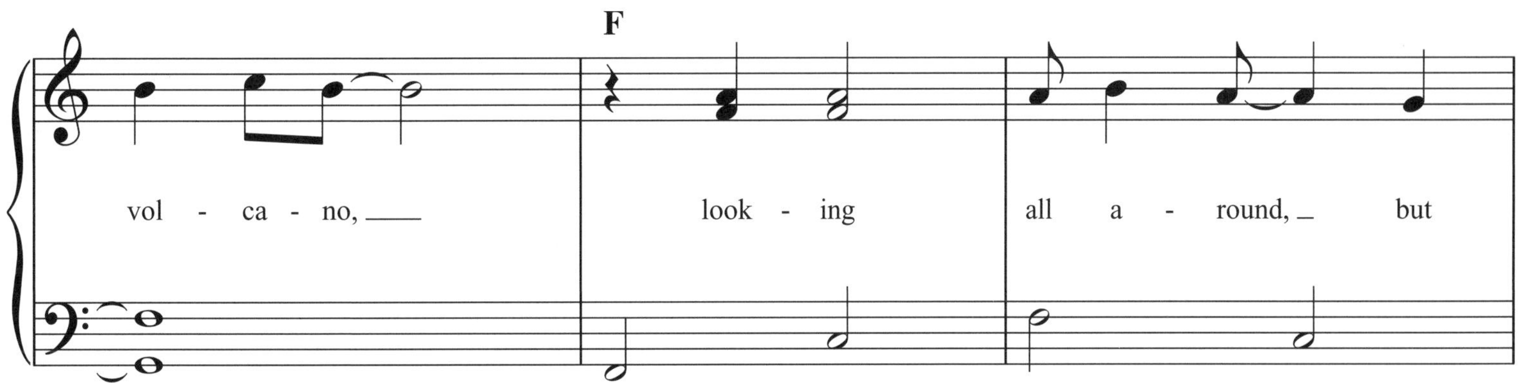
F
vol - ca - no,
look - ing
all a - round,
but

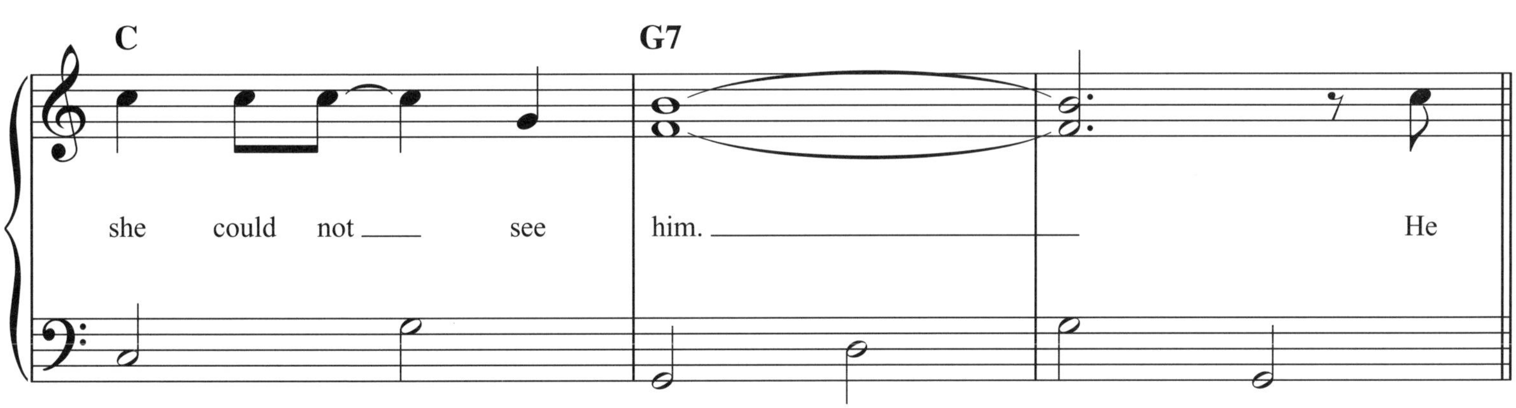
C
G7
she could not see
him.
He

C
G7
tried to sing to
filled the sea
let her know that
with his tears, and
she was not
watched his dreams

F
there a - lone, but
dis - ap - pear as
with no
she re -
la - va his
mem - bered what his

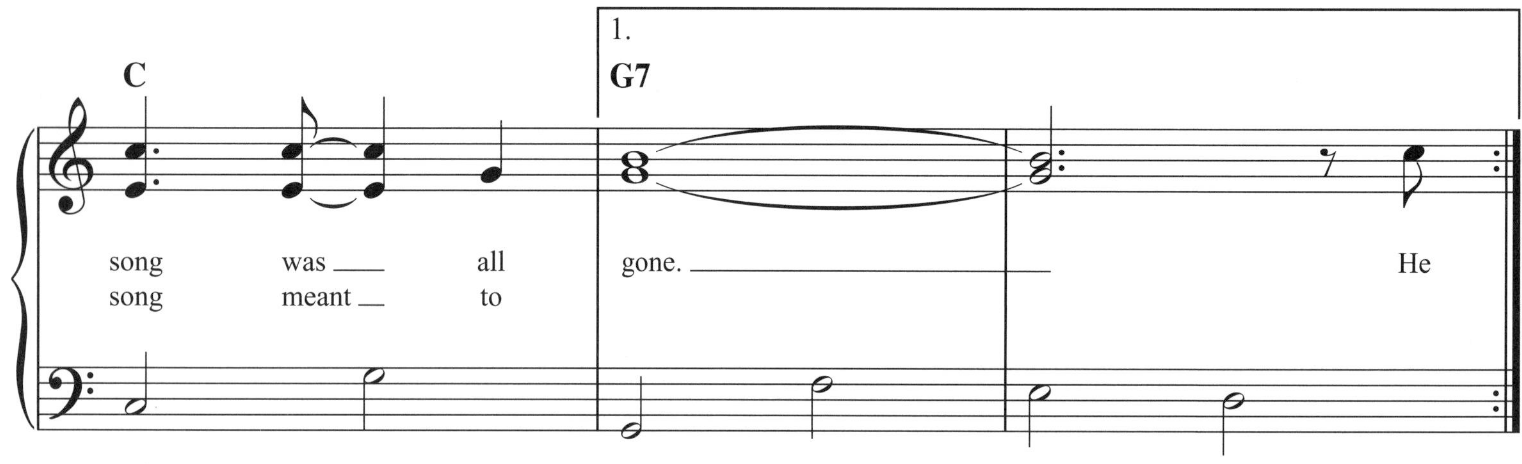
1.
C
G7
song was ___ all gone. ___ He
song meant ___ to

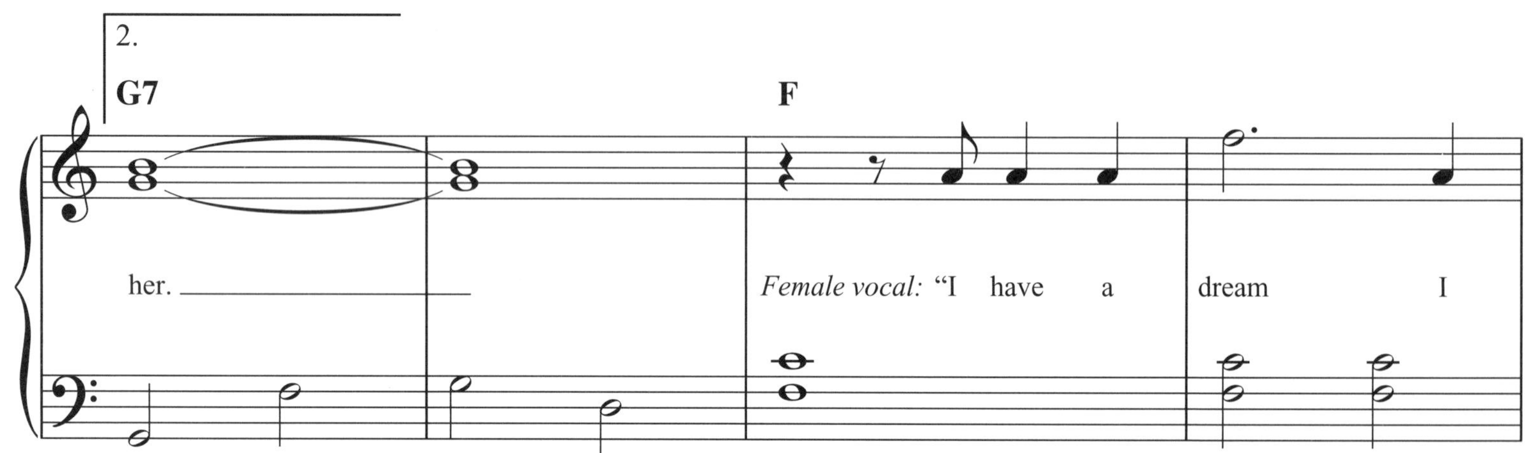
2.
G7
F
her. ___ *Female vocal:* "I have a dream I

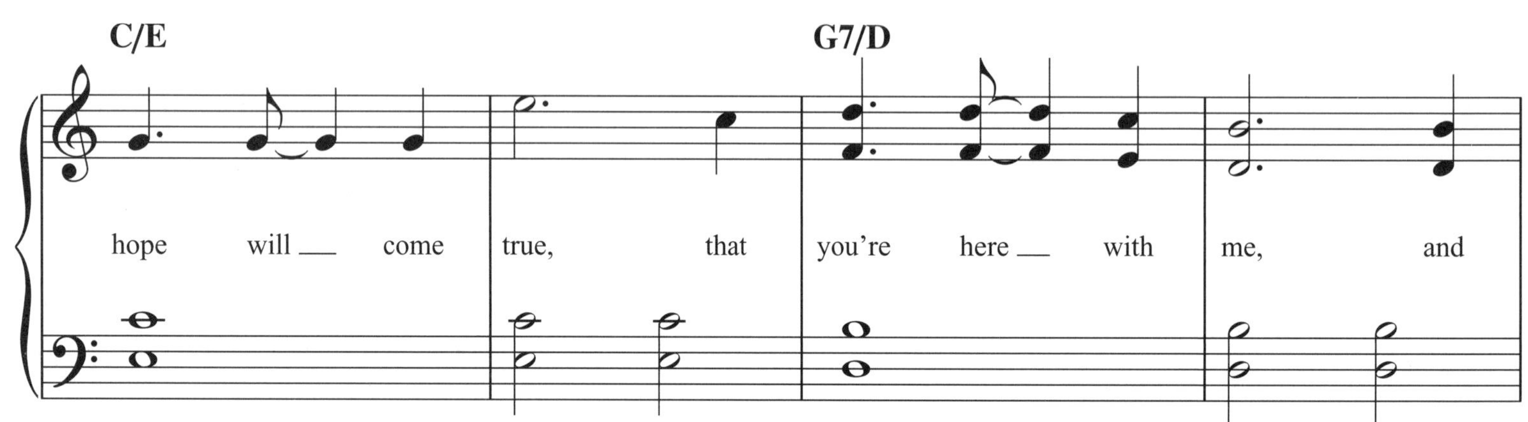
C/E
G7/D
hope will ___ come true, that you're here ___ with me, and

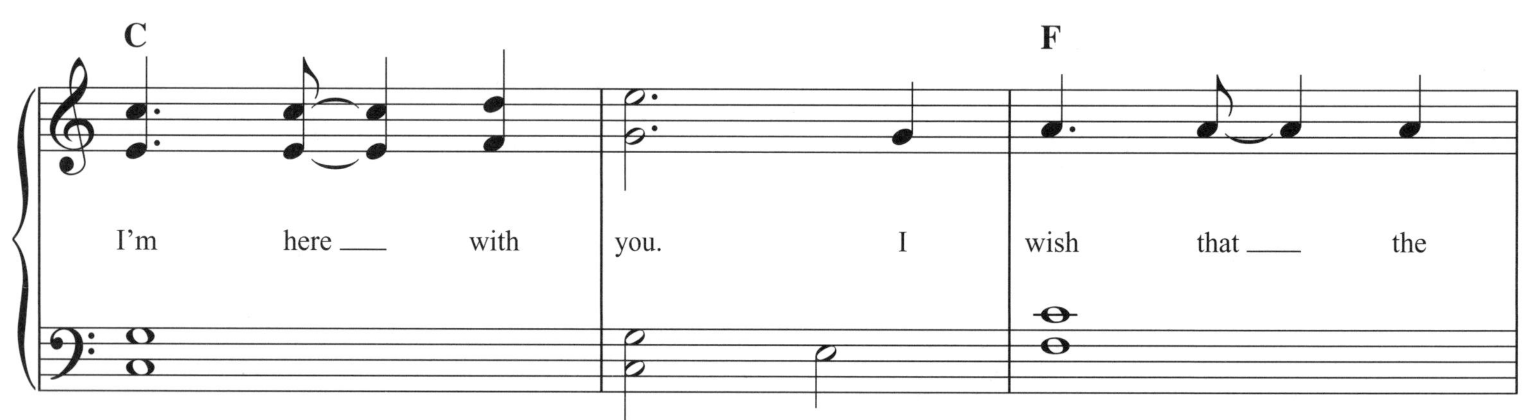
C
F
I'm here ___ with you. I wish that ___ the

C/E
F
earth, sea, and the sky up a - bove - a will send me

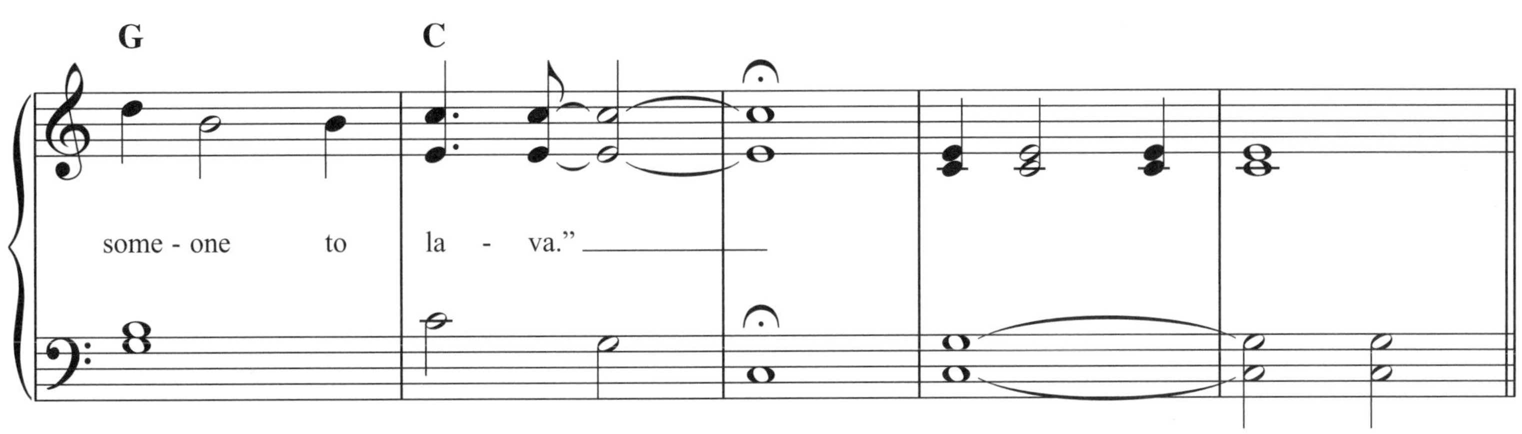
G
C
some - one to la - va."

C
G7
Oh, they were so hap - py to fi - n'lly meet a -
long - er are they all a - lone, with a - lo - ha as

F
bove the sea. All to - geth - er now their
their new home, and when you vis - it them

C
1.
G7
2.
G7
la - va grew and grew.
No
this is what they sing.

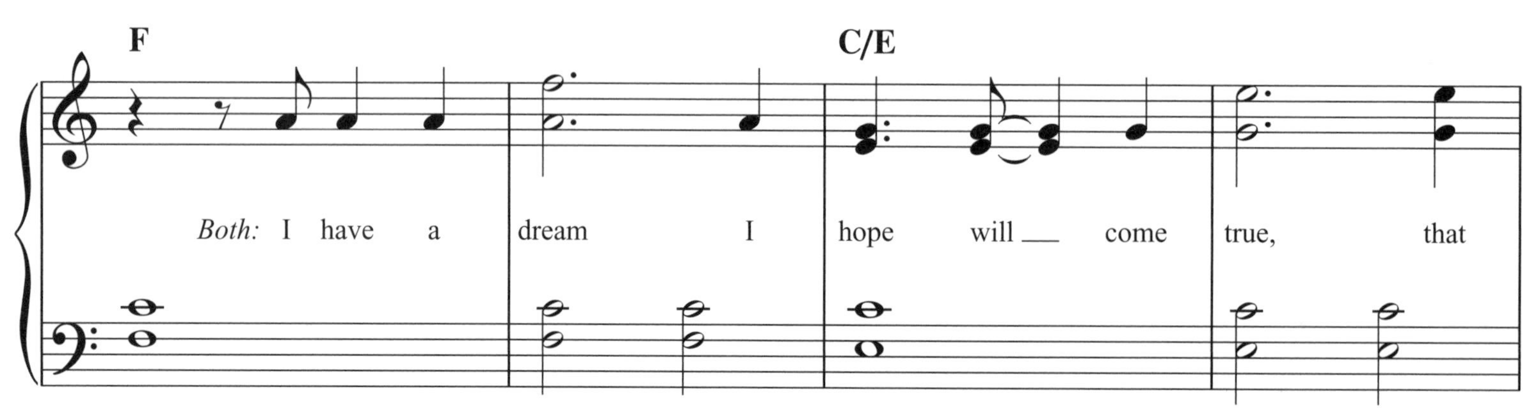
F
C/E
Both: I have a dream I hope will come true, that

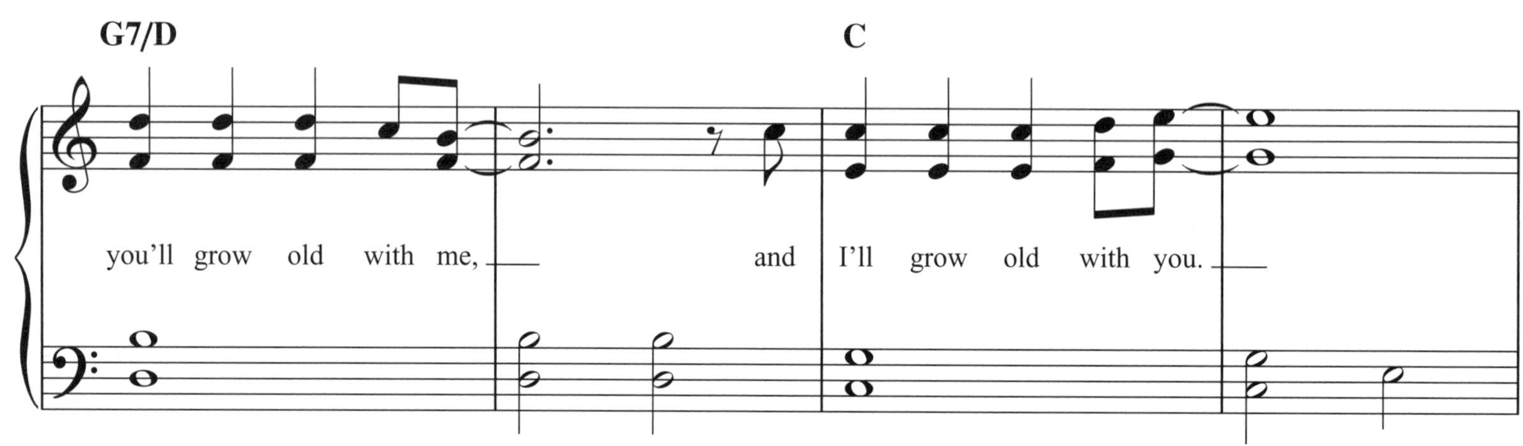
G7/D
C
you'll grow old with me, and I'll grow old with you.

F
C/E
We thank you earth, sea, and the sky we thank

F
G
too,
I
la - va

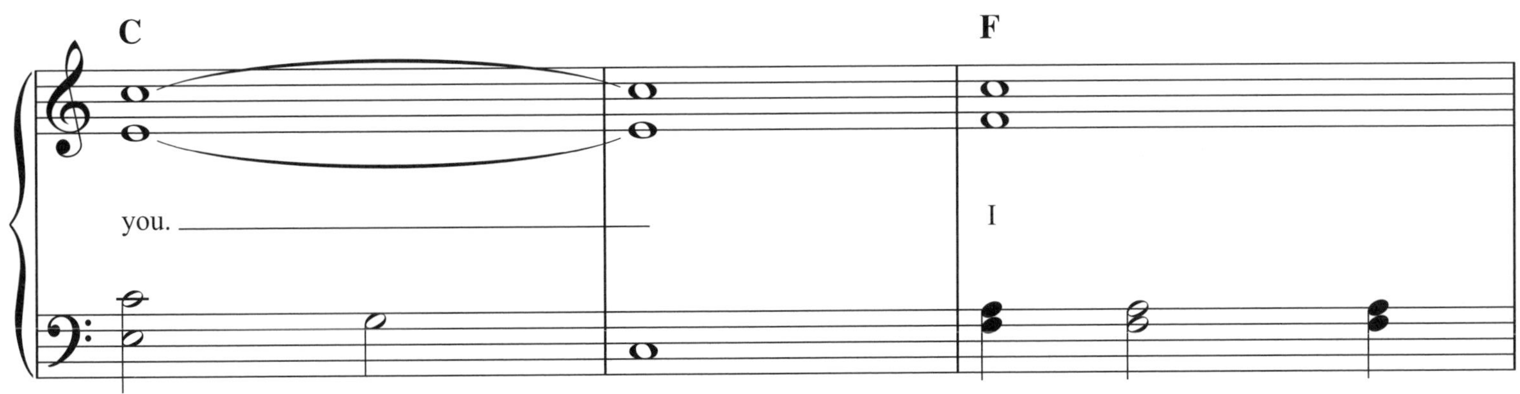
C
F
you.
I

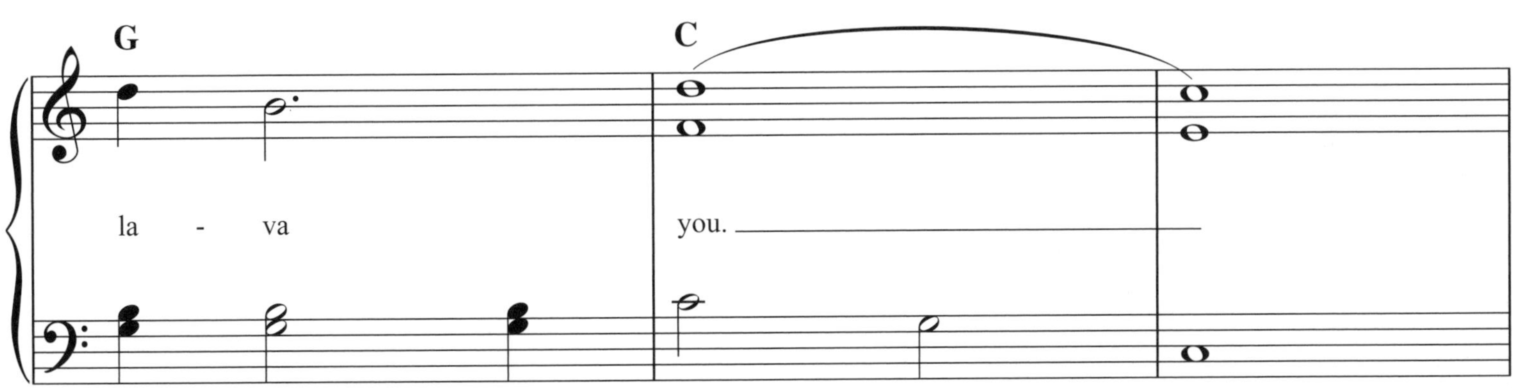
G
C
la - va
you.

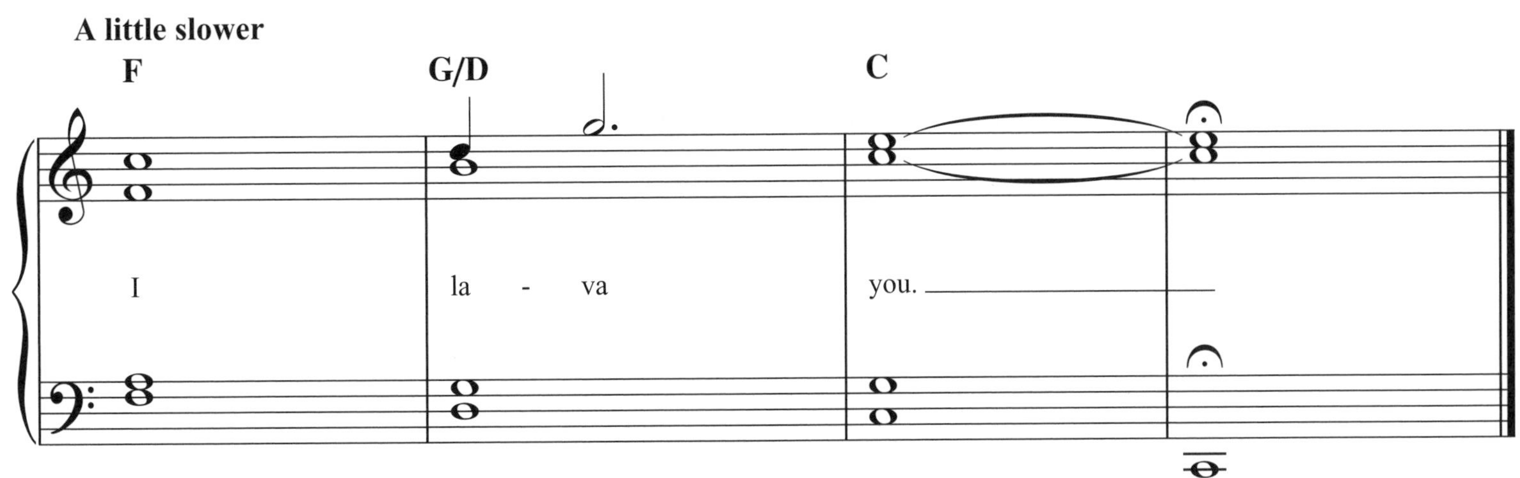
A little slower
F
G/D
C
I
la - va
you.

ONE JUMP AHEAD

from ALADDIN

Music by ALAN MENKEN
Lyrics by TIM RICE

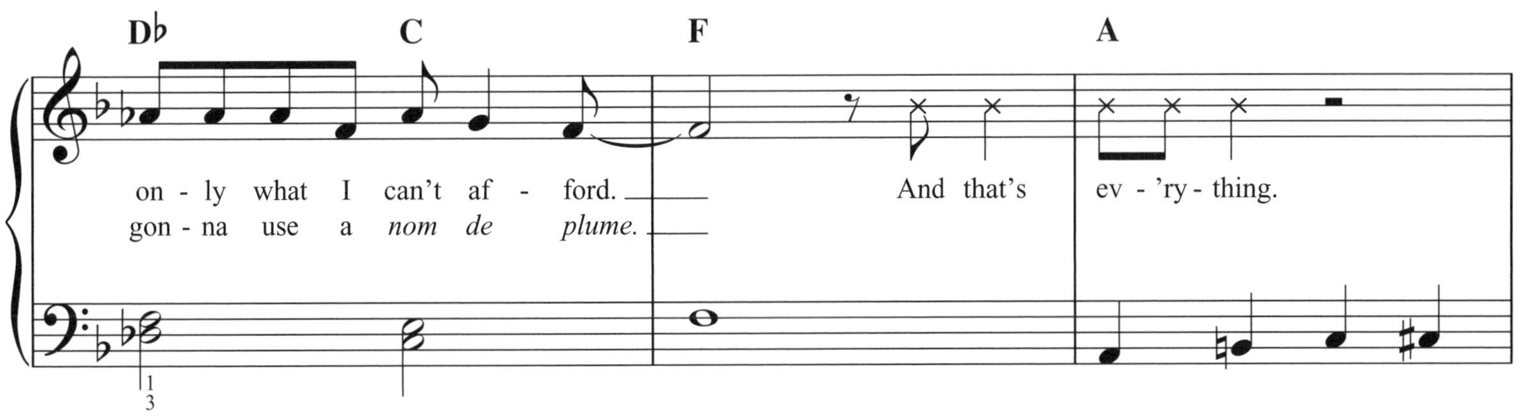
D♭ C F A
on - ly what I can't af - ford.
gon - na use a *nom de plume.*
And that's ev - 'ry - thing.
1
3

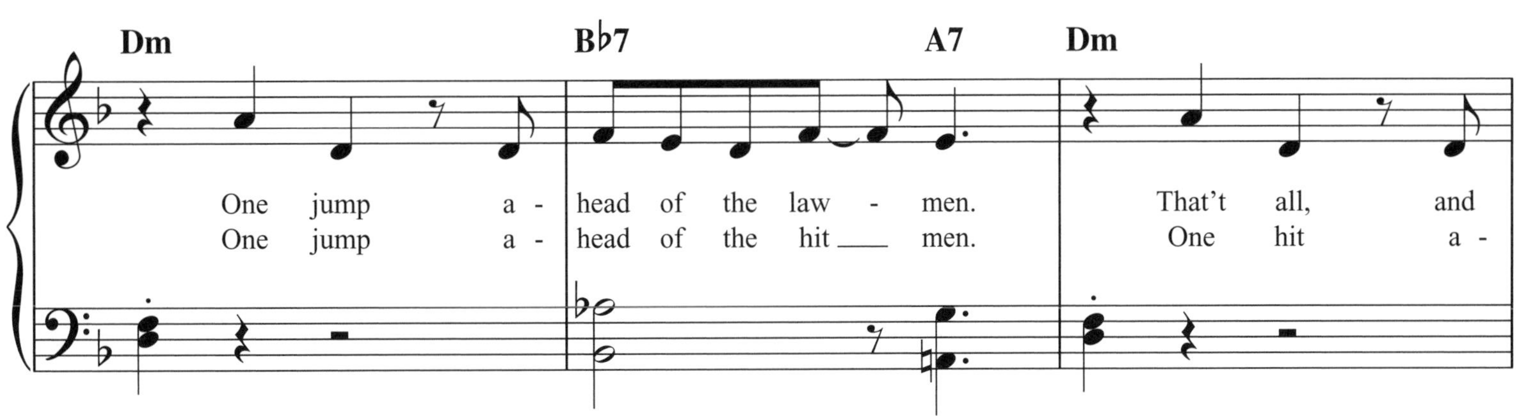
Dm B♭7 A7 Dm
One jump a - head of the law - men.
One jump a - head of the hit men.
That't all, and
One hit a -

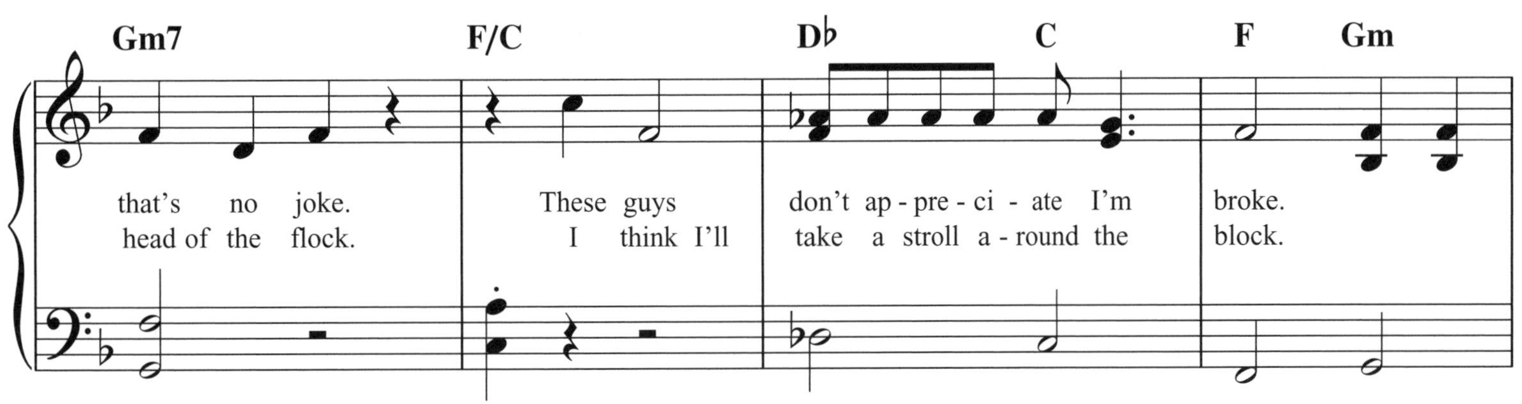
Gm7 F/C D♭ C F Gm
that's no joke.
head of the flock.
These guys don't ap - pre - ci - ate I'm broke.
I think I'll take a stroll a - round the block.

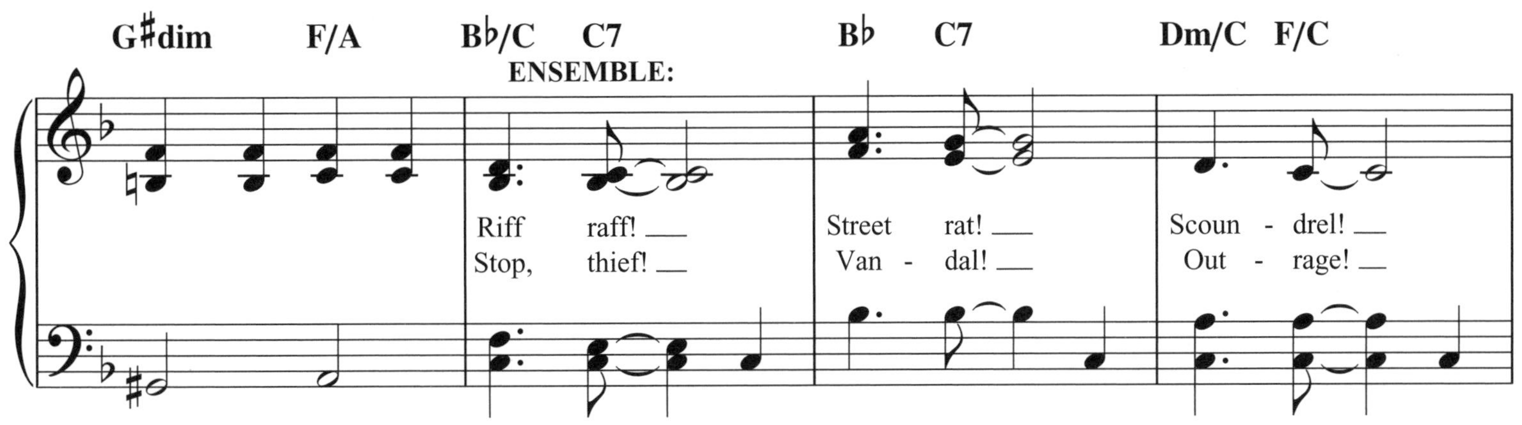
G♯dim F/A B♭/C C7 B♭ C7 Dm/C F/C
ENSEMBLE:
Riff raff! Street rat! Scoun - drel!
Stop, thief! Van - dal! Out - rage!

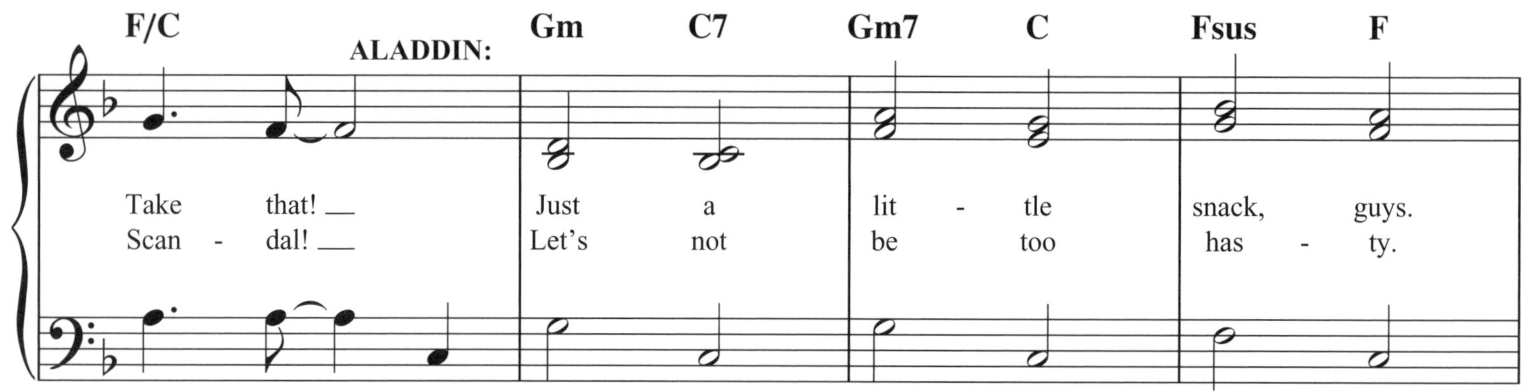
F/C
ALADDIN:
Gm
C7
Gm7
C
Fsus
F
Take that! __ Just a lit - tle snack, guys.
Scan - dal! __ Let's not be too has - ty.

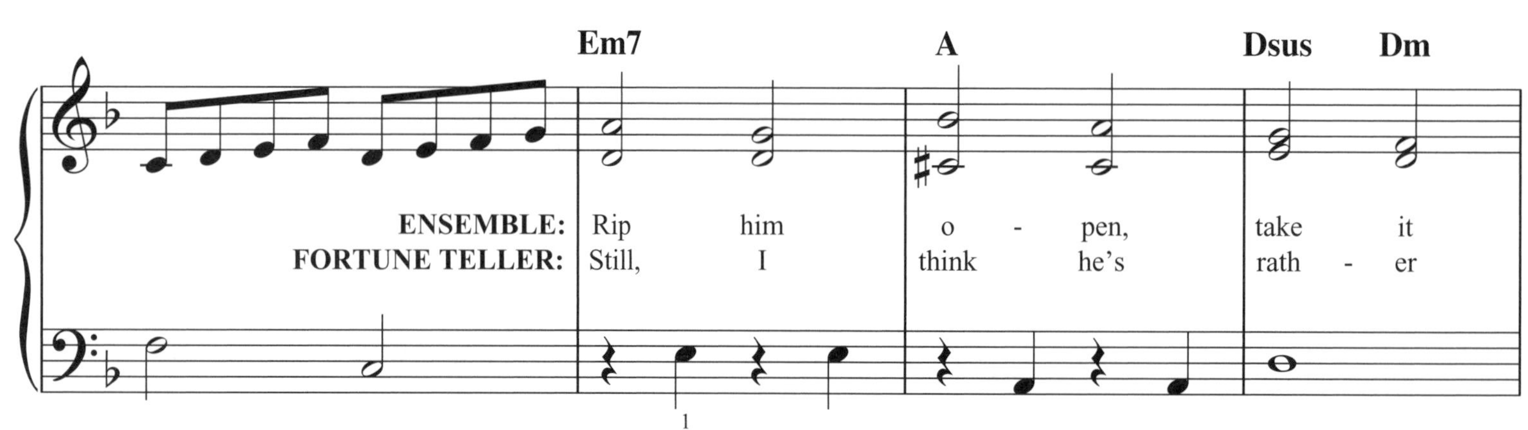
Em7
A
Dsus
Dm
ENSEMBLE: Rip him o - pen, take it
FORTUNE TELLER: Still, I think he's rath - er
1

A/C
Dm/C
B♭7
ALADDIN:
To Coda
back, guys. I can take a hint, got - ta face the facts.
tas - ty. Got - ta eat to live, got - ta steal to eat.
1
2

E7
A
BELLY DANCERS:
Dm
I could use a friend or two! True! Oh, it's sad, A - lad - din's hit the

B♭7 A7 Dm
bot - tom. He's be - come a one - man rise in

G9 Cm
crime. I'd blame par - ents 'cept he has - n't

E7
ALADDIN:
got 'em. Got - ta eat to live, got - ta

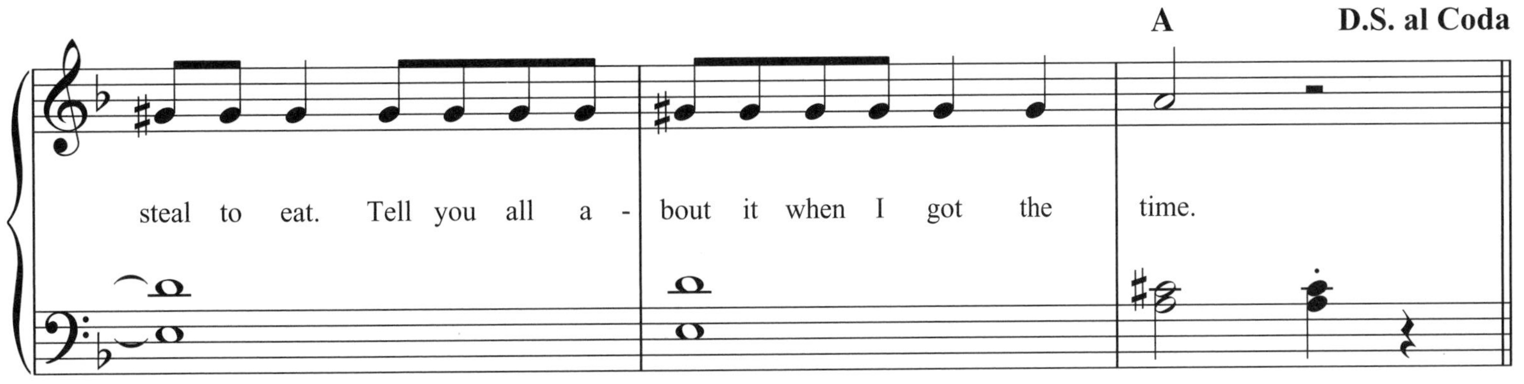
A D.S. al Coda
steal to eat. Tell you all a - bout it when I got the time.

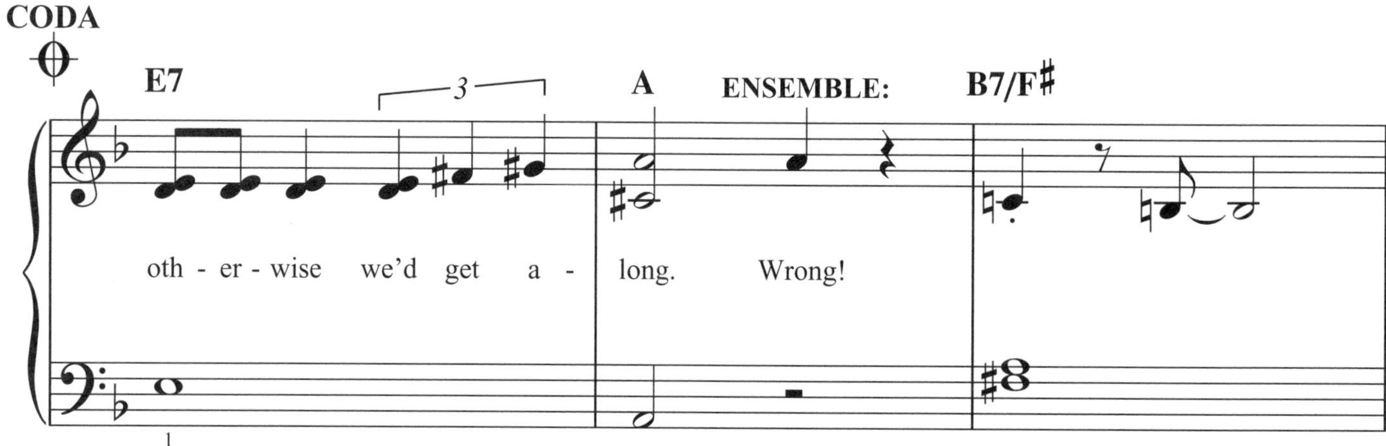
CODA
E7
3
A
ENSEMBLE:
B7/F♯
oth - er - wise we'd get a - long. Wrong!
1

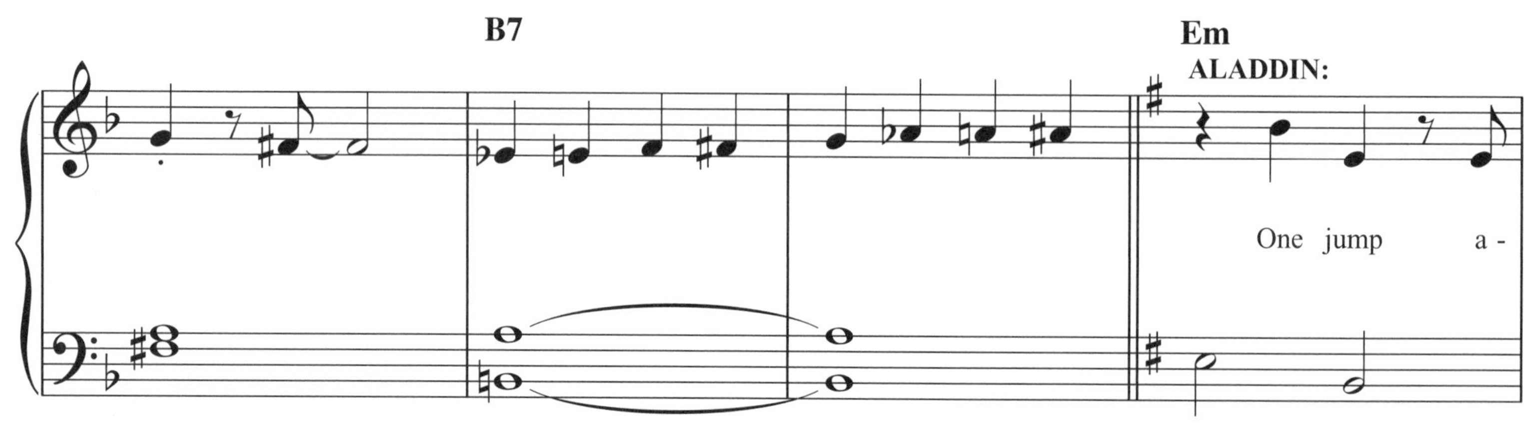
B7
Em
ALADDIN:
One jump a -

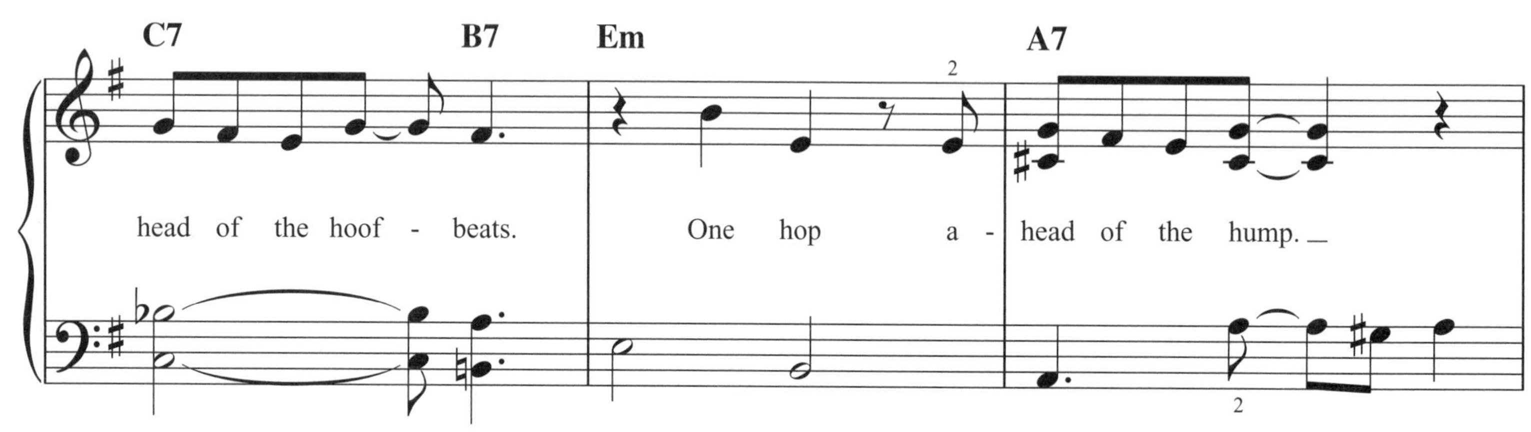
C7
B7
Em
A7
2
head of the hoof - beats. One hop a - head of the hump. _
2

G/D
E♭7
D7
Bm
3
One trick a - head of dis - as - ter. They're quick, but

E7
Am7
C/D
I'm much fast - er.
Here goes,
bet - ter throw my hand in,

N.C.
wish me hap - py land - in'.
All I got - ta do is
jump.

Gm
E♭7
D7
Gm
E♭7
D

Gm
E♭7
D
E♭7
D7
Gm

A SPOONFUL OF SUGAR

from MARY POPPINS

Words and Music by RICHARD M. SHERMAN
and ROBERT B. SHERMAN

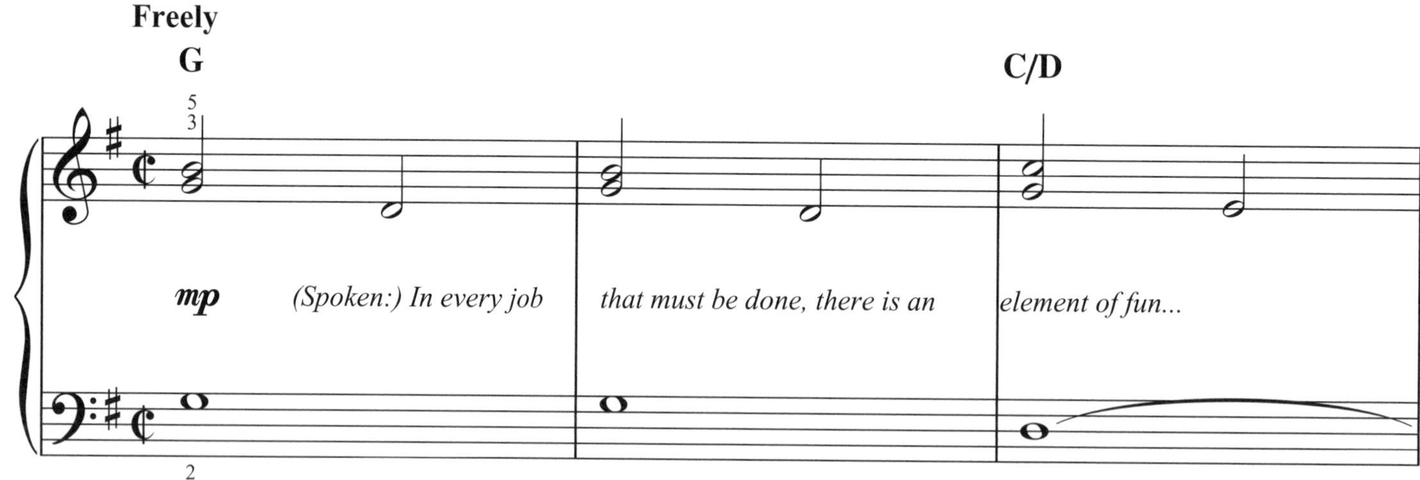

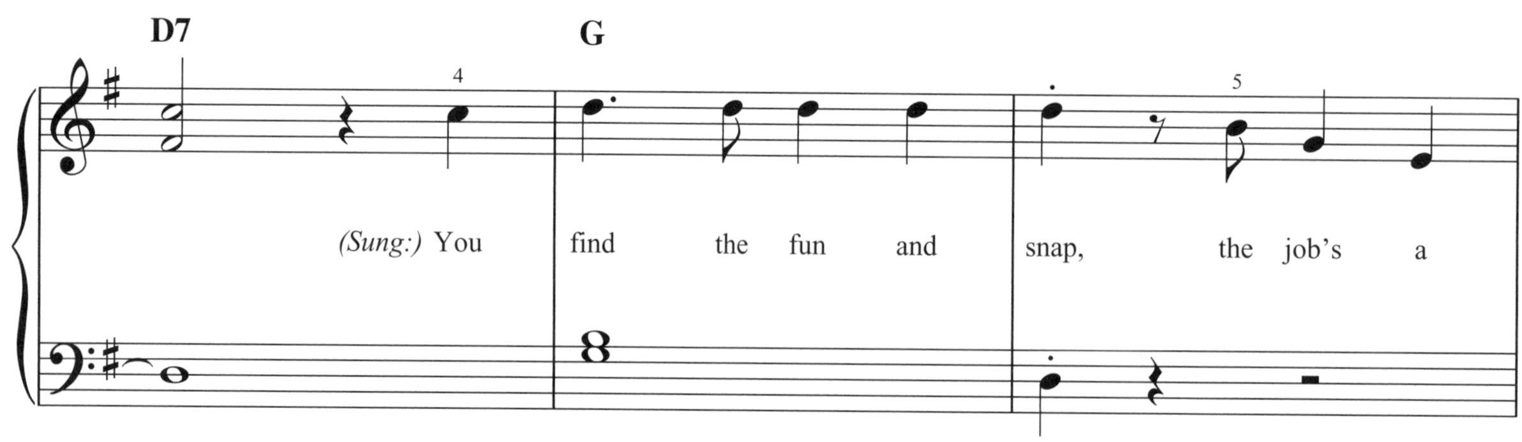

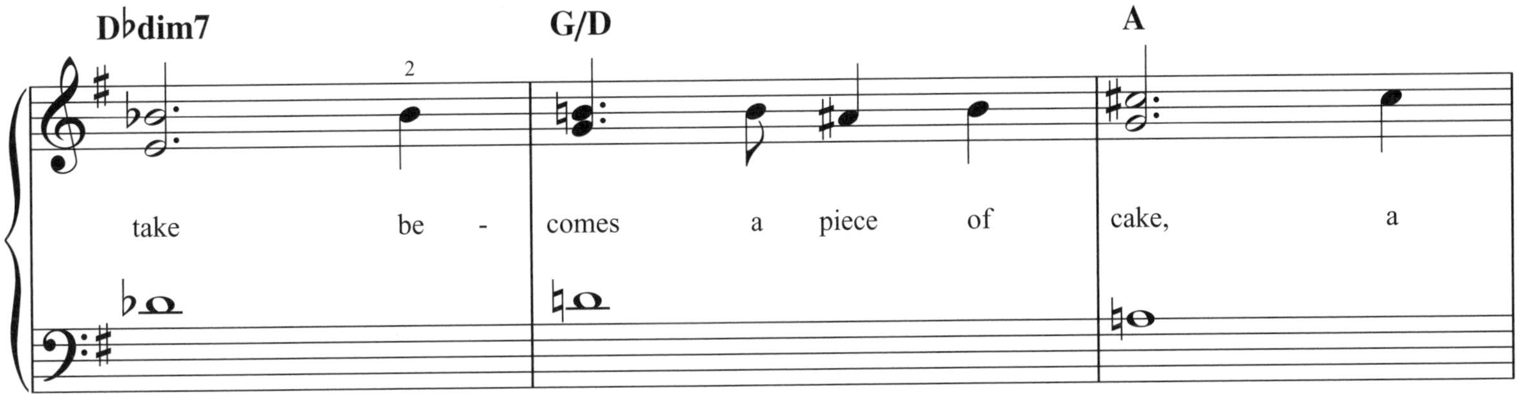
D♭dim7
G/D
A
take be - comes a piece of cake, a

G/B
Gm/B♭
Am7
lark, a spree! It's ver - y clear to

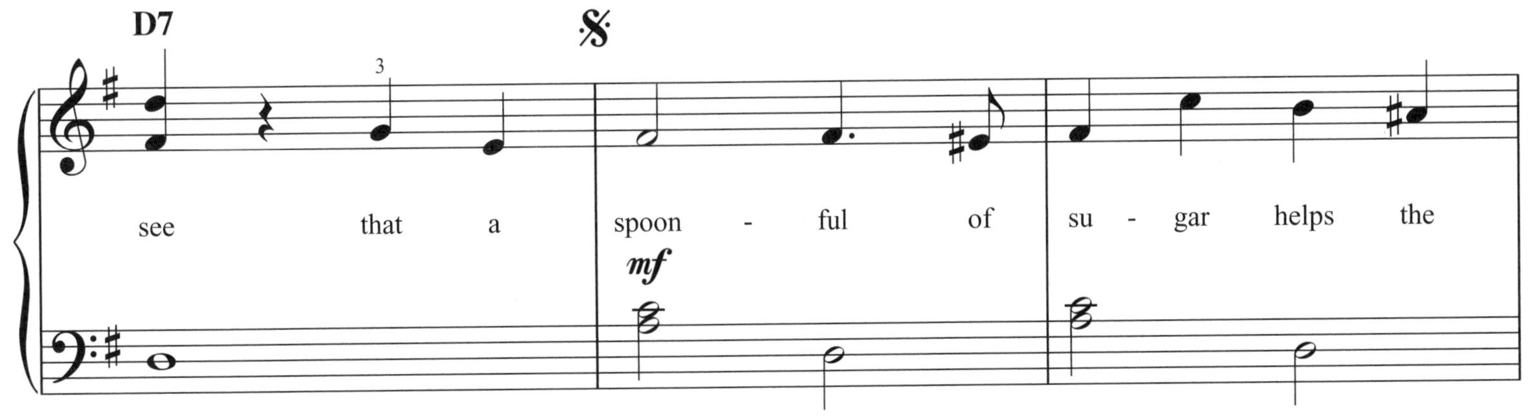
D7
see that a spoon - ful of su - gar helps the
mf

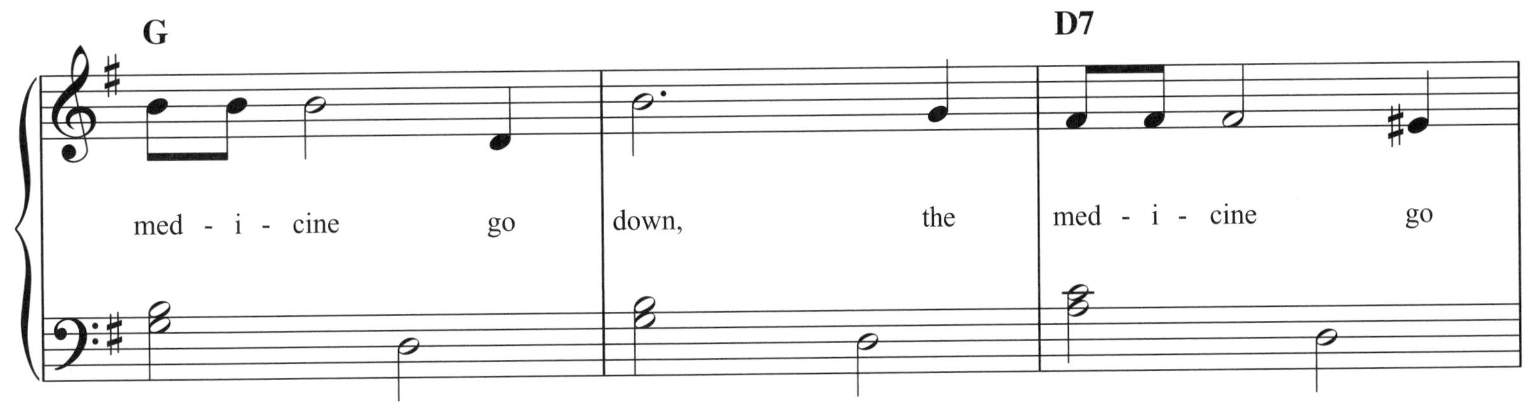
G
D7
med - i - cine go down, the med - i - cine go

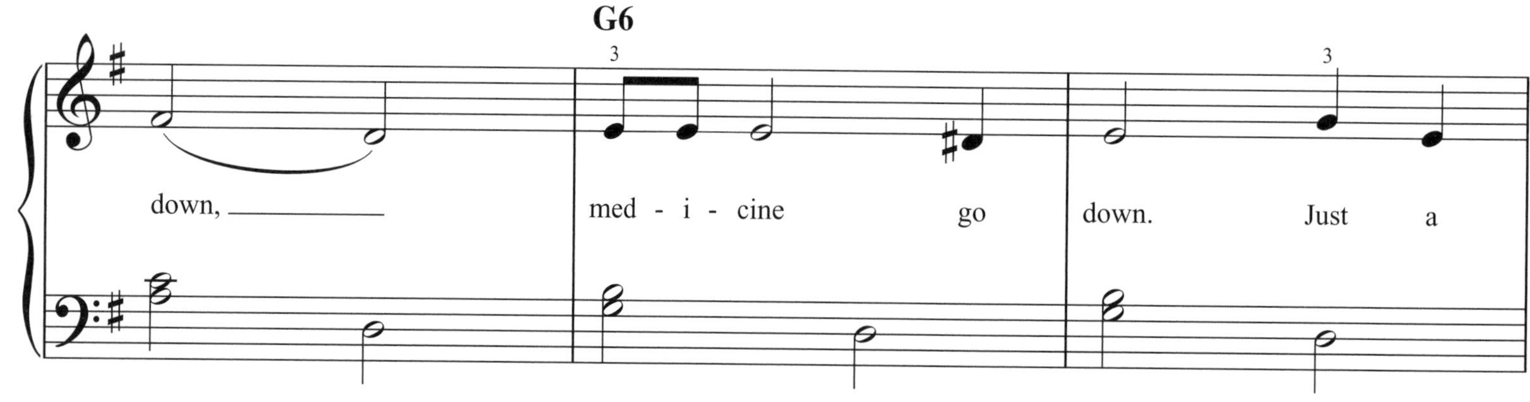
G6
down,
med - i - cine go
down. Just a

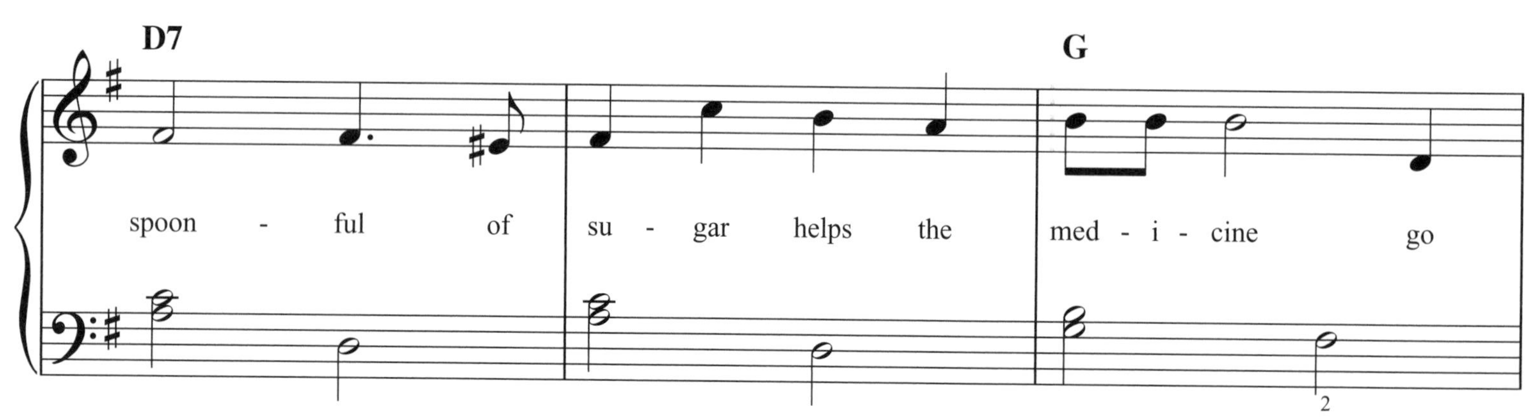
D7
G
spoon - ful of
su - gar helps the
med - i - cine go

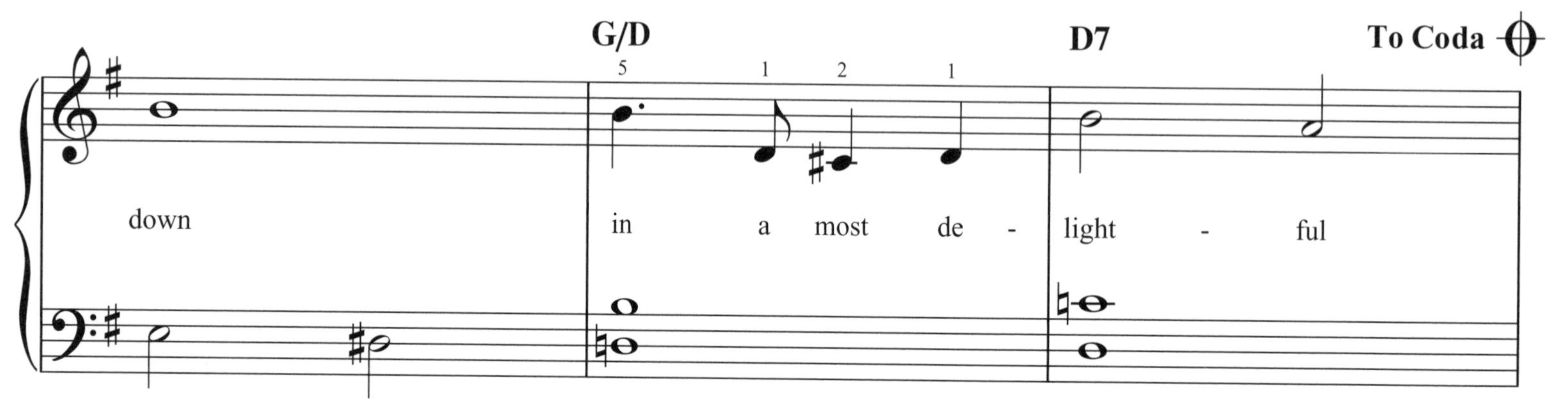
G/D
D7
To Coda
down
in a most de -
light - ful

G
way.
The hon - ey
bees that fetch the

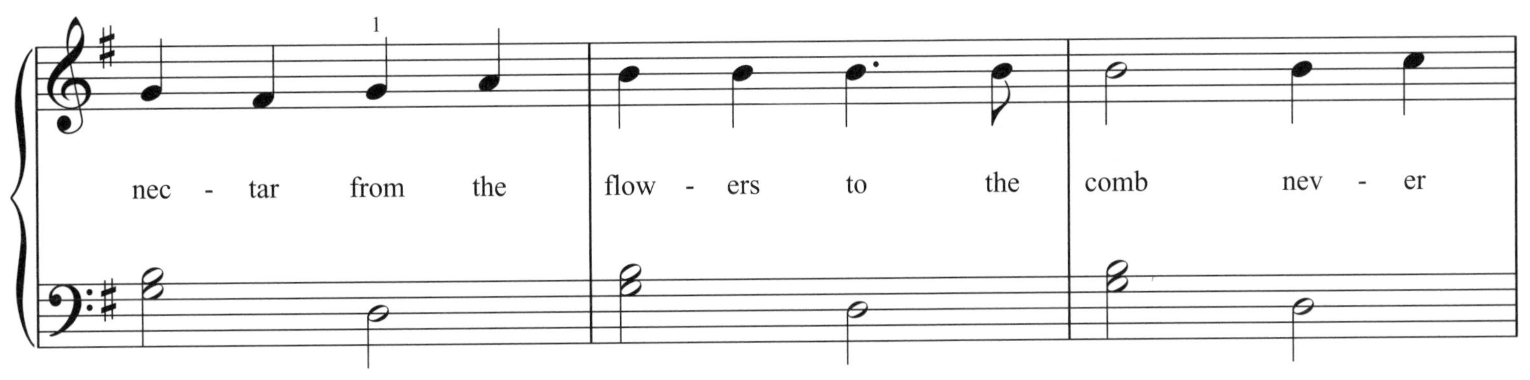
1
nec - tar from the flow - ers to the comb nev - er

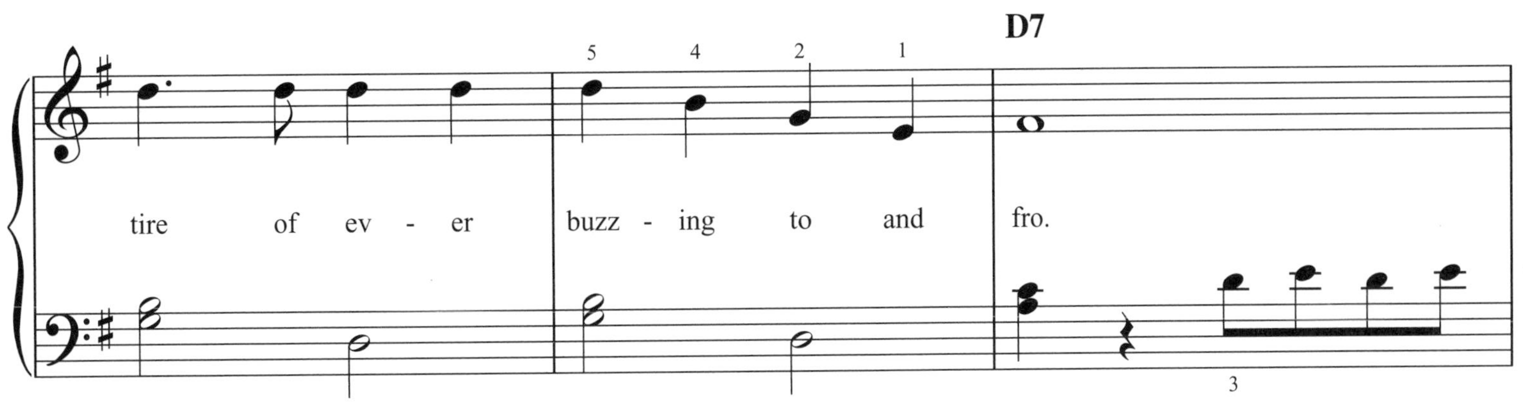
D7
5 4 2 1
tire of ev - er buzz - ing to and fro.
3

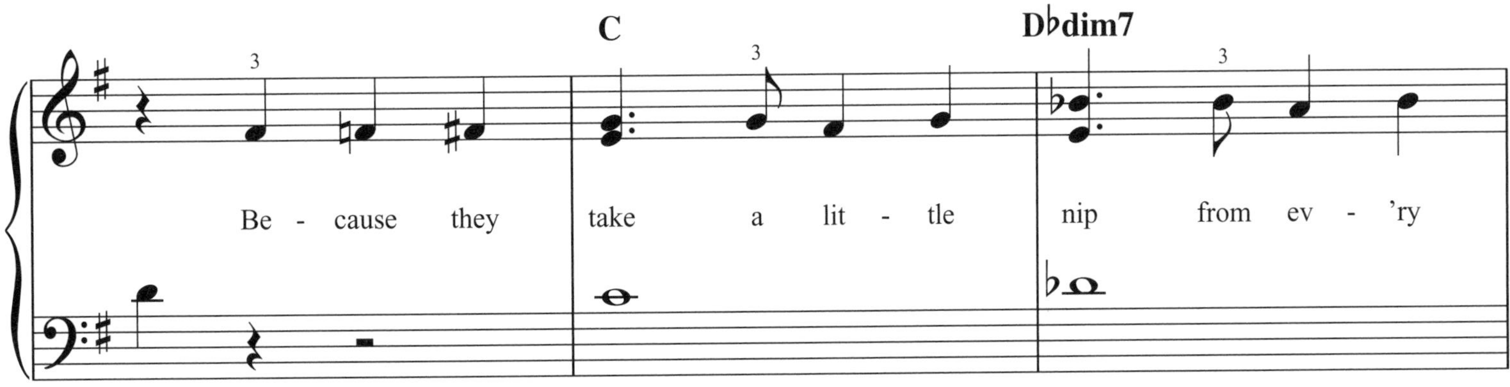
C
D♭dim7
3 3 3
Be - cause they take a lit - tle nip from ev - 'ry

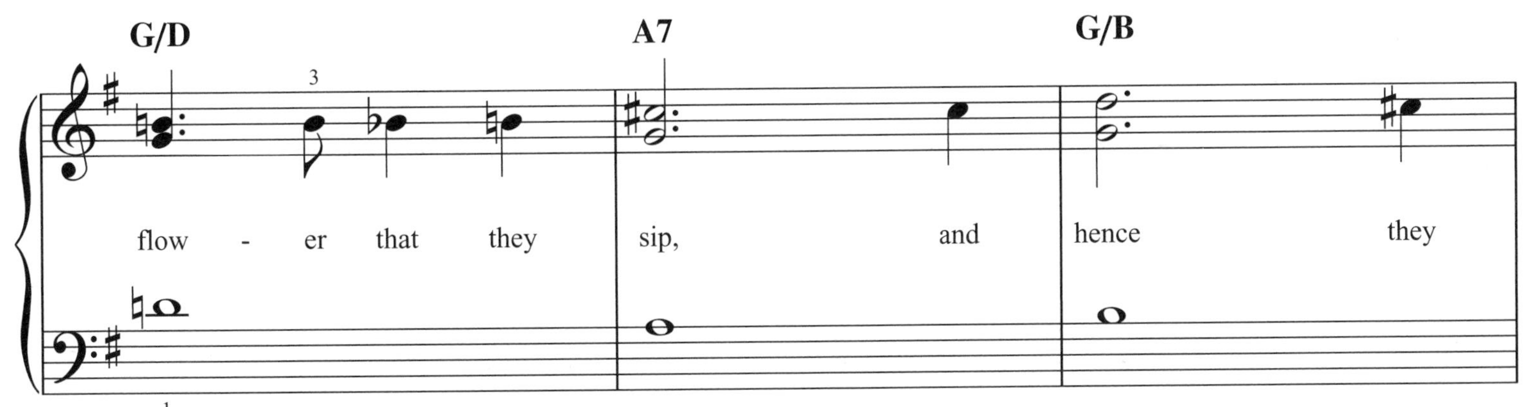
G/D
A7
G/B
3
flow - er that they sip, and hence they
1

Gm/B♭
Am7
D7
D.S. al Coda
find their task is not a grind. For a
1

CODA
G/D
D7
G/D
1 2 1
in a most de - light - ful, in a most
f

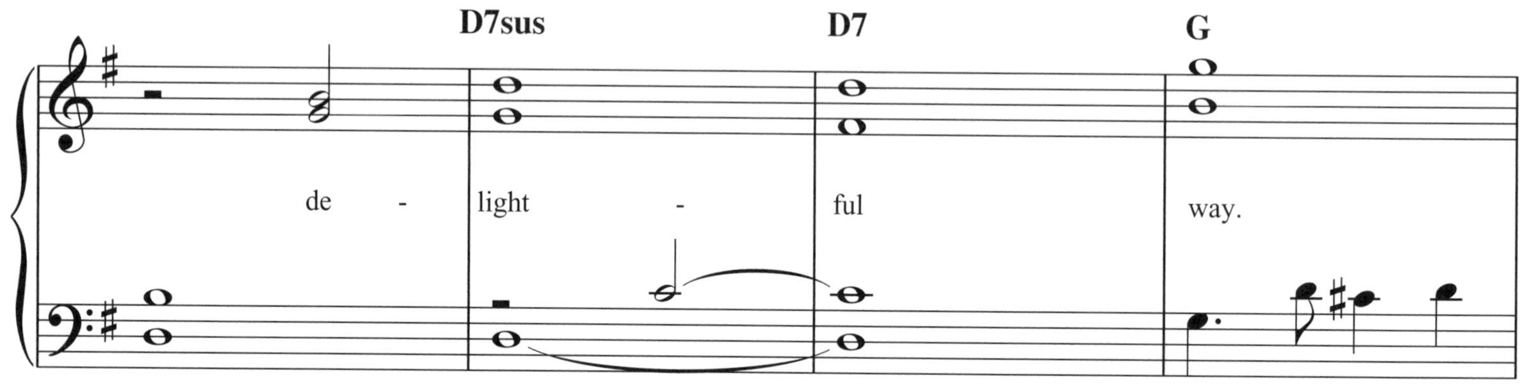
D7sus
D7
G
de - light - ful way.

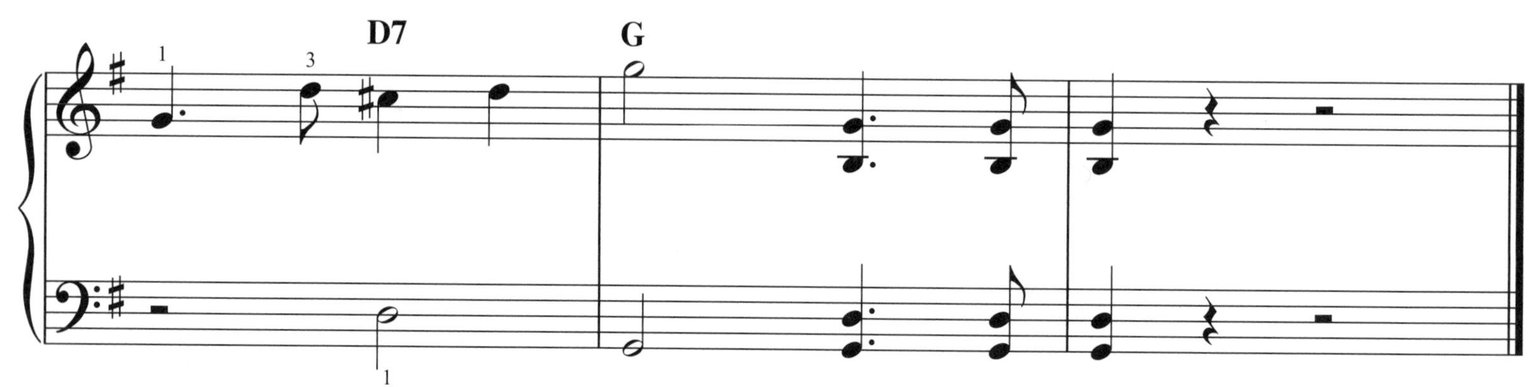
D7
G
1
3
1

UNDER THE SEA

from THE LITTLE MERMAID

Music by ALAN MENKEN
Lyrics by HOWARD ASHMAN

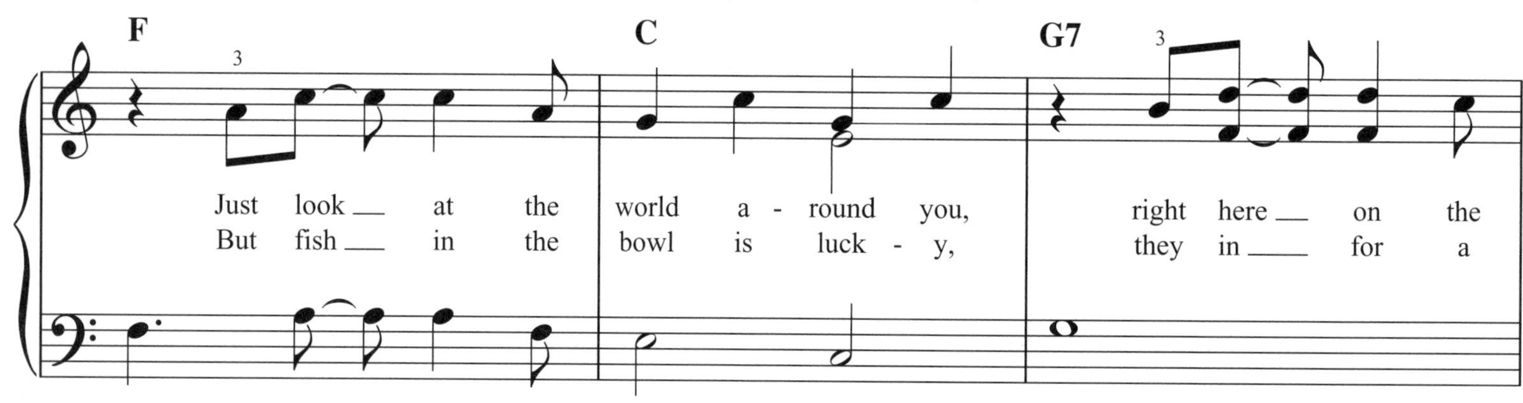
F
C
G7
3
Just look __ at the world a - round you, right here __ on the
But fish __ in the bowl is luck - y, they in __ for a

C
F
C
3
o - cean floor. Such won - der - ful things sur - round you.
wors - er fate. One day __ when the boss get hun - gry

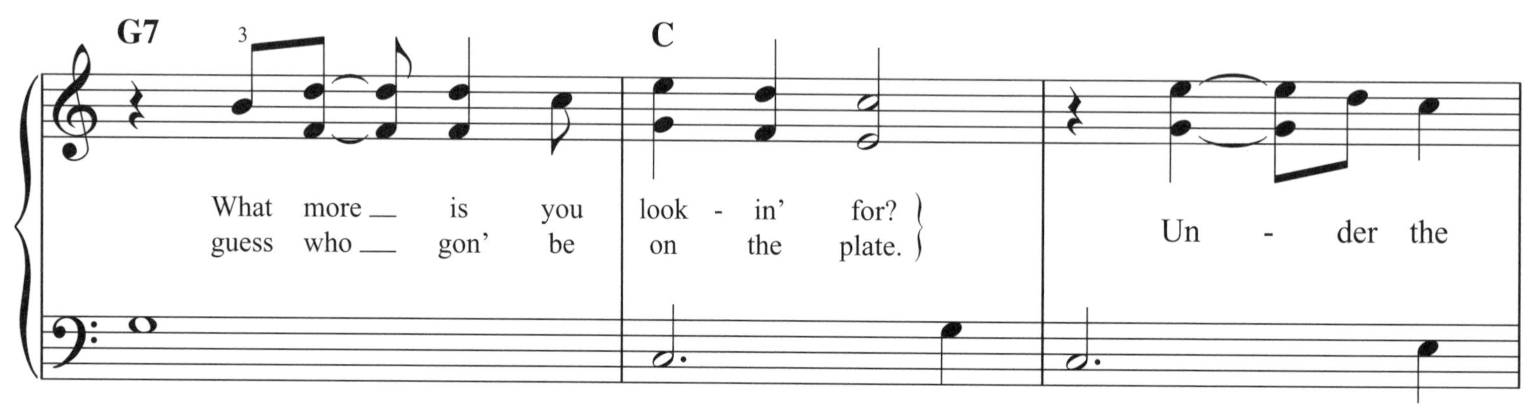
G7
C
3
What more __ is you look - in' for?
guess who __ gon' be on the plate.
Un - der the

F
C
G
2
1
sea, un - der the sea.

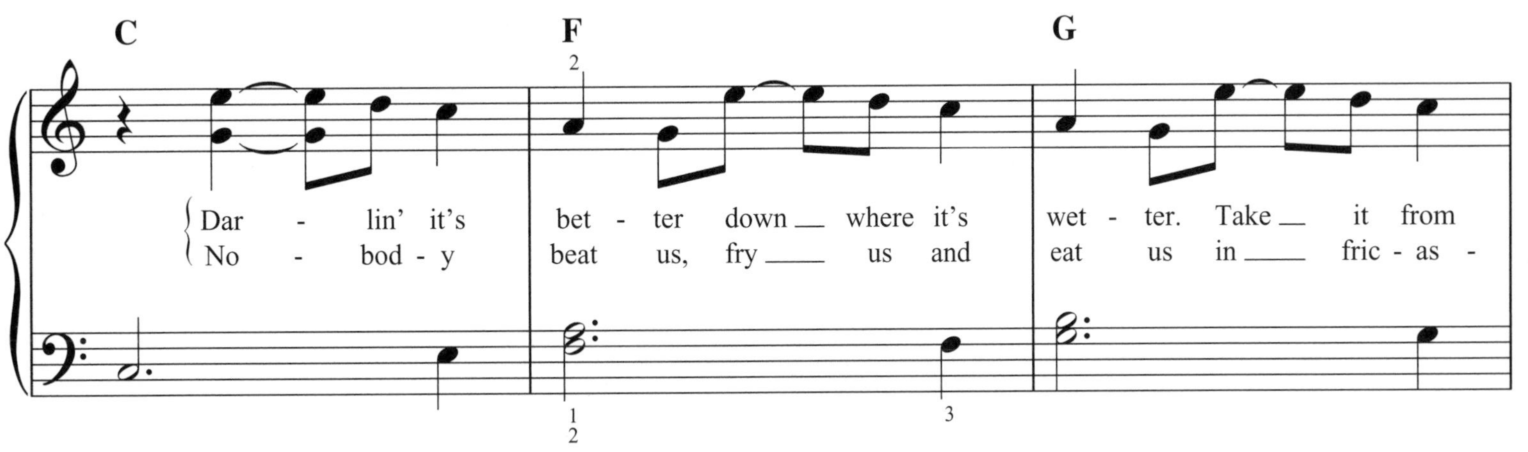
C
F
G
Dar - lin' it's
No - bod - y
bet - ter down where it's
beat us, fry us and
wet - ter. Take it from
eat us in fric - as -

C
C7
F
me.
see.
Up on the
We what the
shore they work all day.
land folks loves to cook.

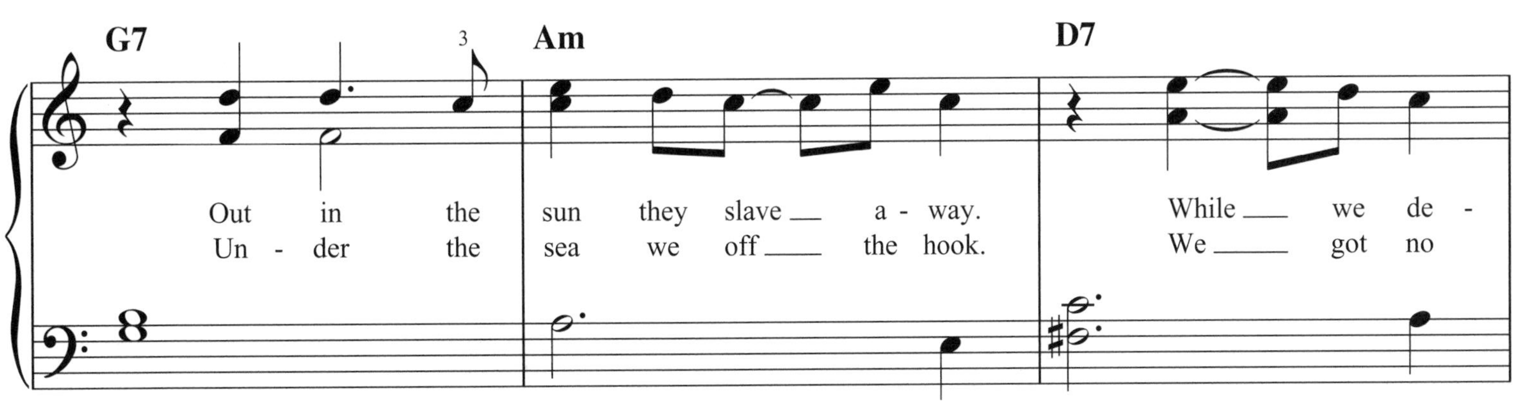
G7
Am
D7
Out in the
Un - der the
sun they slave a - way.
sea we off the hook.
While we de -
We got no

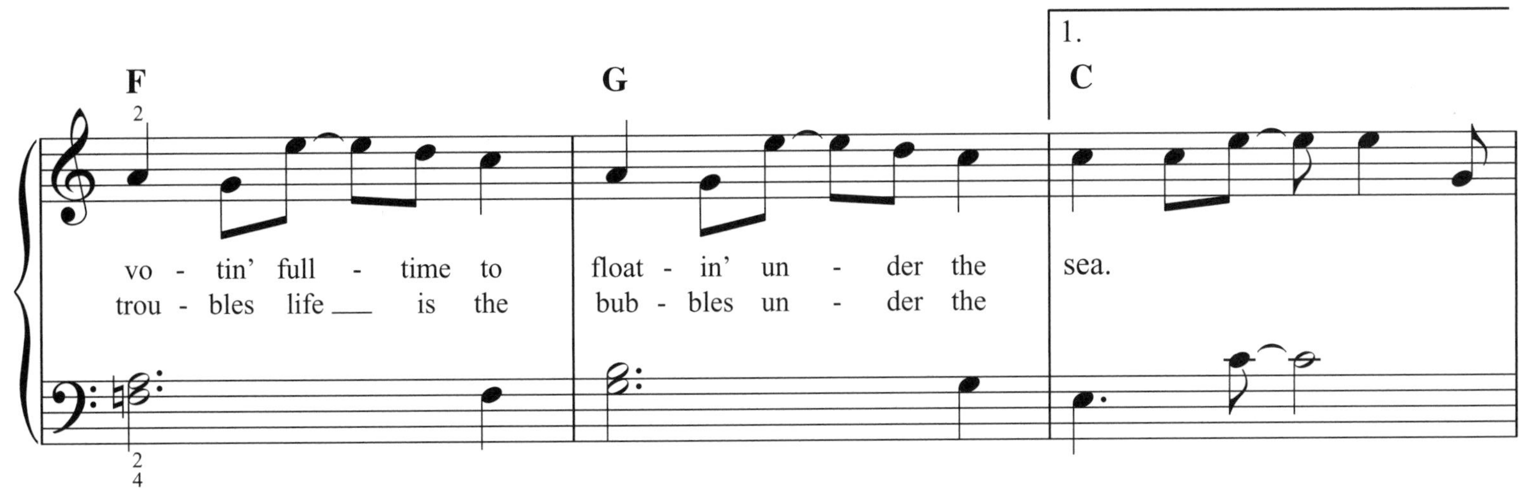
F
G
1.
C
vo - tin' full - time to
trou - bles life is the
float - in' un - der the
bub - bles un - der the
sea.

G7
C
G7
C

2.
F
C
G
sea.
Un - der the
sea.

C
F
G
Since life is
sweet here we got the
beat here nat - u - ral -

C
C7
F
ly.
E - ven the
stur - geon an' the ray

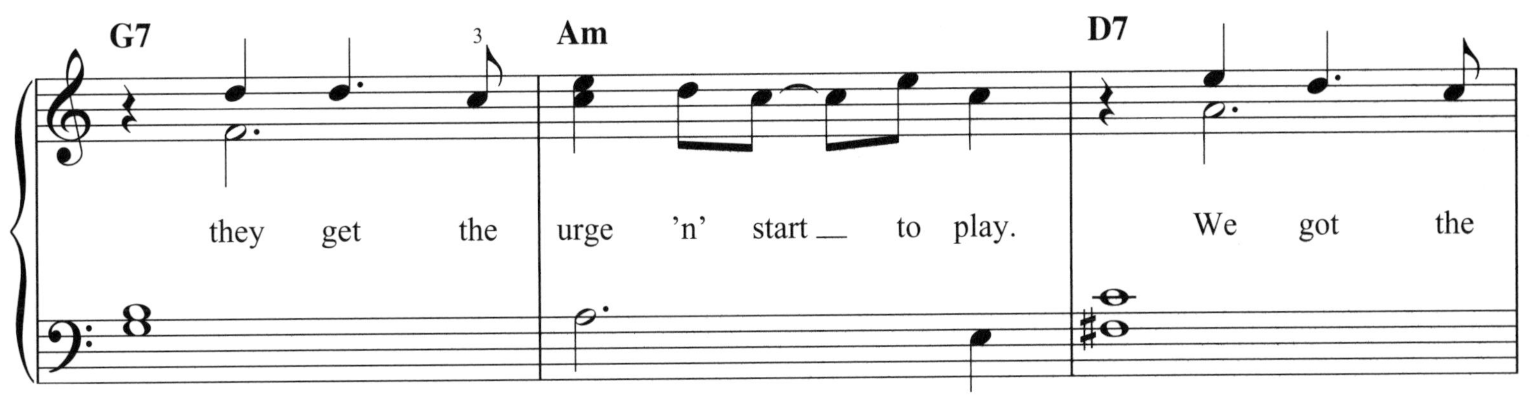
G7
Am
D7
3
they get the urge 'n' start to play. We got the
8

F
G
C
2
spir - it, you got to hear it un - der the sea.

G7
C
G
C
1
3
2
1
The newt play the flute. The carp play the harp. The

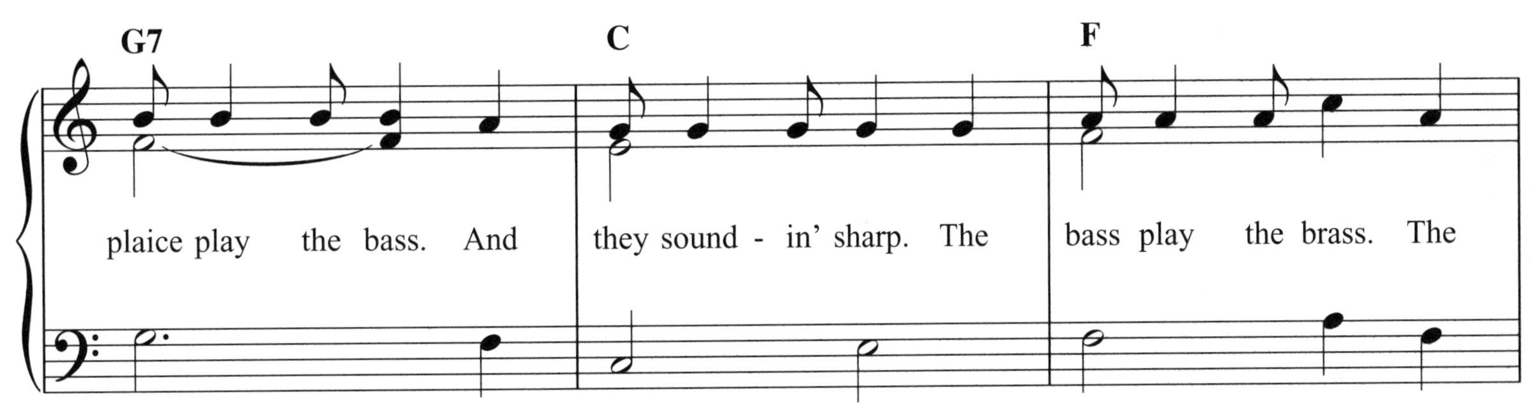
G7
C
F
plaice play the bass. And they sound - in' sharp. The bass play the brass. The

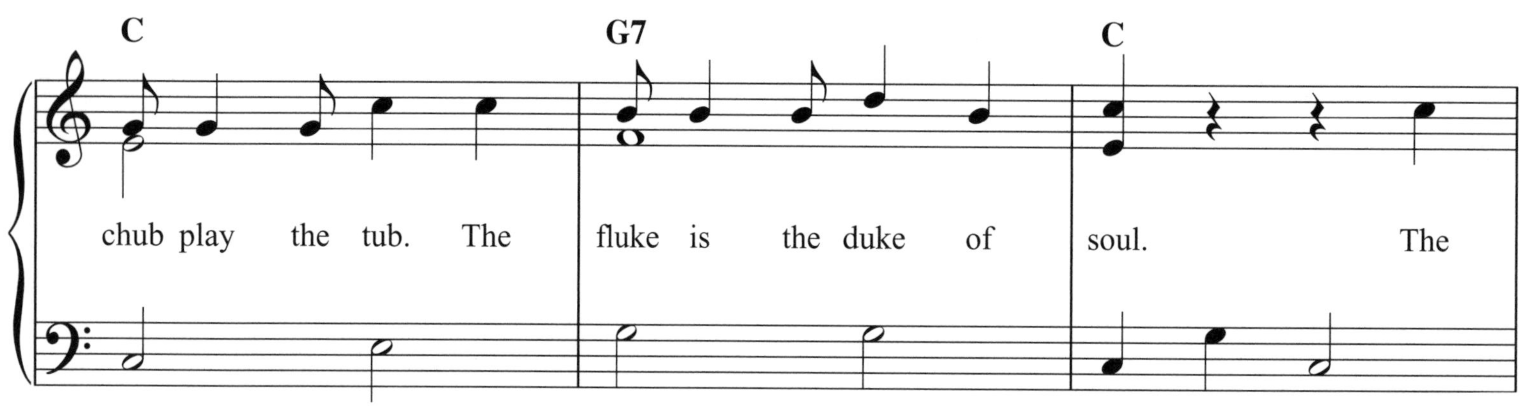
C
G7
C
chub play the tub. The
fluke is the duke of
soul. The

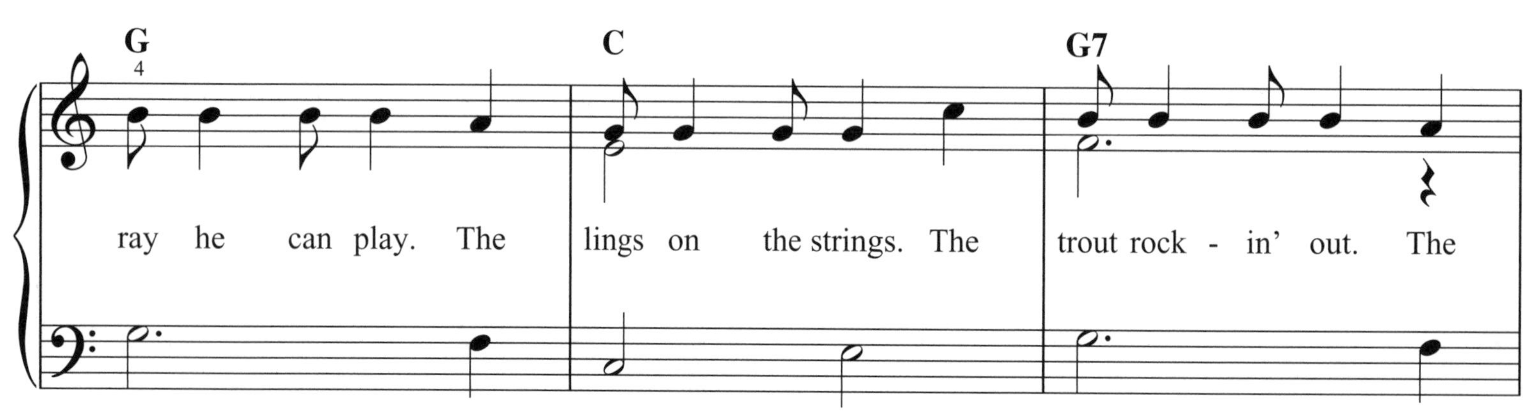
G
4
C
G7
ray he can play. The
lings on the strings. The
trout rock - in' out. The

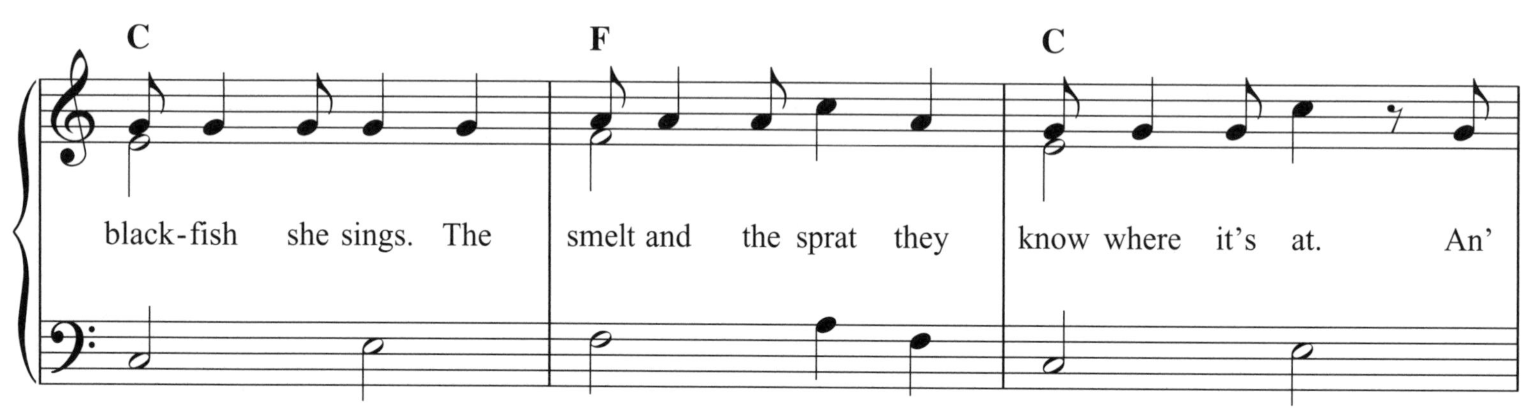
C
F
C
black-fish she sings. The
smelt and the sprat they
know where it's at. An'

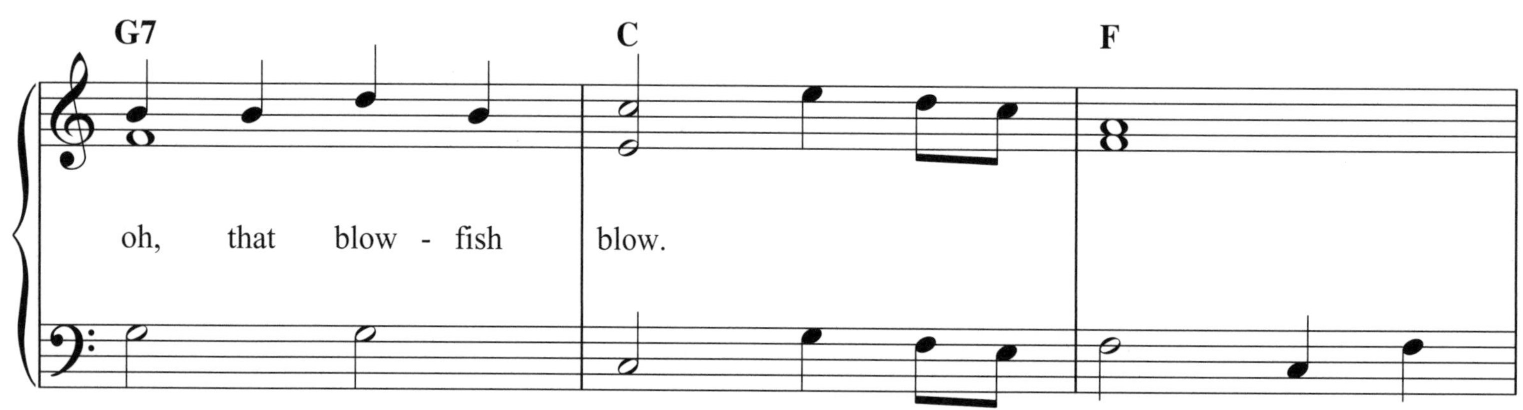
G7
C
F
oh, that blow - fish
blow.

C
G
C
F
G
C
F
G
1
2
Am
D7
F
2
1
4
G7
C
G7
C

G7
C
F
C
Un-der the
sea.
Un-der the

G7
C
F
G
sea.
When the sar - dine be - gin the be - guine it's mu - sic to
3

C
C7
F
me.
What do they got, a lot of sand.
4

G7
Am
D7
We got a hot crus - ta - ce - an band. Each lit - tle

F
G
C
G7
C
clam here know how to
slug here cut - tin' a
jam here un - der the
rug here un - der the
sea.
sea.
Each lit-tle
Each lit-tle

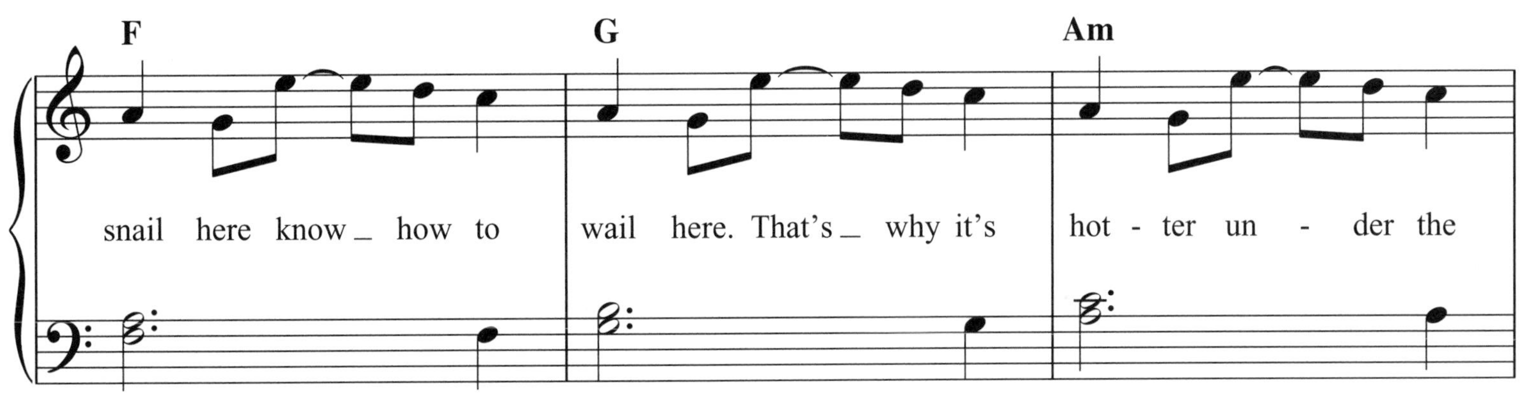
F
G
Am
snail here know how to
wail here. That's why it's
hot - ter un - der the

D7
F
G
wa - ter. Ya we in
luck here down in the
muck here un - der the

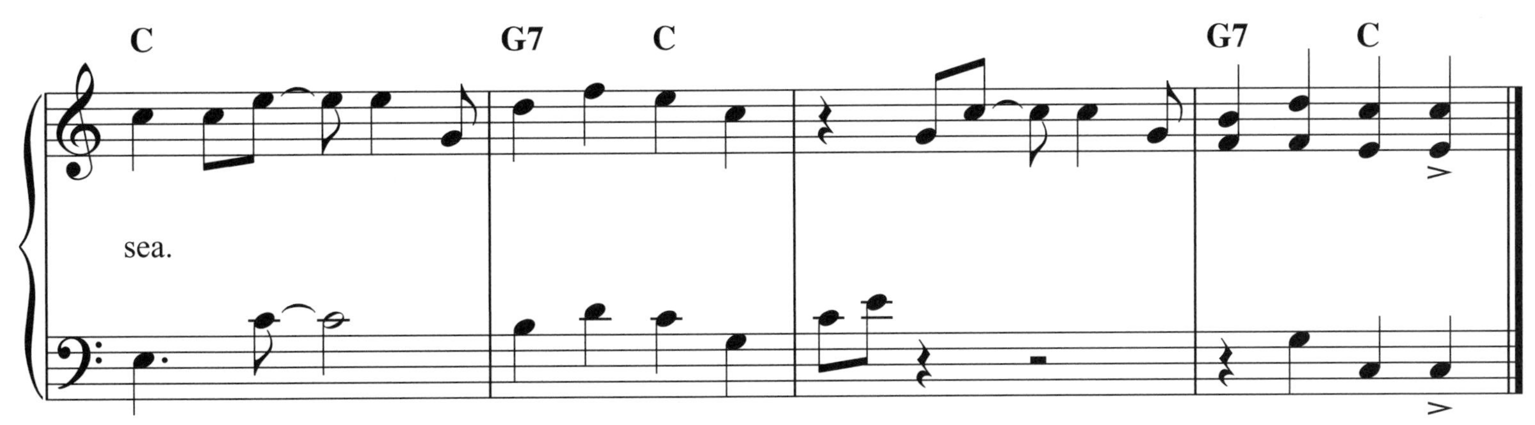
C
G7
C
G7
C
sea.

SUPERCALIFRAGILISTICEXPIALIDOCIOUS

from MARY POPPINS

Words and Music by RICHARD M. SHERMAN
and ROBERT B. SHERMAN

C
G7
C
Pearlies:
Um did - dle did - dle did - dle, um did - dle ay! Um did - dle did - dle did - dle,

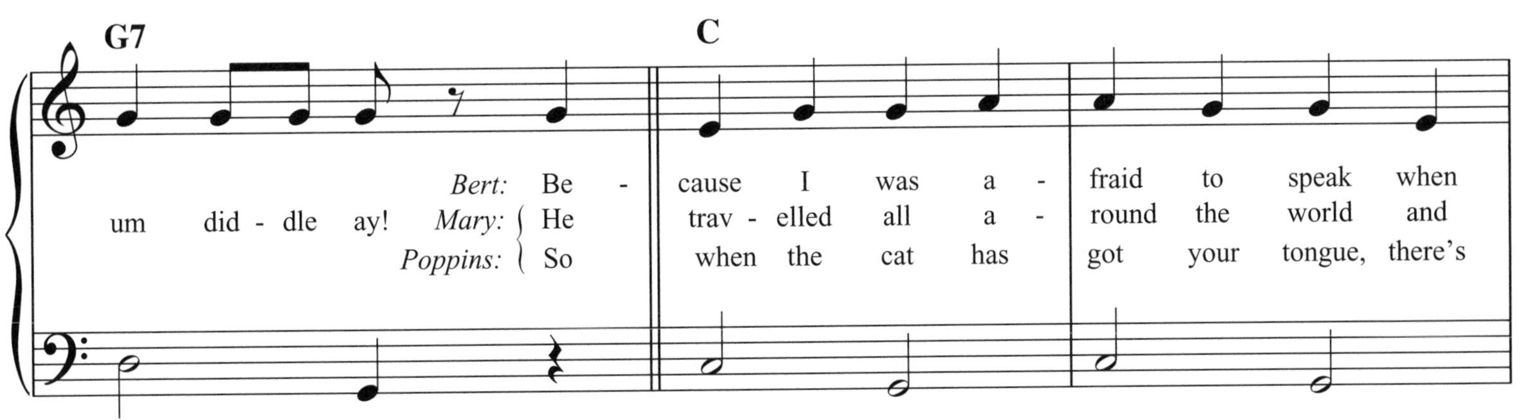
G7
C
Bert: Be - cause I was a - fraid to speak when
um did - dle ay! Mary: He trav - elled all a - round the world and
Poppins: So when the cat has got your tongue, there's

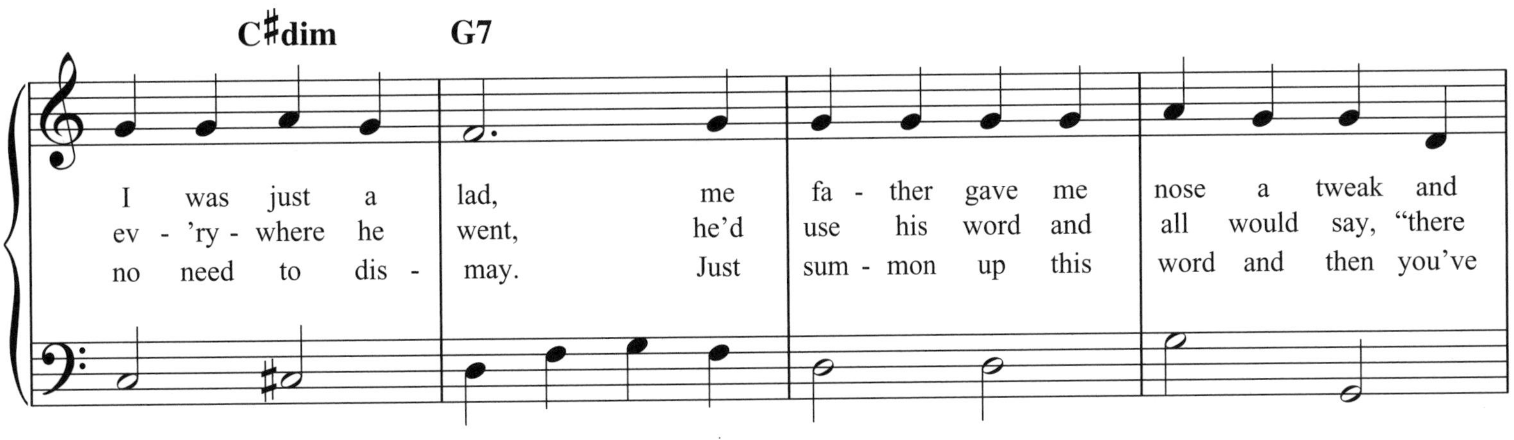
C♯dim
G7
I was just a lad, me fa - ther gave me nose a tweak and
ev - 'ry - where he went, he'd use his word and all would say, "there
no need to dis - may. Just sum - mon up this word and then you've

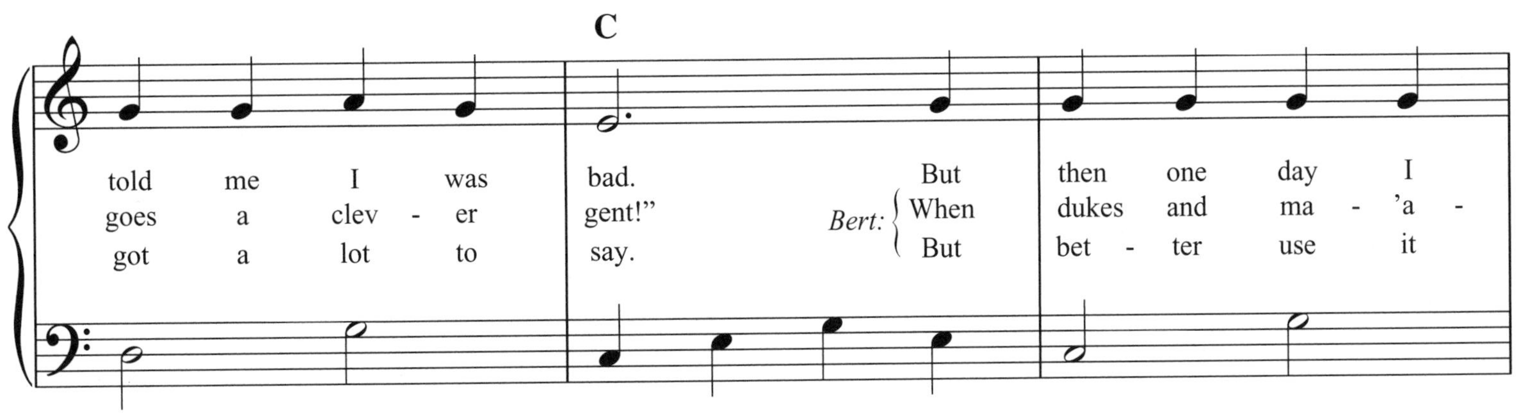
C
told me I was bad. But then one day I
goes a clev - er gent!" Bert: When dukes and ma - 'a -
got a lot to say. But bet - ter use it

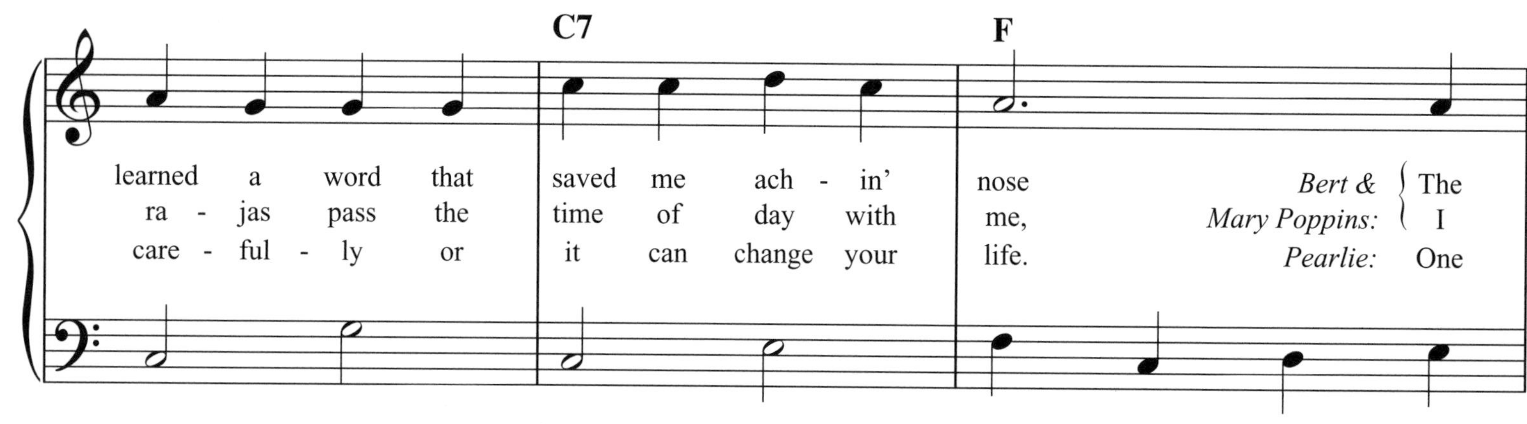
C7
F
learned a word that saved me ach - in' nose
ra - jas pass the time of day with me,
care - ful - ly or it can change your life.
Bert &
Mary Poppins:
The
I
Pearlie:
One

D7
big - gest word you ev - er 'eard and this is 'ow it
say me spe - cial word and then they ask me out to
night I said it to me girl and now me girl's me

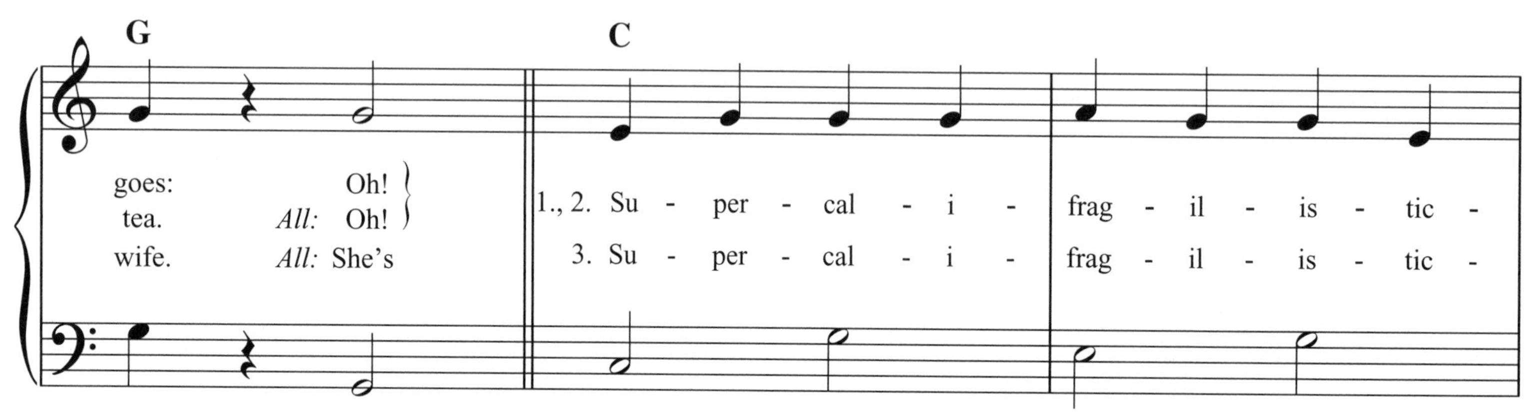
G
C
goes: Oh!
tea. All: Oh!
wife. All: She's
1., 2. Su - per - cal - i - frag - il - is - tic -
3. Su - per - cal - i - frag - il - is - tic -

C♯dim
G7
ex - pi - al - i - do - cious! E - ven though the
ex - pi - al - i - do - cious! Su - per - cal - i -

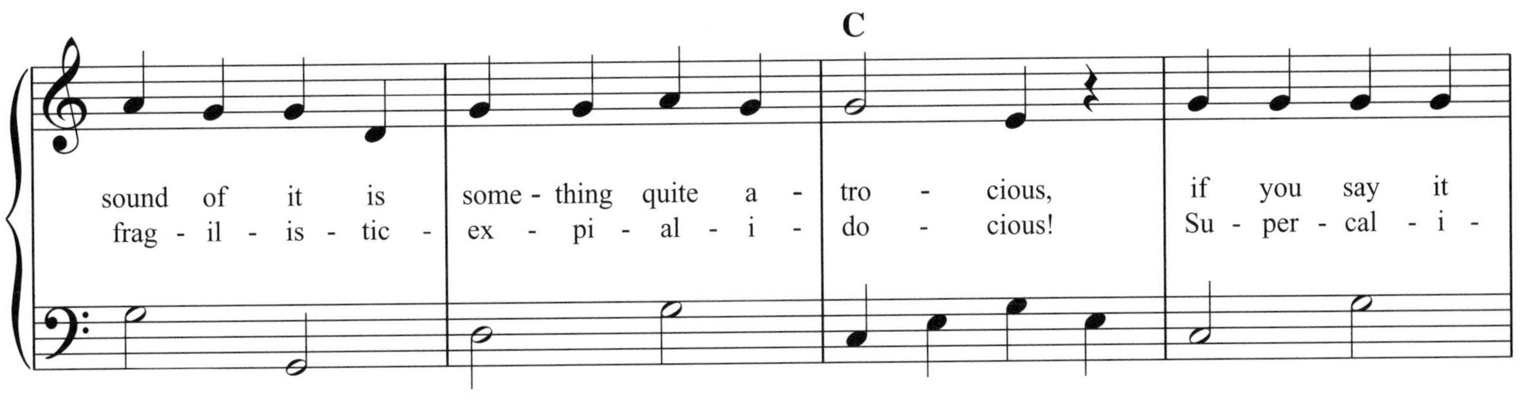
C
sound of it is some - thing quite a - tro - cious, if you say it
frag - il - is - tic - ex - pi - al - i - do - cious! Su - per - cal - i -

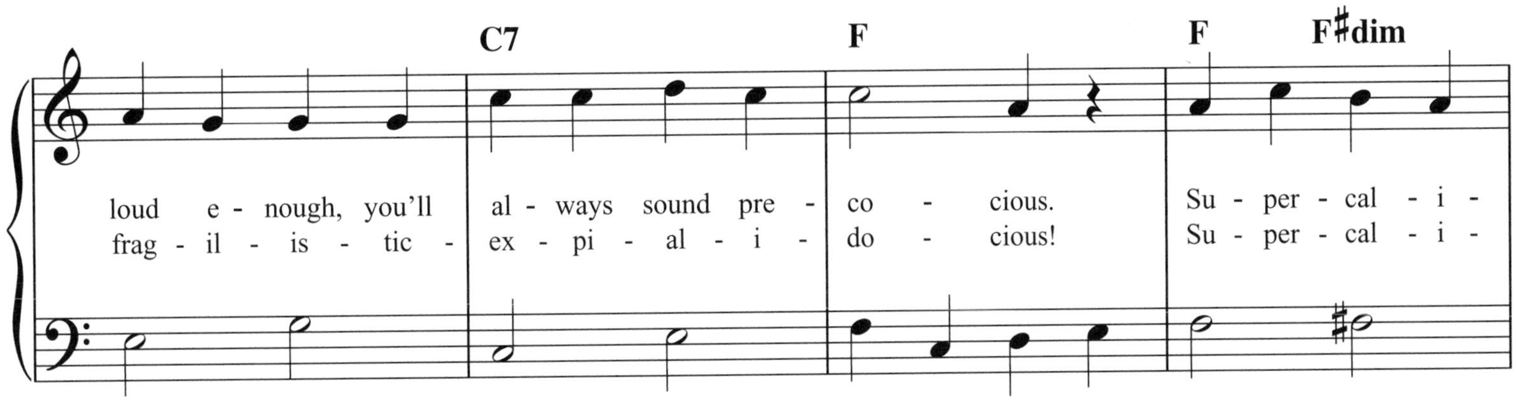
C7
F
F
F♯dim
loud e - nough, you'll al - ways sound pre - co - cious. Su - per - cal - i -
frag - il - is - tic - ex - pi - al - i - do - cious! Su - per - cal - i -

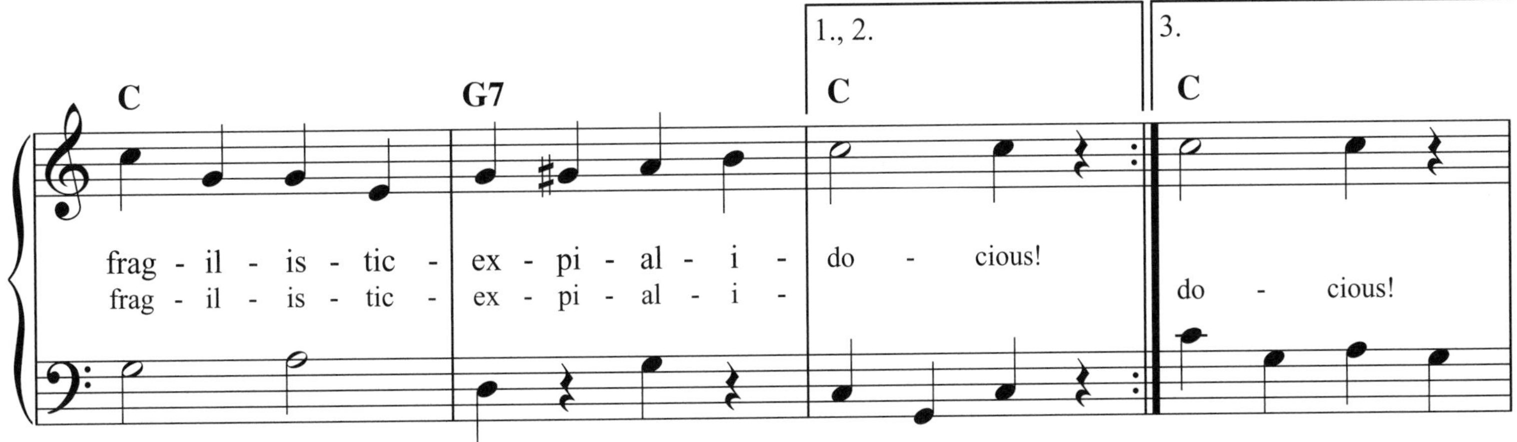
1., 2.
3.
C
G7
C
C
frag - il - is - tic - ex - pi - al - i - do - cious!
frag - il - is - tic - ex - pi - al - i - do - cious!

F
F♯dim
C
G7
C
f

WHEN I SEE AN ELEPHANT FLY

from DUMBO

Words by NED WASHINGTON
Music by OLIVER WALLACE

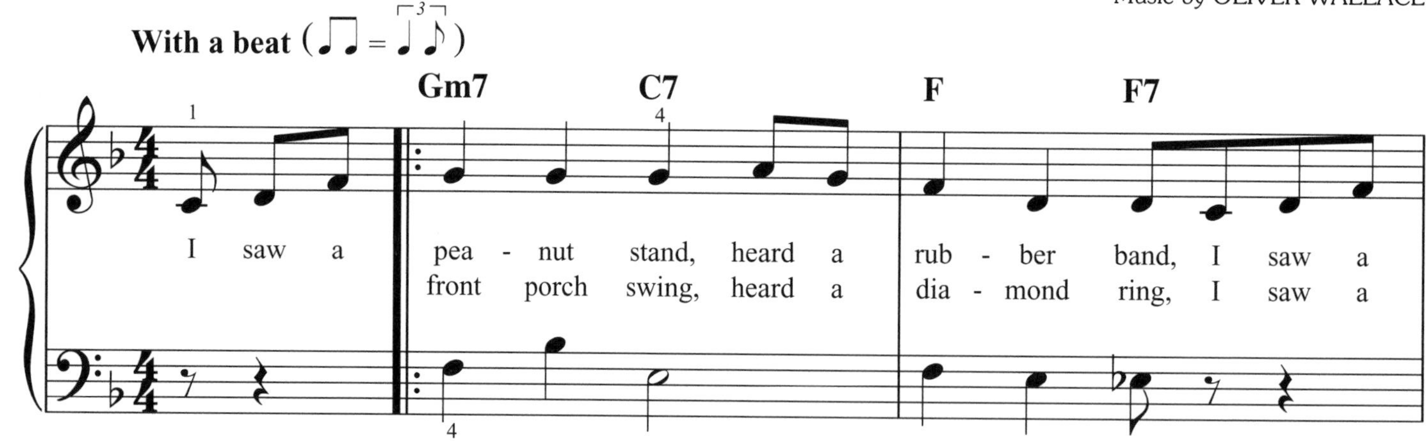

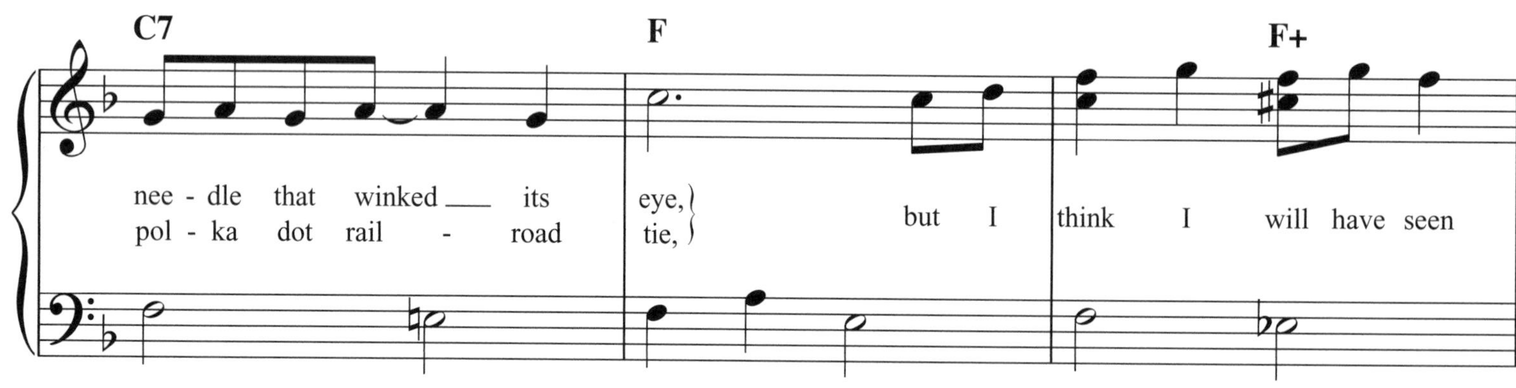

B♭
B♭m7
bi - cy - cle shop. _
You can't de - ny ___ the
things that you see, ___ but

F
G7
C7
Gm7
C7
I know there's cer - tain things that
just can't be. The oth - er
day by chance saw an

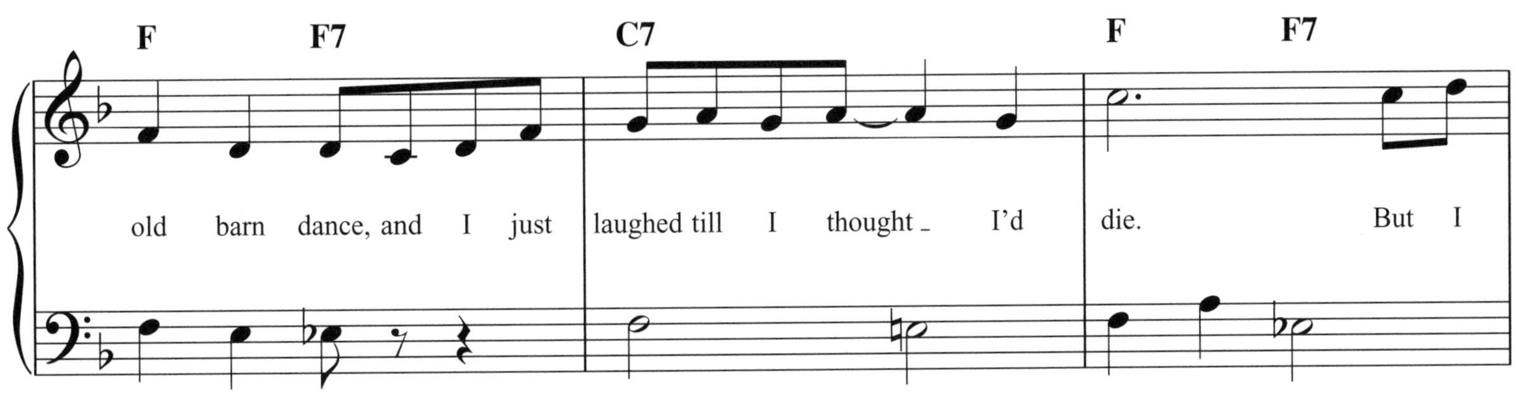
F
F7
C7
F
F7
old barn dance, and I just
laughed till I thought _ I'd
die. But I

F+
B♭
B♭m
F
G7
F
C7
F
think I will have seen
ev - 'ry - thing when
I see an el - e-phant
fly.

WHISTLE WHILE YOU WORK

from SNOW WHITE AND THE SEVEN DWARFS

Words by LARRY MOREY
Music by FRANK CHURCHILL

F
4
there's too much to do, don't let it both - er you. For -
2

Fm
C
C♯dim
Dm
G
4
get your trou - bles, try to be just like a cheer - ful chick - a - dee. And

C
3
5
whis - tle while you work. (Whistle) Come

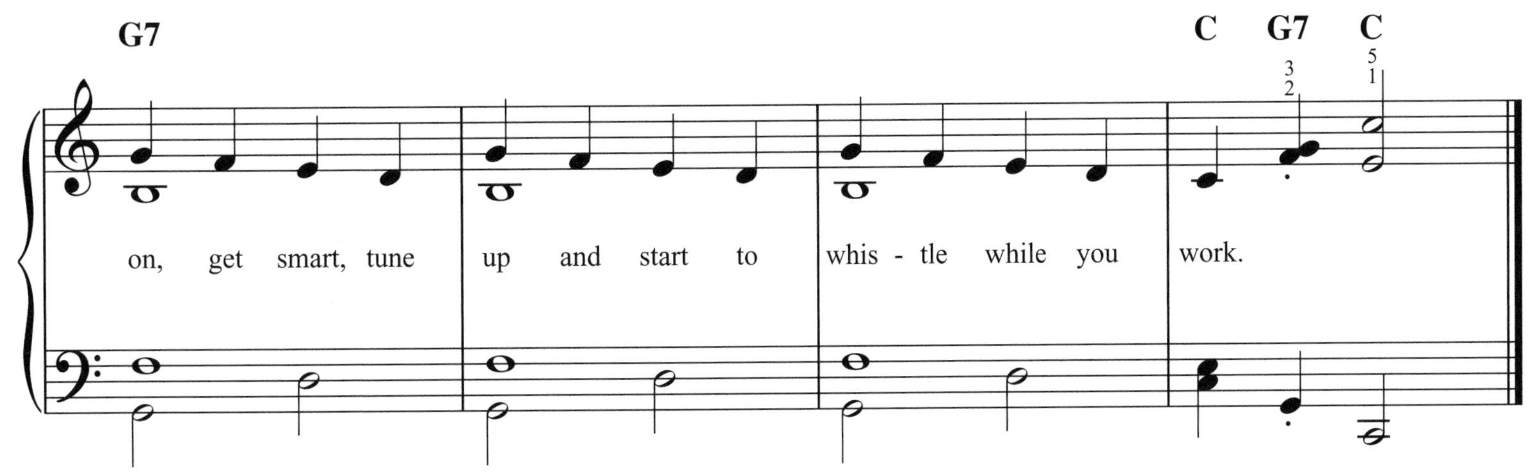
G7
C
G7
C
3
2
5
1
on, get smart, tune up and start to whis - tle while you work.

WHO'S AFRAID OF THE BIG BAD WOLF?

from THREE LITTLE PIGS

Words and Music by FRANK CHURCHILL
Additional Lyric by ANN RONELL

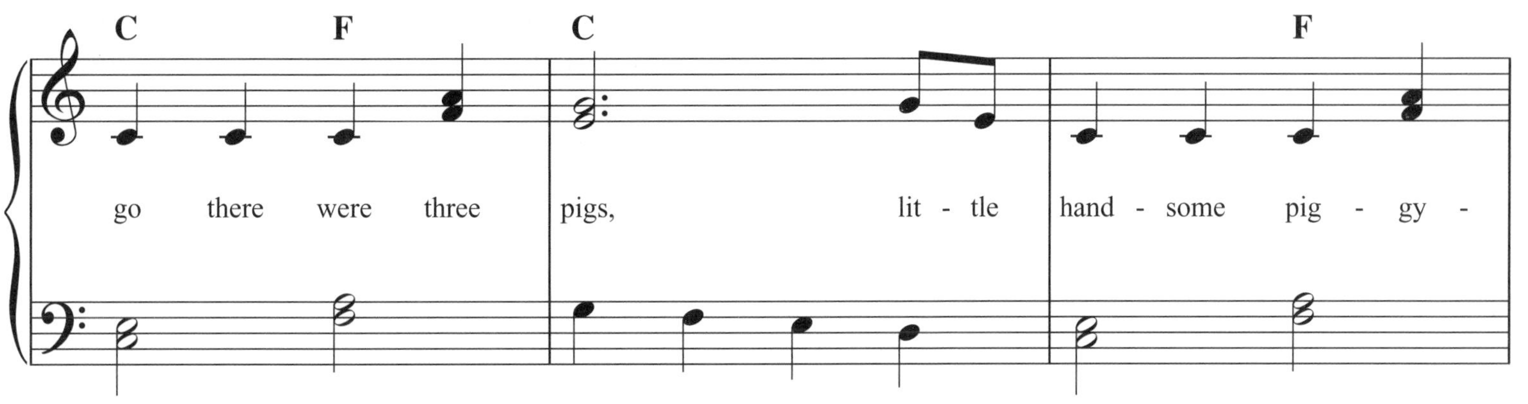
C F C F
go there were three pigs, lit - tle hand - some pig - gy -

C F C/E
wigs. For the big bad, ver - y big ver - y bad wolf, they

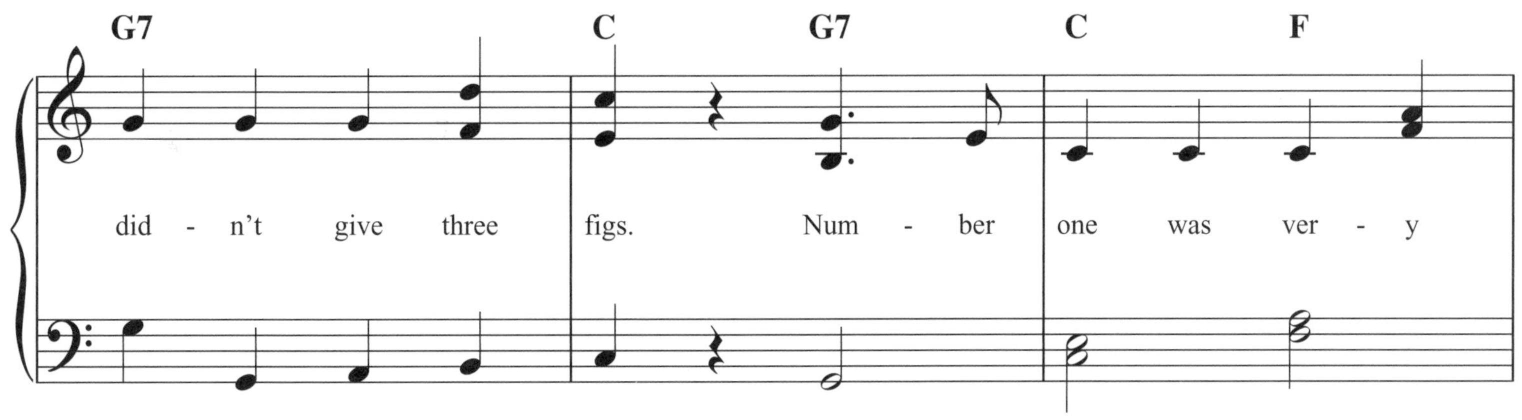
G7 C G7 C F
did - n't give three figs. Num - ber one was ver - y

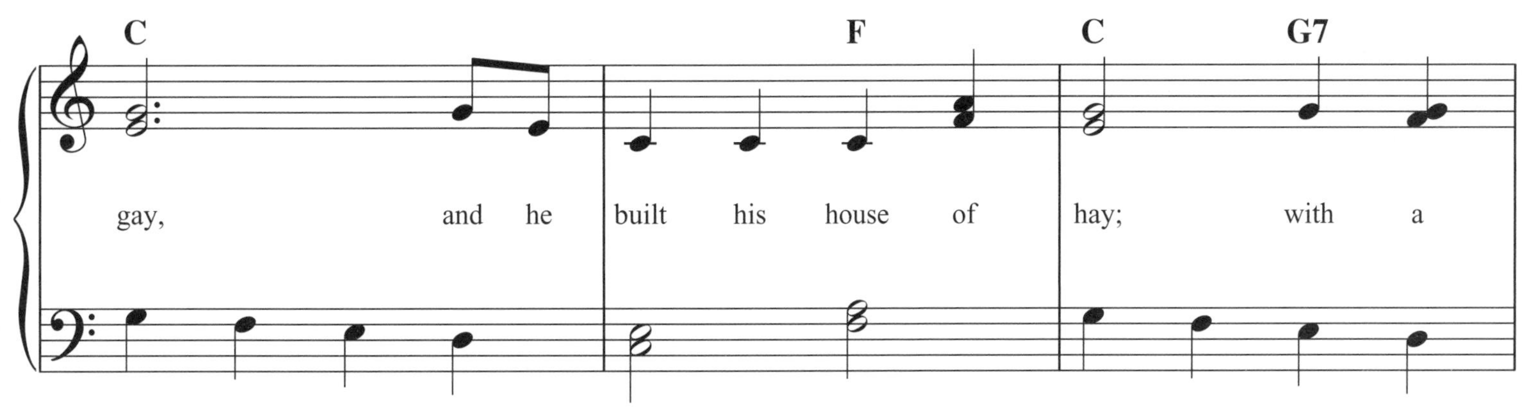
C F C G7
gay, and he built his house of hay; with a

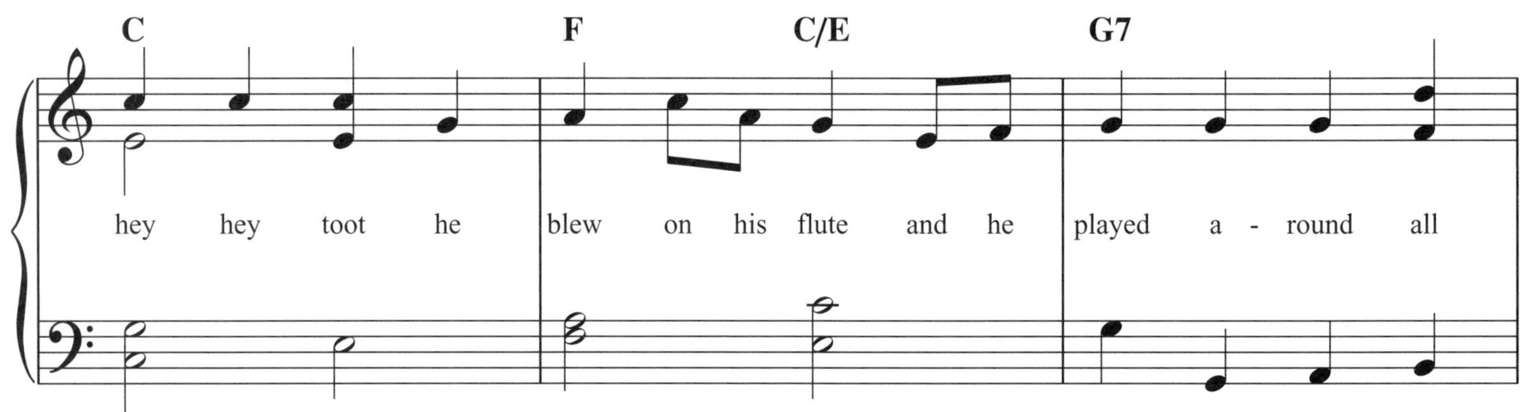
C
F
C/E
G7
hey hey toot he blew on his flute and he played a - round all

C
D7
G
G7
C/E
D7/F♯
day. Who's a - fraid of the big bad wolf,

C/E
D7/F♯
G
G7
big bad wolf, big bad wolf? Who's a - fraid of the

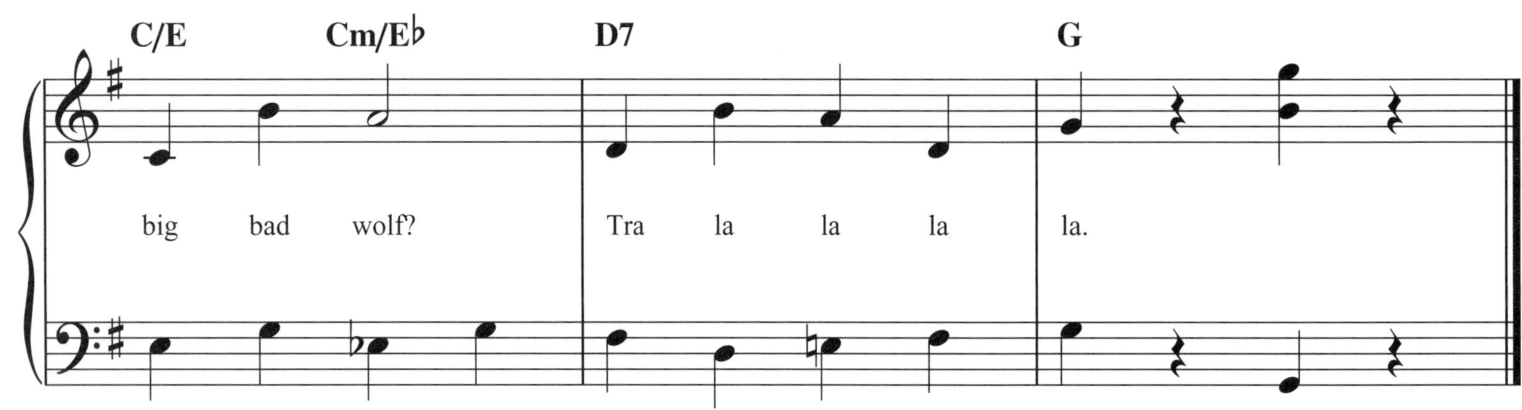
C/E
Cm/E♭
D7
G
big bad wolf? Tra la la la la.

YOU CAN FLY! YOU CAN FLY! YOU CAN FLY!

from PETER PAN

Words by SAMMY CAHN
Music by SAMMY FAIN

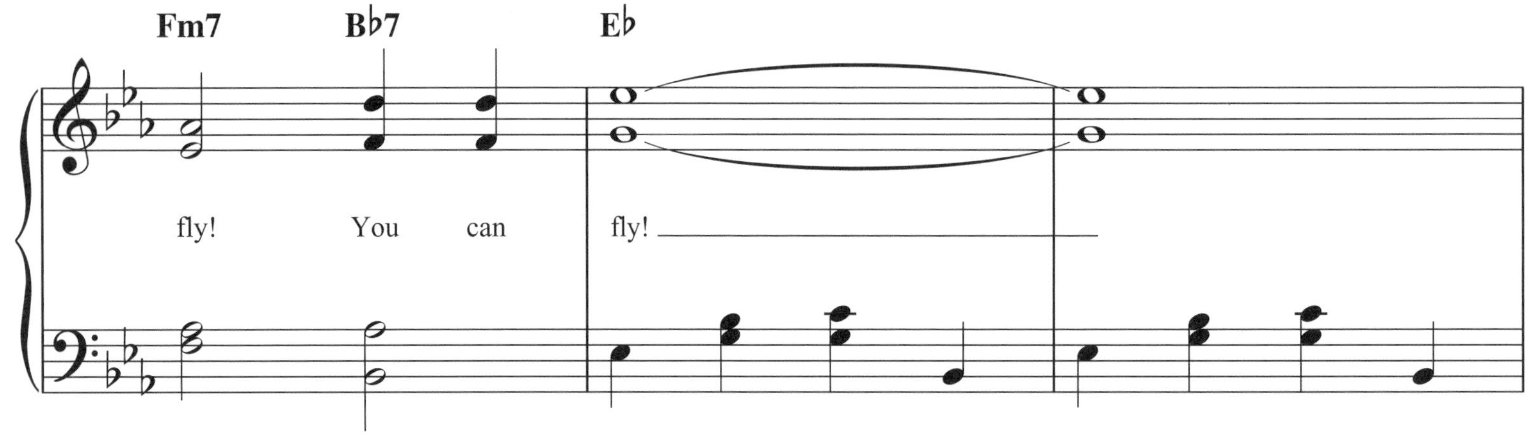
Fm7
B♭7
E♭
fly! You can fly!

Think of the hap - pi - est things, that's the way to get your

B♭7
E♭
wings. Now you own a can - dy store.

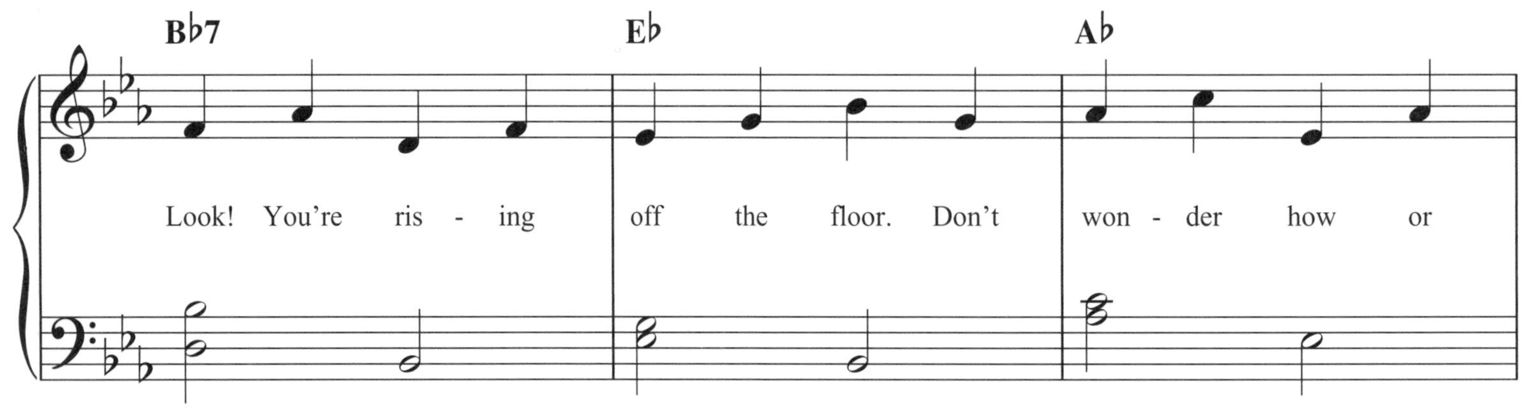
B♭7
E♭
A♭
Look! You're ris - ing off the floor. Don't won - der how or

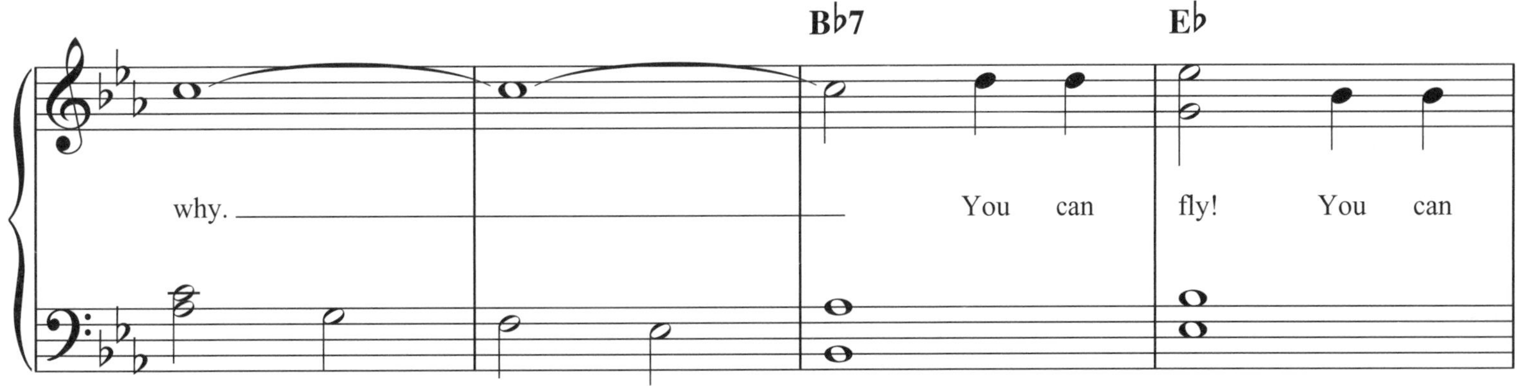
B♭7
E♭
why.
You can
fly! You can

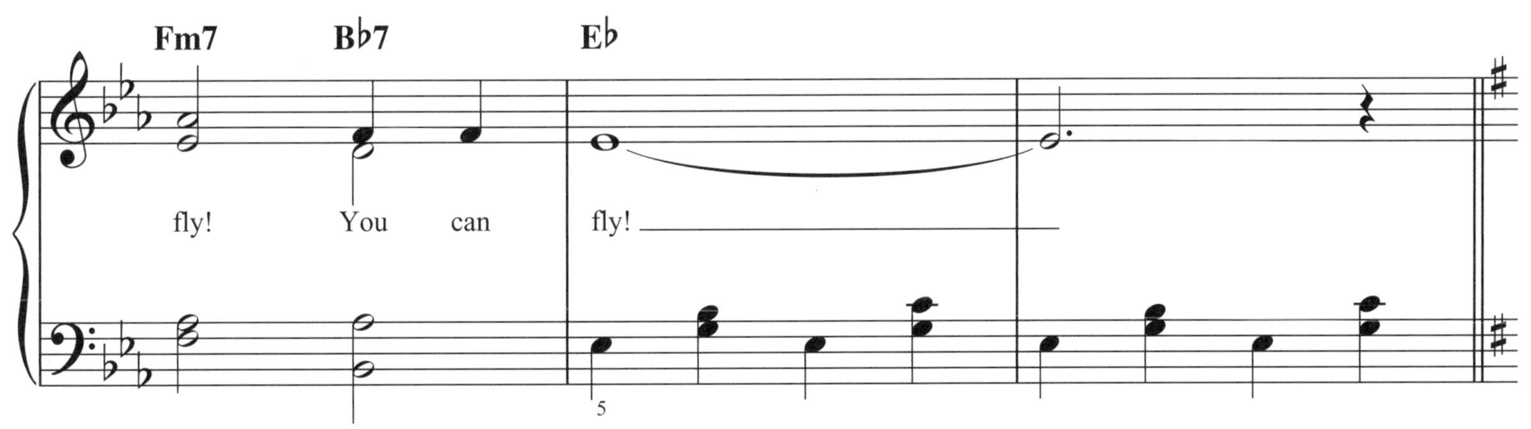
Fm7
B♭7
E♭
fly! You can
fly!
5

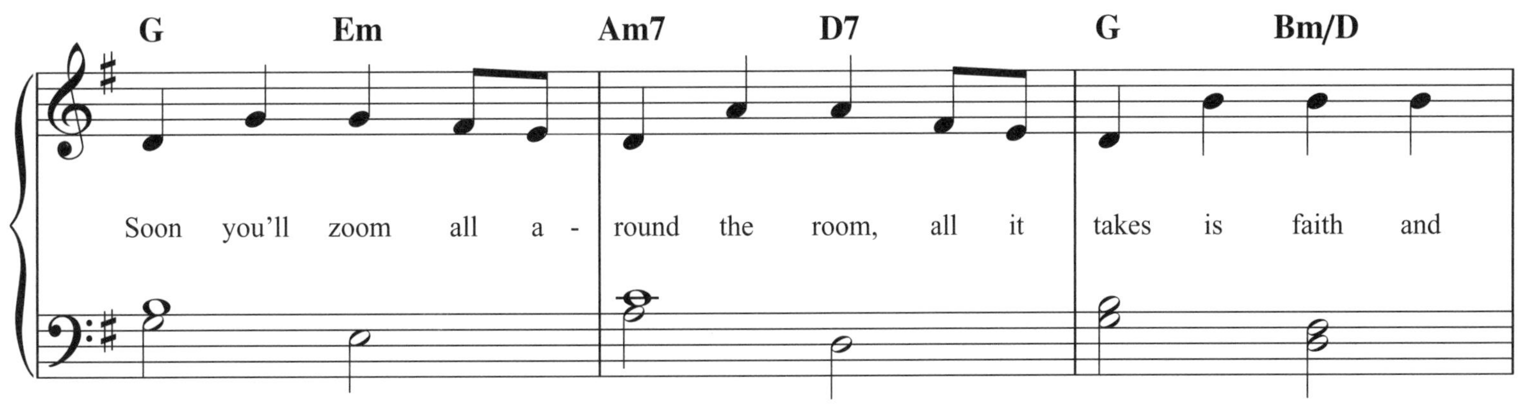
G
Em
Am7
D7
G
Bm/D
Soon you'll zoom all a - round the room, all it takes is faith and

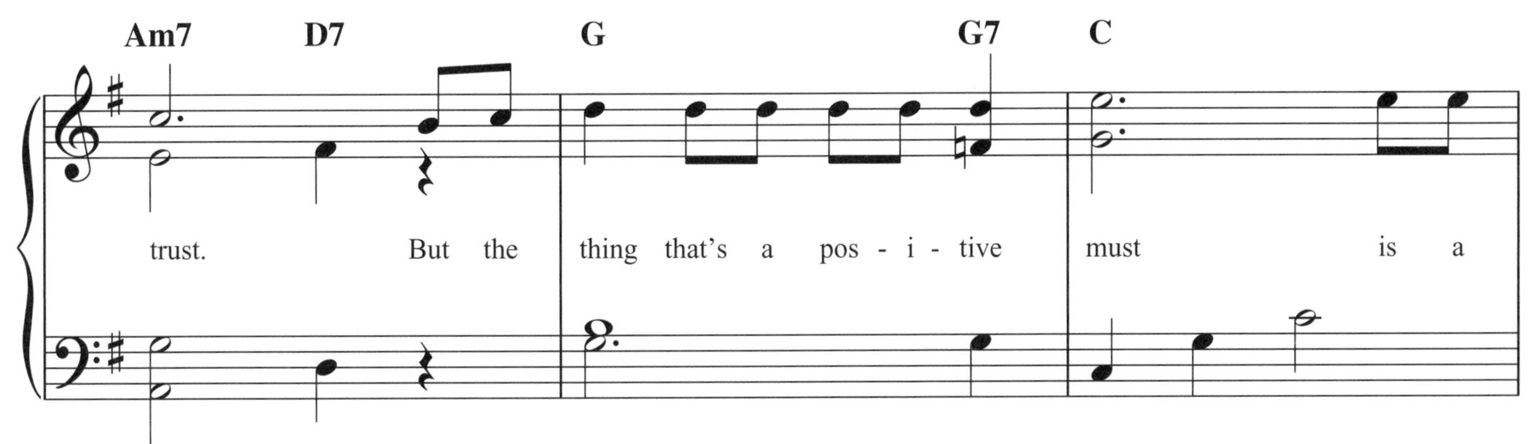
Am7
D7
G
G7
C
trust. But the thing that's a pos - i - tive must is a

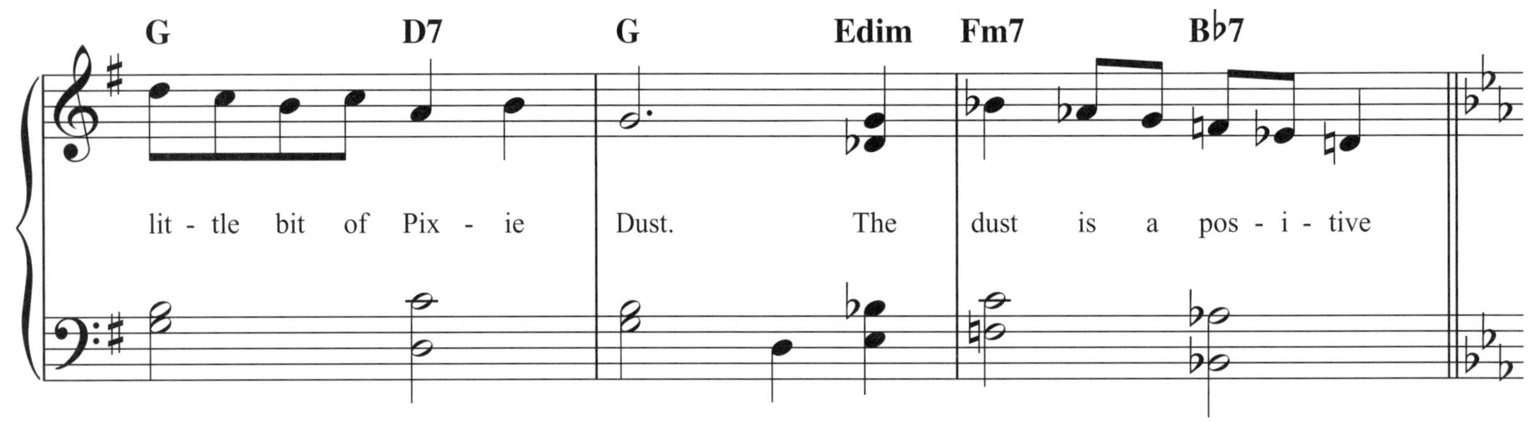
G
D7
G
Edim
Fm7
B♭7
lit - tle bit of Pix - ie
Dust. The
dust is a pos - i - tive

E♭
must!
When there's a smile in your

heart,
there's no bet - ter time to
start.

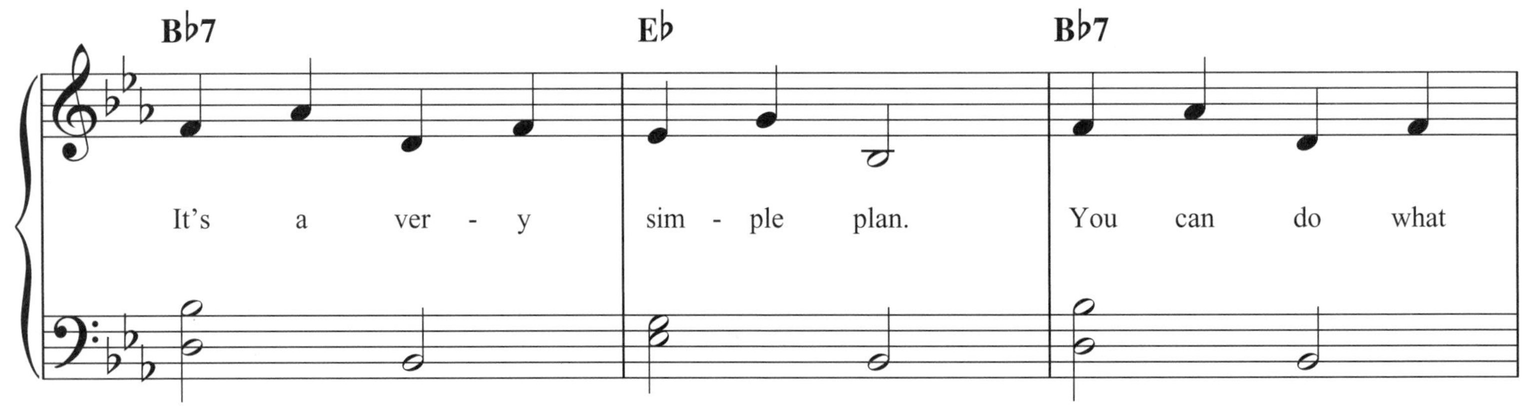
B♭7
E♭
B♭7
It's a ver - y
sim - ple plan.
You can do what

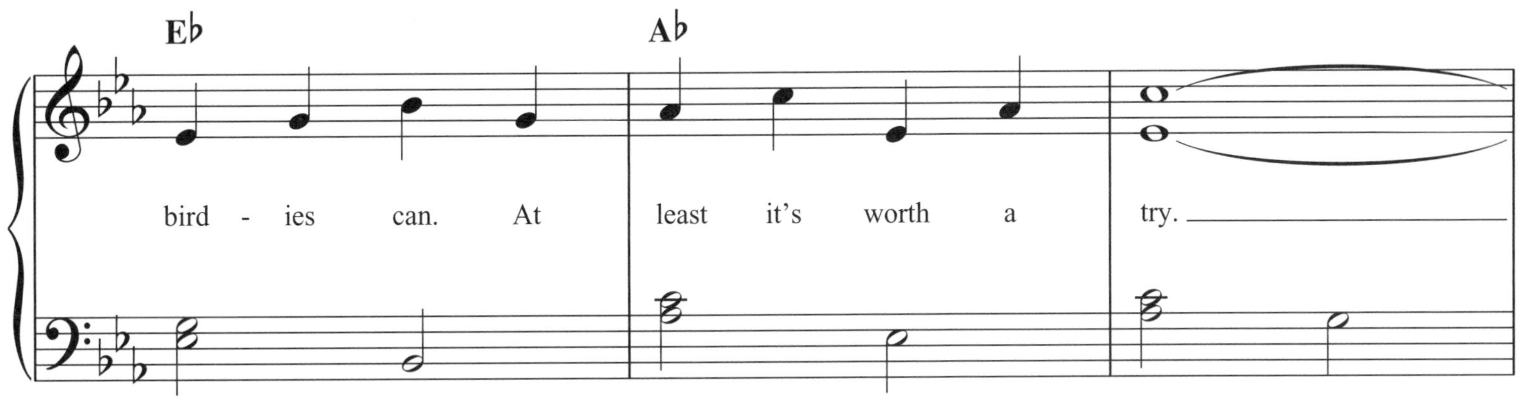
E♭
A♭
bird - ies can. At
least it's worth a
try.

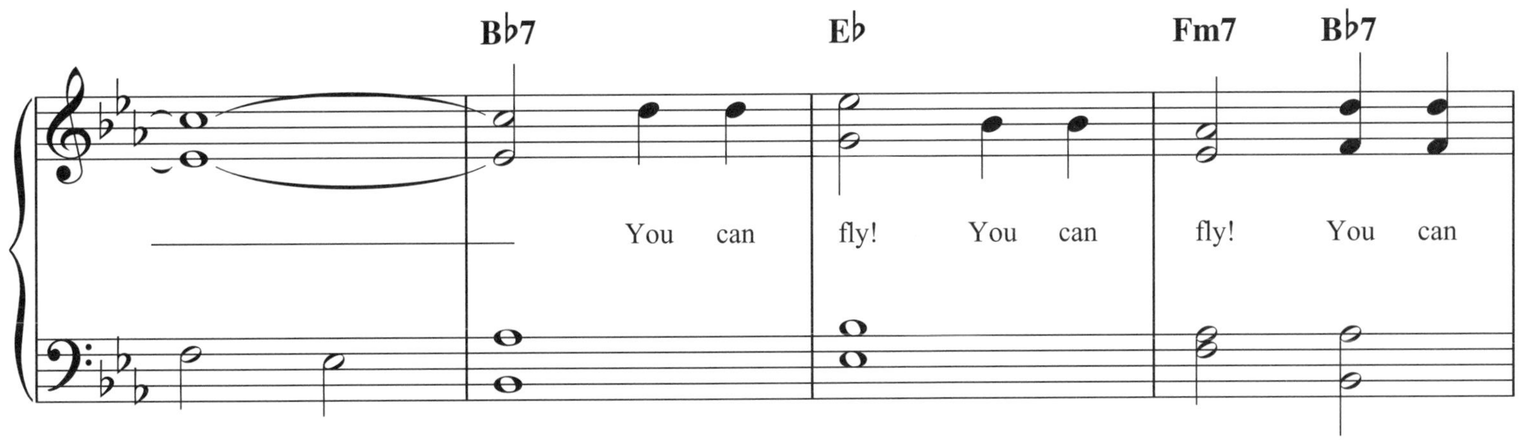
B♭7
E♭
Fm7
B♭7
You can
fly! You can
fly! You can

1.
E♭
Fm7
B♭7
fly!
2.
E♭
Fm7
fly!

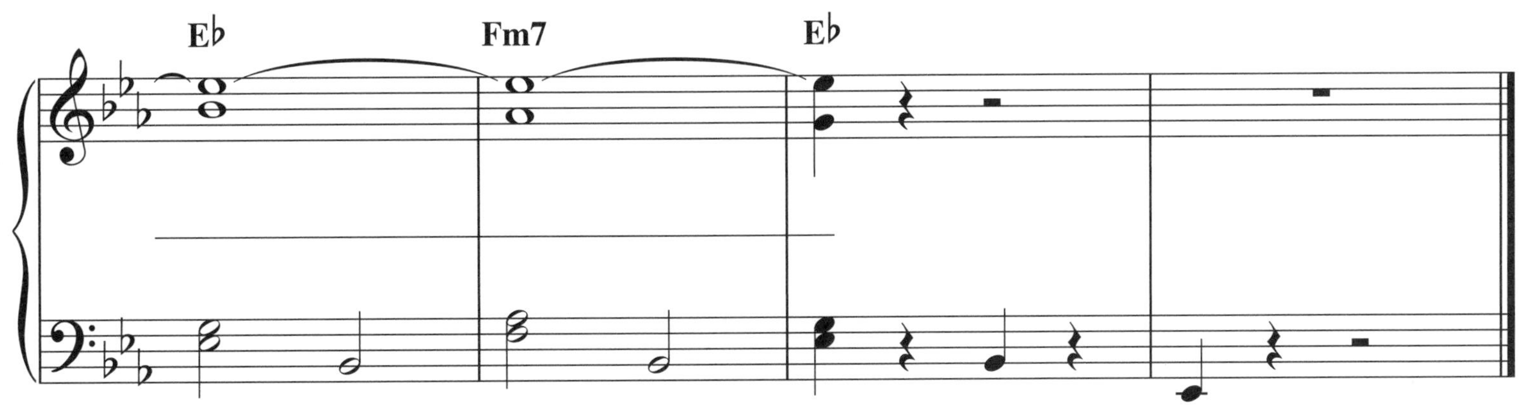
E♭
Fm7
E♭

YO HO
(A Pirate's Life for Me)
from PIRATES OF THE CARIBBEAN® ATTRACTION AT DISNEYLAND® PARK AND MAGIC KINGDOM® PARK

Words by XAVIER ATENCIO
Music by GEORGE BRUNS

In a robust manner

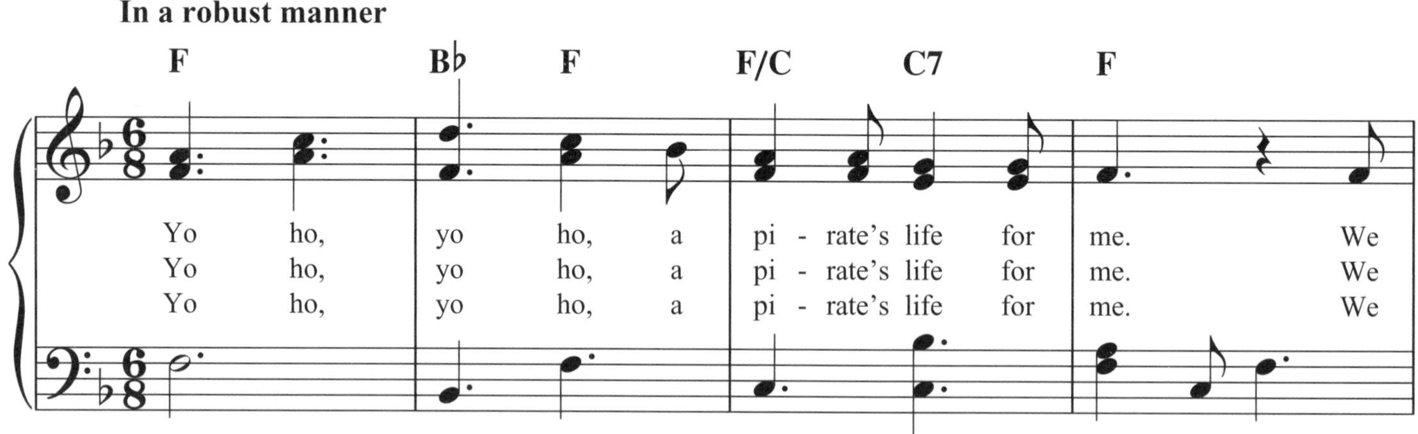
F
B♭
F
F/C
C7
F
Yo ho, yo ho, a pi - rate's life for me. We
Yo ho, yo ho, a pi - rate's life for me. We
Yo ho, yo ho, a pi - rate's life for me. We

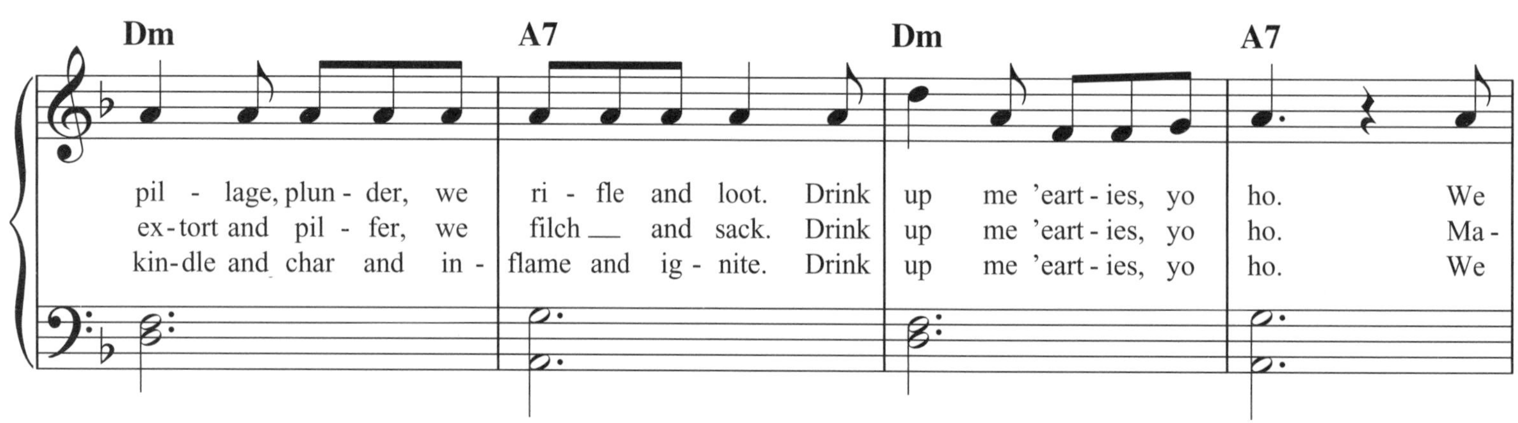
Dm
A7
Dm
A7
pil - lage, plun - der, we ri - fle and loot. Drink up me 'eart - ies, yo ho. We
ex - tort and pil - fer, we filch and sack. Drink up me 'eart - ies, yo ho. Ma -
kin - dle and char and in - flame and ig - nite. Drink up me 'eart - ies, yo ho. We

1., 2.
Gm
C7
F
Dm
G7
C7
kid - nap and rav - age and don't give a hoot. Drink up me 'eart - ies, yo ho.
raud and em - bez - zle and e - ven high - jack. Drink up me 'eart - ies, yo ho.
burn up the cit - y, we're real - ly a fright. Drink

3.
G7
C7
A7
Dm
up me 'eart - ies, yo
ho. We're
ras - cals and scoun - drels, we're
beg - gars and blight - ers and

A7
Dm
A7
Gm
C7
vil - lains and knaves. Drink
ne'er - do - well cads. Drink
up me 'eart - ies, yo
ho. We're
ho. Aye,
dev - ils and black sheep, we're
but ___ we're loved by our

F
Dm
G7
C7
F
real - ly bad eggs. Drink
mom - mies 'n' dads. Drink
up me 'eart - ies, yo
ho.
Yo ho,

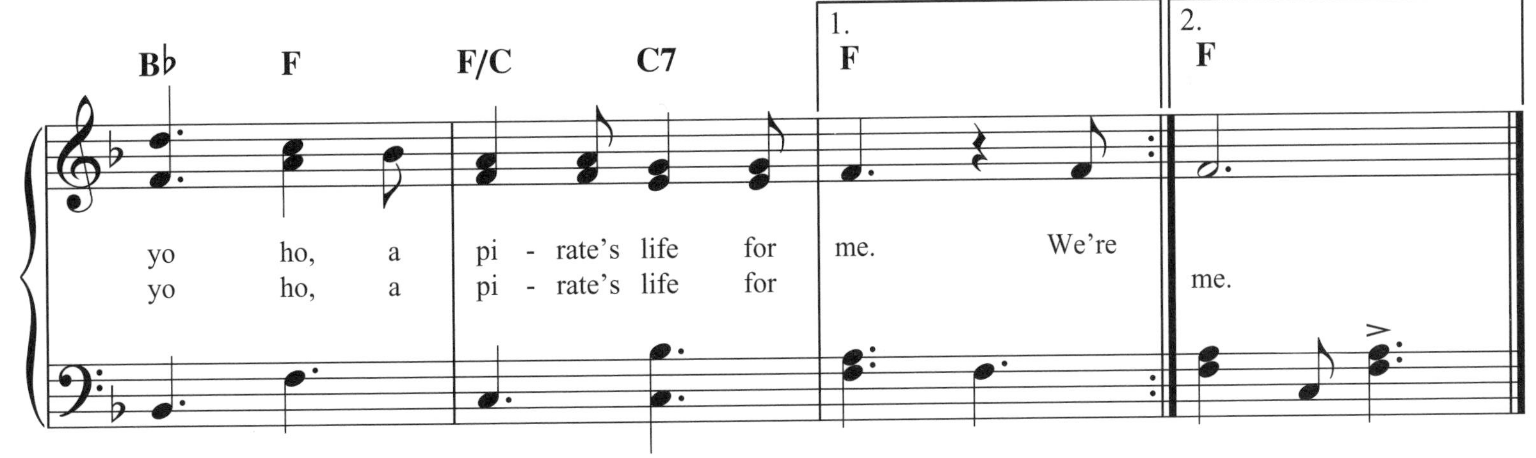
B♭
F
F/C
C7
1.
F
2.
F
yo ho, a
pi - rate's life for
me. We're
me.

YOU'VE GOT A FRIEND IN ME

from TOY STORY

E7
Am
F
B/F♯
C/G
nice warm bed,
I would - n't do for you.
you just re - mem - ber what your
If we stick to - geth - er we can

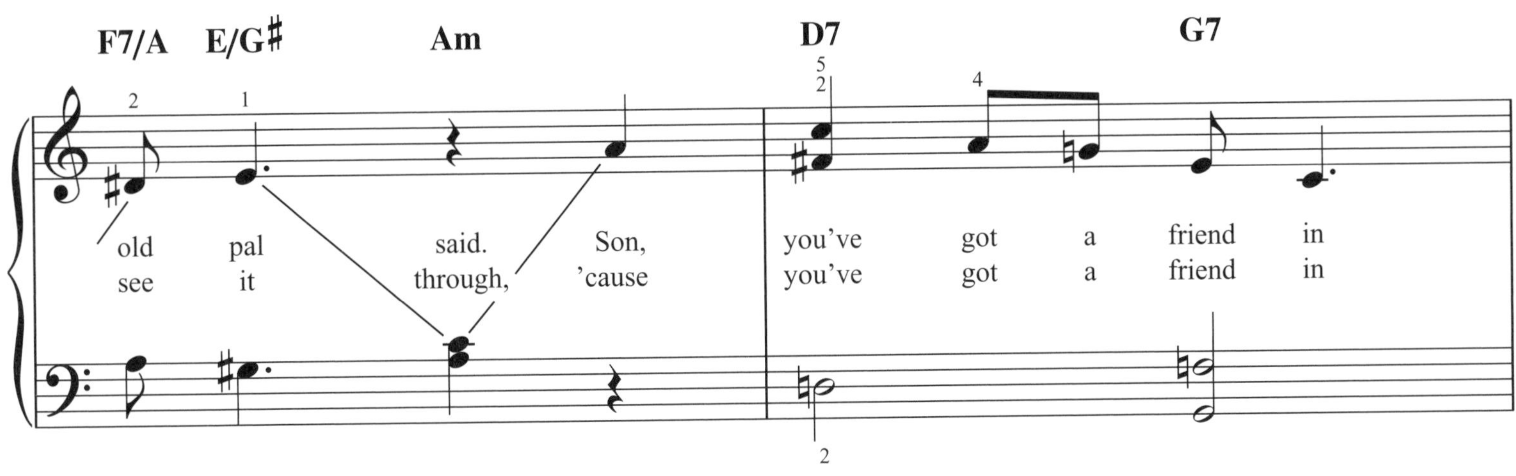
F7/A
E/G♯
Am
D7
G7
old pal said. Son,
see it through, 'cause
you've got a friend in
you've got a friend in

C
A7
D7
G7
1.
C
E7/B
me. Yeah,
me. Yeah,
you've got a friend in
you've got a friend in
me.

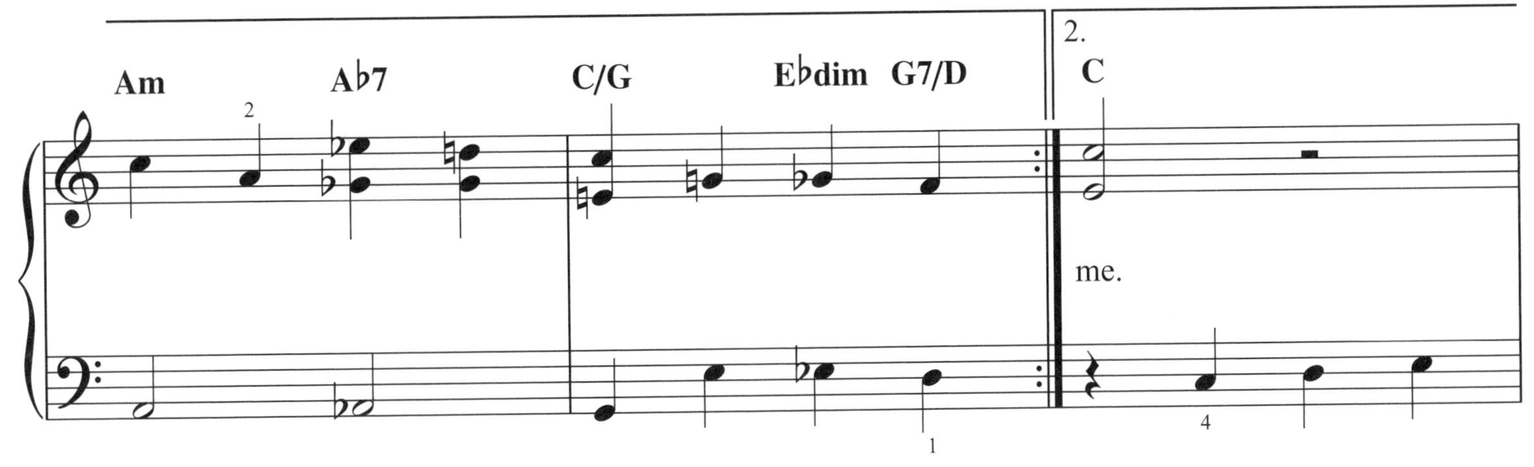
Am
A♭7
C/G
E♭dim
G7/D
2.
C
me.

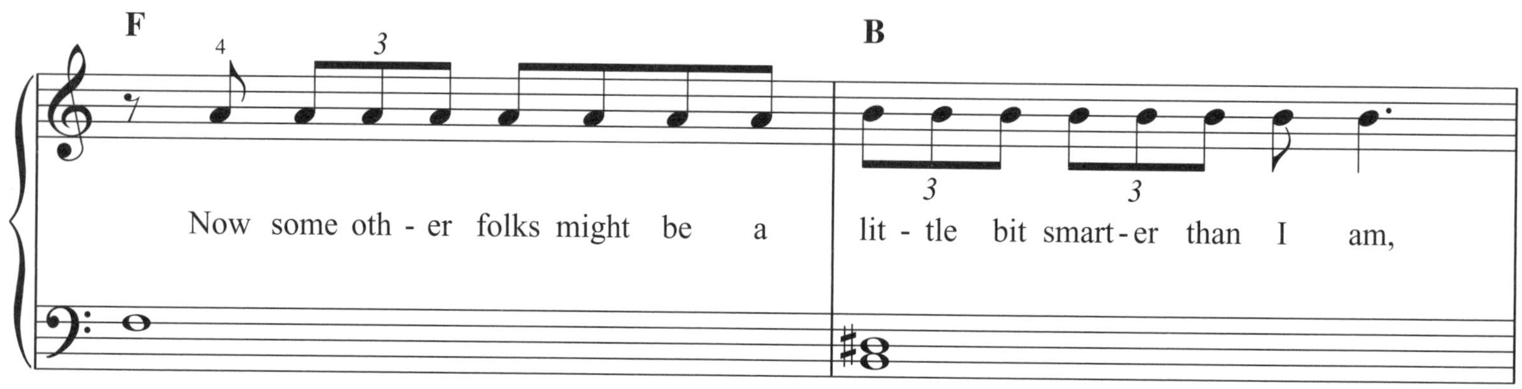
F
B
Now some oth - er folks might be a
lit - tle bit smart - er than I am,

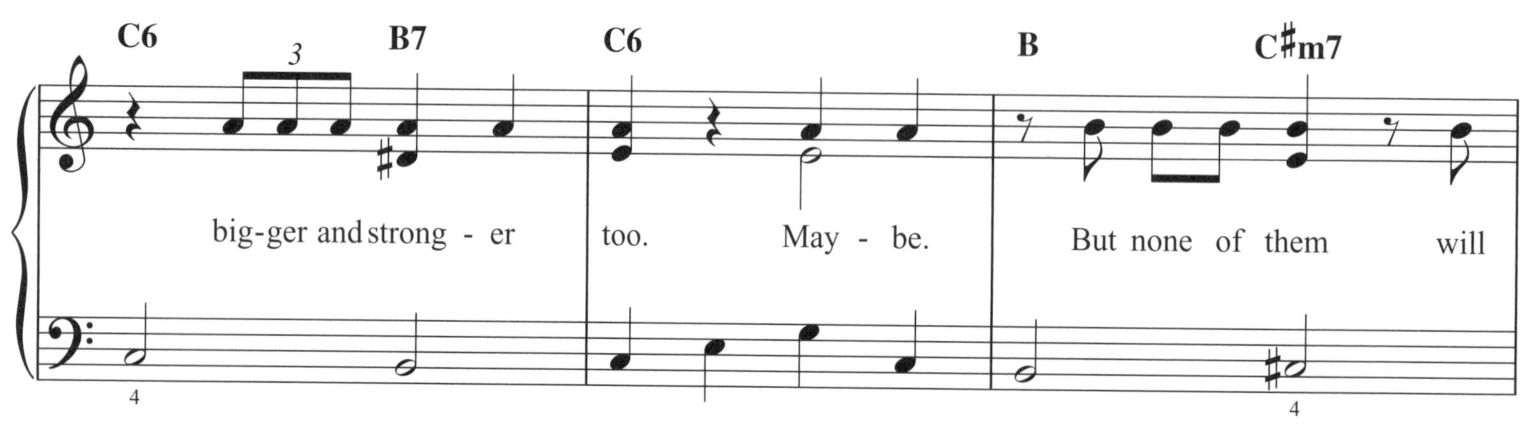
C6
B7
C6
B
C♯m7
big - ger and strong - er
too. May - be.
But none of them will

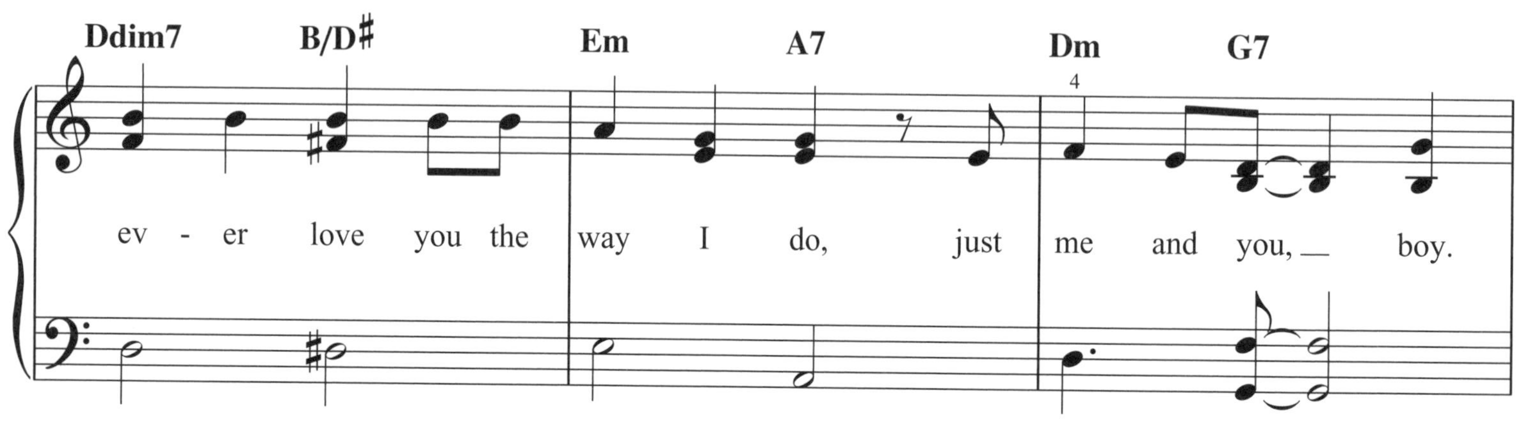
Ddim7
B/D♯
Em
A7
Dm
G7
ev - er love you the
way I do, just
me and you, — boy.

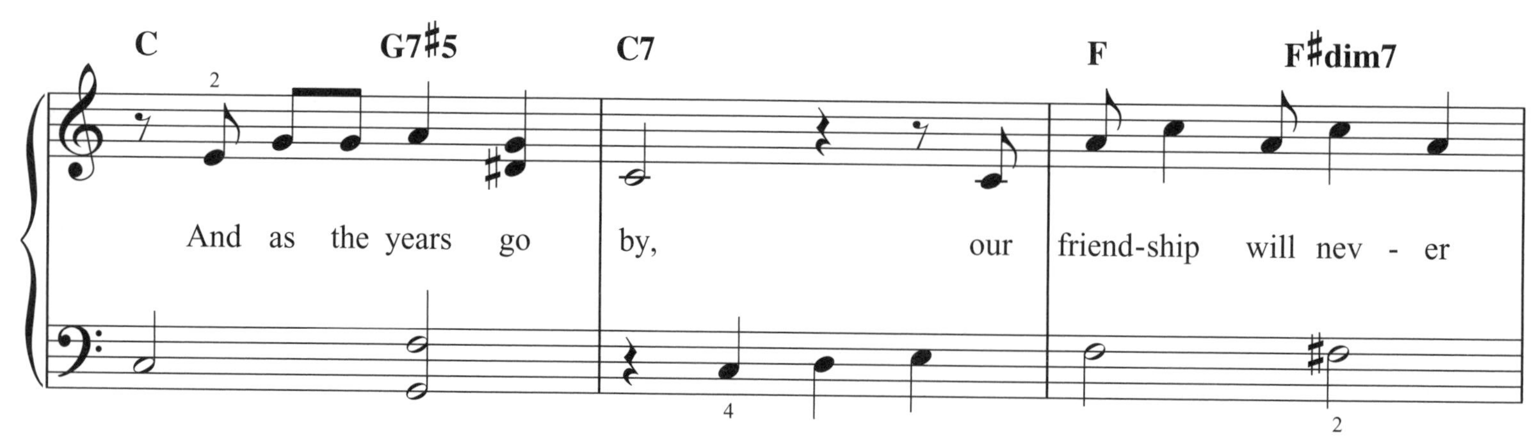
C
G7♯5
C7
F
F♯dim7
And as the years go
by, our
friend - ship will nev - er

C/G
C
F
F♯dim7
C/G
E7/G♯
Am
die.
You're gon - na see it's our des - ti - ny.

D7
G7
C
A7
D7
G7
You've got a friend in me.
You've got a friend in

C
A7
D7
G7
C
E7/B
me.
You've got a friend in me.

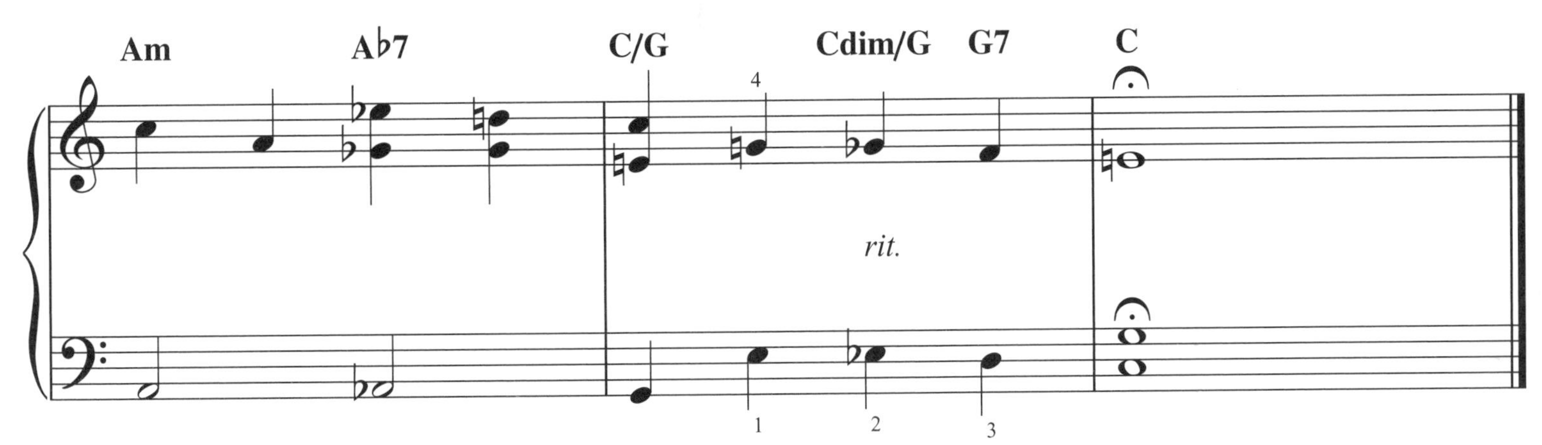
Am
A♭7
C/G
Cdim/G
G7
C
rit.

ZIP-A-DEE-DOO-DAH

from SONG OF THE SOUTH

Music by ALLIE WRUBEL
Words by RAY GILBERT

G7
F
C
Blue - bird on my shoul - der, it's the
D7
G
truth, it's "act - ch'll," ev - 'ry- thing is "sat - is - fact - ch'll."
C
F
C
Zip - a - dee - doo - dah, zip - a - dee - ay!
F
C
Dm/F
G
C
1.
2.
Won - der- ful feel - ing, won - der - ful day. Mis - ter